WOMEN IN ISLAM AND THE MIDDLE EAST

Women in Islam

and the

Middle East

A READER

Edited by Ruth Roded

I.B. Tauris *Publishers*

LONDON • NEW YORK

Revised edition published in 2008 by I.B. Tauris & Co Ltd
6 Salem Road, London W2 4BU
175 Fifth Avenue, New York NY 10010
www.ibtauris.com

In the United States of America and Canada distributed by Palgrave Macmillan
a division of St. Martin's Press, 175 Fifth Avenue, New York NY 10010

First published in 1999 by I.B. Tauris & Co Ltd

ISBN: 978 1 84511 385 8

A full CIP record for this book is available from the British Library
A full CIP record is available from the Library of Congress

Library of Congress Catalog Card Number: available

Typeset in Adobe Minion by Hepton Books, Oxford
Printed and bound in India by Rakesh Press

For my mother
Shoshana

CONTENTS

TABLES AND FIGURES

Tables

Figures

PREFACE

From the first course I taught on women in Islam and Middle Eastern history, the first time I attempted to transmit an understanding of the complex role of women in the history and culture of this part of the world, it was clear to me that the only way to do justice to this controversial subject was to enable students to read primary sources (in translation if necessary) and form their own opinions. Naturally, the first Islamic source was the Quran; the first discussion and debate was about the verses cited to justify the seclusion of women and the Islamic dress code for women. Later, I found that folk tales of Juha, which have circulated in the Middle East for centuries, may contain information about women of the lower strata and may reflect popular attitudes.

A chapter of my previous book *Women in Islamic Biographical Collections: From Ibn Sa'd to Who's Who* opened with a paraphrase of the hagiography of a typical, albeit anonymous, mystic woman; the historical and centenary biographical collections provided information on royal women and women of the ruling dynasties. Thus began my quest for a variety of primary sources spanning different periods of Islamic and Middle Eastern history and reflecting various aspects of women's experience. I myself was surprised to discover how much material has already been translated into English whether for scholarly purposes, for the use of European colonial administrators or for the millions of Muslims whose mother tongue is English or for whom English has become a lingua franca. Since Hebrew is my chosen language and the language of most of my teaching, I was particularly sensitive to translations of Middle Eastern material into Hebrew. These translations often deal with subjects of Jewish interest but they also serve to cement and disseminate our cultural ties to the region. When I deemed it necessary, I translated primary sources myself.

I have been fortunate to be associated with the Department of the History of Islam and the Middle East, The Institute for Asian and African Studies, at The Hebrew University of Jerusalem for over twenty-five years. This affiliation has given me access to an excellent research library, The Israel National and University Library, in which I found an obscure nineteenth-century ethnographic work and many other more recent sources. My colleagues at the Hebrew University, and at other institutions of higher education in Israel, have served as a veritable encyclopaedia of Islam and Middle Eastern history, a human anthology of Middle Eastern languages and literature, without whose assistance a work of this scope would not be possible.

Among my colleagues, I must express my gratitude to a great many people who have helped me in numerous ways, and yet I may fail to mention them all. My premier Arabic teacher, Avraham Yinon, continues to assist me in language and literature. Eytan Kohlberg tutors me in Quran, guides me in numerous questions relating to Islam and has taught us all about the history of the Shi'a. Yitzhak Hasson and Arnikam Elad are unstinting with their time and knowledge, defined as the Umayyad and Abbasid periods but surpassing the constraints of time. My friend and colleague, Miriam Hoexter, assists me with her expertise and supports me in my endeavours. Haim Gerber delved into his store of knowledge to recall that Khasseki Sultan's endowment deed was published in English in the 1940s. A volume of Halide Edib's memoirs was located at Tel Aviv University thanks to the computer people and librarians who are expanding our electronic search capabilities. The professionals at the Mount Scopus Computer Centre, Julia in particular, taught me the peculiar logic of scanning texts.

In the autumn of 1993, on a mini-sabbatical at Villanova University, I had an opportunity to broaden my intellectual horizons in interchanges with the faculty and staff of the History Department and The Centre for Arab and Islamic Studies. Returning to Jerusalem, I received support for my work from The Harry S. Truman Institute for the Advancement of Peace, in particular the Maurice J. and Fay B. Karpf Foundation. The students in my graduate seminar at the Rothberg School for Overseas Students were the guinea pigs upon whom most of this material was first tested. Their astute questions and comments undoubtedly contributed to the lucidity of this work. Some of my Israeli students have also added to my knowledge and understanding of Islam and Middle Eastern history.

My family - my husband, Roby, and my children, Micha, Alona and Lea - have shared the ups and downs of this as well as my other work. They have also contributed insights I might have missed, each from his or her own perspective. My mother, Shoshana, has again proven the truth of the maxim 'Behind every successful women there is a supportive mother.'

The growing interest in women in Islam and Middle Eastern history as well as the variety of primary sources available in English translation have paved the way for non-specialists to receive an introduction to this subject. This volume aims to meet that need and to challenge its readers to continue their quest for more knowledge about Middle Eastern Muslims, women and men. In that sense, this book is for Sara, Christina, Herbert and Robyn, for Tamar and Eleazer and for Gideon, Suha and Muhammad.

Ruth Roded
Jerusalem, 1998

ACKNOWLEDGEMENTS

I would like to express my gratitude to the following for granting permission to reprint excerpts from the works cited:

A. Guillaume, *The Life of Muhammad: A Translation of lbn Ishaq's Sirat Rasul Allah* by permission of Oxford University Press.

Muhammad Muhsin Khan, *The Translation of the Meanings of Sahih al-Bukhari* distributed by Kazi Publications, Inc.

Jere L. Bachrach, editor, *A Middle East Studies Handbook,* Cambridge University Press, 1984, Table: "Umayyad Caliphs."

C.E. Bosworth, *The History of Al-Tabari: Volume XXX* by permission of the State University of New York Press.

Amnon Cohen and Elisheva Simon-Piqali, editors, *Jews in the Moslem Court: Society, Economy and Communal Organization in Sixteenth Century Jerusalem* (in Hebrew), Yad Yitzhak Ben Zvi, 1993.

St. H. Stephan, translator, "An Endowment Deed of Khasseki Sultan, Dated the 24th May 1552," *The Quarterly of the Department of Antiquities in Palestine,* volume 10 (1944), Israel Antiquities Authority.

Rahamim Rejwan, editor, *Juha* (in Hebrew), Zmora, Bitan Publishers.

Justin McCarthy, *The Arab World, Turkey and the Balkans (1878-1914): A Handbook of Historical Statistics.* (Boston: G. K. Hall, 1982.), pp. 116-7,123-5, 134.

Selim Deringil, The Well-Protected Domains: Ideology and the Legitimation of Power in the Ottoman Empire, 1876-1909 (London: I.B.Tauris, 1998)

Halide Edib, *The Memoirs of Halide Edib,* copyright by John Murray (Publishers) Ltd.

Halide Edib, *The Turkish Ordeal,* copyright by John Murray (Publishers) Ltd.

Margot Badran and Miriam Cooke (eds), *Opening the Gates: A Century of Arab Feminist Writing,* Indiana University Press.

Nawal El Saadawi, "The Arab Women's Solidarity Association," in Nahid Toubia (ed.) *Women of the Arab World,* copyright by Zed Books Ltd.

Fatima Mernissi, *Doing Daily Battle: Interviews With Moroccan Women,* (translated by Mary Jo Lakeland), copyright c 1989 by Rutgers, The State University. Reprinted by permission of Rutgers University Press.

Marcia Hermausen, translator, *Fatime Fatima Ast* by Ali Shari'ati in *Women and Revolution in Iran,* ed. Guity Nashat, Westview Press, 1983.

Reuven Paz, translator, *The Islamic Covenant* (in Hebrew) Moshe Dayan Center for Middle Eastern and African Studies, Shiloah Institute.

Other authors, translators and publishers, spread out on three continents and working over more than a century, proved difficult to contact but have been cited alongside their work.

INTRODUCTION

What is the proper dress for a devout Muslim woman in public? Should a Muslim woman appear in public at all, or must she be secluded from men who are not members of her immediate family, restricted to a harem? Can women achieve positions of political leadership in a traditional Muslim state? What roles do women have in Islamic law as legal experts, litigants and witnesses? How does Islamic law affect different aspects of women's lives? What economic rights do Muslim women have and to what extent have they been able to exercise them? What is the attitude of Islam to woman and female sexuality?

These are not new questions. They have been addressed by Muslim scholars and non-Muslim observers of Islamic society for centuries. They are becoming more and more relevant to the lives of modern Muslims and non-Muslims alike because of the growing contact between different societies and cultures. Westerners in large numbers are visiting the Muslim Middle East for business, pleasure or military objectives. At the same time, Europeans and Americans are beginning to realize that a growing proportion of the citizens of their countries are practising Muslims. Fame and notoriety have been achieved by Muslim leaders and elites, sparking interest in their societies. Islamic and Middle Eastern themes - such as the harem princess - continue to permeate popular culture.[1]

The role of women in Islam and Middle Eastern society is not a neglected subject as some scholars would have us believe. On the contrary, the subject has been addressed by Muslim scholars through the ages; it has fascinated Western travellers since they first came in contact with the East; and it has been dealt with by Islamic scholars and Middle East experts since the advent of oriental studies. The problem is that the literature on women is extremely valueladen, informed by stated and latent assumptions derived from the culture and society of the author and the audience. This is true not only of popular and polemical literature but of scholarly works as well. These assumptions

1

influence the choice of topic, the source material selected, the methodology used and, of course, the evaluation and presentation of the material. For this reason, it is important to return to the primary sources, to try to place data on women in the proper perspective, to search for alternative meanings and to attempt to critically evaluate them.

The problem is complicated by the richness and variety of Islamic culture on the one hand, and the authority of a divinely-revealed religion (albeit humanly-transmitted) on the other. The ethical message and legal injunctions embodied in the Quran and the normative words and deeds of the Prophet Muhammad were framed in a certain language, at a discrete time and in a specific place. In the course of time, and as Islam spread to different geographical and cultural regions, Muslims interpreted these sources in various ways and applied them to their everyday needs. Alternative interpretations of Islam often led to diverging religious and political movements, but the premium placed on the unity of the community of believers frequently set off efforts to reach a consensus, at least in the religious realm. Variations of local custom were legitimized at a fairly early stage, limiting conflicts between theory and practice, but a common body of traditional wisdom also evolved. Thus, all Muslims will agree that Islam has a definitive position on issues relating to the status of women, but they will disagree over the precise definition of that position. What is important here is that the differing Muslim attitudes toward the role of women all derive from similar if not identical sources.

A related problem encountered in evaluating Islamic theories or Middle Eastern practices regarding the status of women is the explicit or more often implicit criteria of judgement. Does the status of women in Islam reach the level of the ideal, egalitarian society to which many of us aspire but few of us attain? How does it compare to the position of women in other contemporary societies? How did the roles of women in traditional Middle Eastern societies compare to that in the West before the advent of the feminist, women's liberation and equal rights movements? How did the condition of women in Islam differ from that in the pre-Islamic Middle East? Delving into the status of women in society at the time and place of the advent of Islam not only provides historical background and illuminates potential influences but also indicates the extent to which certain practices and attitudes were universal. Recalling the situation of women in the West during the nineteenth and twentieth centuries helps define what 'modernized' or 'Westernized' meant when applied to Middle Eastern women. In reading the source material of Islam and Middle Eastern history, we aim to understand the original intent of the author but also seek alternative meanings.

In order to underscore the importance of the religious and historical source material, a survey of the various ideological influences which have impinged on the literature on women in Islam and Middle Eastern history will serve as an introduction to this collection of readings. At the end of this introductory chapter, the criteria of selection of the excerpts and the problems this process engenders will be discussed. A short section will deal with differing approaches to translation - attempting to transmit both the meaning and the style. In conclusion, the format of the book and the order of the selections will be explained.

Classical Islamic Sources

Classical Islamic literature, like the works of other great religions and cultures, contains material which reflects woman's subservient position, depicts woman as a danger to society, and regards men and women as equal in certain realms. An oft-quoted verse from the Quran states:[2]

> Lo! men who surrender unto Allah, and women who surrender, and men who believe and women who believe,
> and men who obey and women who obey,
> and men who speak the truth and women who speak the truth, and men who persevere (in righteousness) and women who persevere,
> and men who are humble and women who are humble,
> and men who give alms and woman who give alms,
> and men who fast and women who fast,
> and men who guard their modesty and women who guard (their modesty),
> and men who remember Allah much and women who remember - Allah hath prepared for them forgiveness and a vast reward.

In the past, this verse has been quoted to indicate that men and women are equal in the eyes of Allah and have the same religious duties. Other excerpts from the Quran have been cited to prove that women's equality in Islam is spiritual but not social or economic (see: selection 1 below). Recently, an African-American Muslim feminist has claimed that this verse is merely an artifact of the language of the Quran, Arabic, which is gender-specific. Her approach is that all of the revelation, even if it is couched in the masculine gender, applies to men and women equally.[3]

Similarly, the Prophet Muhammad is quoted as saying: 'A people whose affairs are managed by a woman, will not prosper.'[4] This normative statement or *hadith* has traditionally served as the justification for excluding women from positions of political leadership and authority (see: selections 3 and 9). No wonder that the Moroccan feminist Fatima Mernissi chose this saying of the Prophet as one of two hadiths which she tried to prove were baseless, using classical Islamic critical methods.[5] On the other hand, the Prophet also said: 'How excellent the women of the Ansar [supporters of Muhammad in Medina] are! They do not feel shy while learning sound knowledge in religion,'[6] a dictum which has been used to support women's education.

The biography of the Prophet Muhammad, one of the oldest extant Islamic sources, portrays active and passive women, positive and negative role models. The biographies of some twelve hundred women who came in contact with Muhammad, women who serve as role models for Muslims to this day, project conflicting messages on the proper behaviour of believing women.[7]

Early Islamic mystical literature was based on ascetic ideals, and like other ascetic movements, it had a misogynist bent. Woman was compared to the base personality that incites to evil, the *nafs* in Arabic, because this word is in the feminine gender. Woman is the epitome of the *nafs* that seduces man to the sensual pleasures of this world (the *dunya,* also feminine). But the Prophet's lifestyle and other factors lead Islam to decry celibacy, and the life stories of devout Muslim women of the eight and ninth centuries offset the negative view of woman. The idea became prevalent that 'Allah does not look at the external form. The external form is not important, but the internal goal of the heart,' according to the thirteenth century Persian mystic Attar.[8] 'When a woman walks in the path of Allah like a man, she should not be called a woman,' Attar said, describing the noted mystic woman Rabi'a al-Adawiyya.[9] Modern feminists may not regard Attar's words as a compliment, implying that when a woman achieves excellence, she becomes like a man. This simile is common in many cultures to this day.[10]

In short, classical Islamic sources comprise a variety of attitudes toward women's role in society. Some modern scholars have attempted to differentiate between earlier and later Islamic positions on women, or between mainstream, orthodox Islam and alternative, more egalitarian movements.[11] The richness of the primary sources on women in Islam and Middle Eastern history, however, seems to point to a far more complex cluster of influences on women's roles and the attitudes of men to them. These primary texts are open to various alternative readings as the reader will see throughout this book. The alternate readings also fuel the endless debate about the role of women in contemporary Islam.

European Travel Literature

From their first contact with the Islamic Middle East, Europeans were fascinated, one might even say obsessed, with the different status of women in that society. Westerners who visited the Middle East for any length of time rarely failed to note the conspicuous differences between the status of women in the East as they saw it and women's position in the West in their day. They often devoted at least a section of their travel books if not a chapter or an entire volume to unique eastern institutions such as polygamy, concubinage, seclusion of women, etc. Most of the European travellers and authors of memoirs and travel literature were men, and they brought to their meeting with Middle Eastern women their own conceptions of the 'proper' roles of women.

In the Middle Ages, although large numbers of Europeans came in contact with Middle Eastern Islamic society, the literature on this subject in European languages was written almost exclusively by Christian clerics. Perhaps this is the reason for the scholastic interest in varying translations of verse 223 in the second chapter of the Quran, the passage most often translated in the Middle Ages. The Quranic verse, which reads 'Your wives are your tillage; go therefore unto your tillage in what manner so ever ye will,' was understood by Europeans to refer to varying sexual positions. The frequently-made accusation that Islam permits, even encourages 'unnatural' sexual intercourse was based not only on textual analysis but also on hearsay evidence about the intimate practices of Muslim couples.[12] (It is interesting to compare this view of human sexuality with that expressed in selection 15.)

In the course of time, European merchants, consuls, missionaries, speculators, adventurers and tourists visited the Middle East and wrote about their impressions and experiences. Henry Harris Jessup, for example, a Protestant missionary in Syria for seventeen years in the mid-nineteenth century, wrote a book on *The Women of the Arabs* dedicated to 'the Christian women of America.' In his preface, he cites a number of scholarly works and Arabic written and oral sources. Despite Jessup's knowledge and familiarity with life in Syria, his attitude to the subject is revealed in the early pages of the book.

Mohammedans cannot and do not deny that women have souls, but their brutal treatment of women has naturally led to this view. The Caliph Omar said that 'women are worthless creatures and soil men's reputations.' In Sura iv. [of the Quran] it is written: 'Men are superior to women, on account of the qualities with which God has gifted the one above the other, and on account of the outlay they make, from their substance for them. Virtuous women are obedient ... But chide those for whose refractoriness ye have cause to fear ... and *scourge them.*

The interpretation of this last injunction being left to the individual believer, it is carried out with terrible severity. The scourging and beating of wives is one of the worst features of Moslem domestic life. It is a degraded and degrading practice, and having the sanction of the Koran, will be indulged in without rebuke as long as Islamism as a system and a faith prevails in the world. Happily for the poor women, the husbands do not generally beat them so as to imperil their lives, in case their own relatives reside in the vicinity, lest the excruciating screams of the suffering should reach the ears of her parents and bring the husband into disgrace. But where there is no fear of interference or of discovery, the blows and kicks are applied in the most merciless and barbarous manner. Women are killed in this way, and no outsider knows the cause. One of my Moslem neighbours once beat one of his wives to death. I heard her screams day after day, and finally, one night, when all was still, I heard a dreadful shriek, and blow after blow falling upon her back and head. I could hear the brute cursing her as he beat her. The police would not interfere, and I could not enter the house. The next day there was a funeral from that house, and she was carried off and buried in the most hasty and unfeeling manner. Sometimes it happens that the woman is strong enough to defend herself, and conquers a peace; but ordinarily when you hear a scream in the Moslem quarter of the city and ask the reason, it will be said to you with an indifferent shrug of the shoulder, 'that is only some man beating his wife.'

That thirty-eighth verse of Sura iv. is one of the many proofs that the Koran is not the book of God, because it violates the law of love. 'Husbands love your wives,' is a precept of the Gospel and not of the Koran. Yet it is a sad fact that the nominal Christians of this dark land are not much better in this respect than their Moslem neighbours. The Greeks, Maronites and Papal Greeks beat their wives on the slightest provocation.[13]

A man's right to physically chastise his wife is in fact mentioned in the Quran, and Muslim exegetes throughout the ages took great pains to delimit this rule in order to protect women from undue violence (see: selection 1). In his book on *The Women of the Arabs,* however, Jessup chose this reference to symbolize Islam's attitude toward women and reified it through a dramatic story of contemporary Middle Eastern life. By his own evidence, Christians in Syria beat their wives as often as Muslims which might lead us to conclude that we are dealing with social custom rather than religious precept. Moreover, a man's right and even obligation to punish women and children in his care by beating if necessary was widely recognized in the West as well as the East until very recently. Yet Jessup depicts wife-beating as a principle of the Islamic faith to be compared to the ideal of Christian love not to common practice or abuses in the Christian West. This uneven comparison is a fitting opening to Jessup's book most of which is devoted to the work of American missionary women in Syria from 1820 and, in particular, details about the conversion of a small number of Druze girls. Clearly, the book aimed to marshal support in the United States for these missionaries by depicting Islam in the most negative light, local Christians of other denominations as 'nominal Christians,' and Syria as a 'dark land.'

At the time that Henry Jessup was living in Syria, the American author Mark Twain participated in a 'grand tour' by steamer to Europe and the Holy Land, stopping off at Constantinople (as Istanbul was still called by Europeans), visiting Damascus and journeying to Cairo by rail. The description of this trip, *The Innocents Abroad or The New Pilgrims Progress,* does not contain much more information on nineteenth-century Middle Eastern women than Jessup's book. Mark Twain's keen eye and ironic criticism, however, show that even a tourist could make some astute observations not only about the Middle East but about American views of the East as well.

Describing his visit to the great bazaar of Istanbul, Mark Twain mentions among the strange-looking throng, the presence of 'high-born Turkish female shoppers.' In another passage, he relates in his typically ironic style to prevalent Western ideas about the harems of the East while not sparing his barbs for objectionable Eastern customs.

They say the Sultan has eight hundred wives. This almost amounts to bigamy. It makes our cheeks burn with shame to see such a thing permitted here in Turkey. We do not mind it so much in Salt Lake, however.

Circassian and Georgian girls are still sold in Constantinople by their parents, but not publicly. The great slave marts we have all read so much about - where tender young girl were stripped for inspection, and criticised and discussed just as if they were horses at an agricultural fair - no longer exist. The exhibition and the sales are private now. Stocks are up, just at present, partly because of a brisk demand created by the recent return of the sultan's suite from the courts of Europe; partly on account of an unusual abundance of breadstuffs, which leaves holders untortured by hunger and enables them to hold back for high prices; and partly because buyers are too weak to 'bear' the market, while sellers are amply prepared to 'bull' it. Prices are pretty high now, and holders firm; but, two or three years ago, parents in a starving condition brought their young daughters down here and sold them for even twenty and thirty dollars, when they could do no better, simply to save themselves and the girls from dying of want. It is sad to think of so distressing a thing as this, and I for one am sincerely glad the prices are up again.[14]

Most Western visitors to the Middle East were not social critics of the calibre of Mark Twain. Moreover, attempts to describe women's lives accurately involved multiple cultural, social and gender barriers.

The quality of European contact with Middle Eastern women was dictated by the gender of most of the travellers, their class and the purpose of their travel to the Middle East. Upper and upper-middle class men would have little opportunity to meet urban Middle Eastern women of their stratum since these were precisely the women who were secluded. The only reports from inside the harem that we have were written by the few women who ventured to the Middle East, often wives or sisters of consuls. Some of these women's descriptions of the shallow, child-like women of the harem whose lives revolved solely around their beauty, clothing and jewels, are suspiciously similar. One cannot avoid the hypothesis that they were copied from each other (a common practice among authors of travel literature).[15] A woman like Lucy Garnett (1893), however, could write of the inner workings of the Ottoman harem accurately and intelligently.[16]

Women of the 'lower classes,' like their male counterparts, were usually described in European travel literature in stereotypes, if they were described at all. More often, they were just part of the scenery. The general absence of women from the streets and public spaces was sometimes noted; the appearance of a female peddler or a 'woman of the lower classes' was considered unique enough to warrant mention. Men like Edward Lane (who lived in Egypt 1825-49) and women like Lucy Garnett did manage to provide us with some reliable information on urban middle class and lower class women, and even on rural women. Lane not only learned Arabic but made an effort to associate almost exclusively with Muslims of various social strata. Lane's preface still stands as an excellent guide to studying a foreign culture and society. His book is an extremely detailed description (with illustrations) of many aspects of Egyptian life including much material relevant to the lives of women. In his chapter on domestic life, he mentions:

> The portion of the dowry which has been paid by the bridegroom, and generally a much larger sum (the additional money, which is often more than the dowry itself, being supplied by the bride's family), is expended in purchasing the articles of furniture, dress, and ornaments for the bride. These articles which are called 'gahaz,' are the property of the bride; and if she be divorced, she takes them away with her. She cannot, therefore, with truth be said to be *purchased*.

Lane notes: 'Among the peasants, however, the father, or other lawful guardian of the bride, receives the dowry, and gives nothing in return but the girl, and sometimes a little corn, etc.[17]

European travel literature may serve as a source for information on women in Islam and Middle Eastern history but, like any other source, it must be read critically. Far too often, it teaches us more about European views on gender at the time the book was written than about Middle Eastern realities.[18] The influence of these works on European public opinion, including decision-makers, cannot be exaggerated. The portrayal of Middle Eastern women was part, perhaps even a major part, of a larger picture of the primitive, Islamic East.

Reaction to the West and the Woman's Rights Movement

Whether by chance or not, the growing exposure of Middle Easterners to Western culture occurred more or less at the time that the European and American women's rights movements were gaining public attention. This heightened the perceived differences between Western ideals of womanhood and Islamic norms, and between Middle Eastern customs and European practices. Initial Middle Eastern reactions to the status of women in European society was far from enthusiastic. But the military and material power of the West as well as the incessant European attacks on the ills of Middle Eastern culture required a more variegated response.

The conservative, apologetic approach was (and still is) that the contemporary status of Muslim women is no worse than that of Western women. On the contrary, women in the Middle East are respected, cared for and guarded compared to the licentiousness which characterizes Western relations between the sexes.

Another approach emerged from the Salafiyya movement (referred to as Islamic reform by European scholars) founded by Jamal al-Din al-Afghani (1838–97) and developed by his Egyptian disciple Muhammad Abduh (1849–1905). The Salafiyya aimed to return to the authentic, original Islam of the Prophet and the first four rightly-guided caliphs and to eliminate negative, foreign accretions that had corrupted Islam through the centuries. This led to a heightened interest in the status of women during the pre - and early Islamic periods and the female figures of these times. It also generated historical and pseudo-historical research into the sources of such customs as veiling and the seclusion of women.

The Salafis also advocated a renewed, critical study of the Quran and the *hadith* (sayings of the Prophet). Shaykh Muhammad Abduh is considered the first Muslim scholar to reinterpret the verse of the Quran permitting a man to marry up to four women simultaneously. The Quran requires men to treat all their wives equally – a concept which was interpreted by most classical exegetes in the narrow, material sense. Abduh argued that the meaning of the Quran encompassed equality in feelings, and since no human could love more than one wife absolutely equally, in fact, the Quran forbade polygamy.

A third reaction to Western attacks on the status of women in Islam, adopted by the Westernized-liberal elite, was to internalize European frames of reference, whether on principle, or more frequently, for instrumental reasons. This approach informed the positions of the nationalist movements (and the socialist movements) in the Middle East on the woman question. The main argument in this case was that eastern countries must improve the status of women in line with the Western model because of liberal principles of equality and justice, and in particular, to strengthen their societies and liberate their peoples from European colonialism.

Qasim Amin, an Egyptian lawyer who was one of the first to call for the liberation of women (at the end of the nineteenth century), argued explicitly that the status of women in Europe should be the norm for the Middle East as well. Women's liberation, and in particular education, was imperative for the entire society. In his book, *Liberation of the Woman* he wrote:

It is not possible to raise successful men if their mothers are not capable of preparing them for success. This is the noble profession that civilization has placed in the hands of the woman of our generation. She undertakes this heavy burden in all of the civilized countries where we see her giving birth to children and moulding them into men.[19]

Westernized-liberal positions on the status of women tended toward a secular sub-text but many of the spokespersons of this ilk claimed that they did not oppose the true religion and relied on Salafi interpretations of Islam.

Nationalist leaders often attacked the call for women's liberation as a blind imitation of the West. Mustafa Kamil, for example, the Egyptian nationalist leader of the early twentieth century, opposed the appearance of women in public, linking this to the preservation of the national personality.[20] Other nationalist leaders wanted to use women for political activities, and established women's auxiliaries to their parties or associations. They did not, however, regard women's liberation as a top priority compared to the foremost goal of national liberation.

A good example of the nationalist approach to women's roles may be seen in a book written by Mrs Matiel Mogannam, *The Arab Woman and the Palestine Problem*, published in 1937 shortly before the arrival of the British Royal Commission to Palestine. Introducing her work, Mogannam writes:

The aim of this book is twofold: to present a faithful picture of the Arab woman and to explain the true facts of the Arab case in Palestine. The first parts deals with the Arab woman from two aspects. In addition to a brief study of the Arab woman in the early days of the Moslem era, it explains the social and cultural position which she has attained. It attempts to give a vivid picture of the Arab woman in Palestine, particularly in connection with her national achievements, and explains what little, but useful I hope, work she has done in furtherance of her country's cause since the establishment of the Administration under the British Mandate, abandoning, as she did, the old-aged traditional restrictions in her endeavour to take part in the national movement, at the occasional risk of severe hardships which amounted, in some cases, to personal injury and loss of life.[21]

Mogannam's book contains interesting and important details about women's organizations in Palestine, Syria and Lebanon. In the first part of the book, she cites women who played important roles in the early centuries of Islam in various fields - culture, warfare, politics, religion, etc. Among the female warriors, she mentions 'Hind bint Attabeh' who fought vigorously at the battle of Yarmuk, the seventh-century battle which resulted in Syria and Palestine falling under Muslim rule.[22] Clearly, Hind is meant to be a role model for Palestinian women of the 1930s, but Mogannam does not include some of the less savoury and more controversial aspects of Hind's career (see: selection 2).

The Western women's rights movement did not only influence the writing of Middle Eastern thinkers and political leaders, but Western scholarship on Islam and Middle Eastern history as well. From 1928 (corresponding roughly to the high-point of the Western women's rights movement) until 1946, five scholarly books (and numerous articles) were published by female classical orientalists.[23] These studies are serious works of scholarship that have withstood the test of time but they are not lacking an explicit ideological message. Margaret Smith, for example, in her book on the female mystic Rabi'a al-Adawiyya, writes:

The women saints, a great host, out of whom it has been possible to mention only a few of the most outstanding in the foregoing pages, certainly represent the greatest height to which Muslim womanhood has attained, and in the reverence accorded them by Muslim men and the example which they offer to Muslim women, lies the real hope for the attainment of a higher standard, religious and social, for Muslim women of today ... The modern Muslim woman, even more than man, is outgrowing orthodox Islam. The tendency is, on the one hand, towards religious indifference, on the other towards mysticism, which offers a living religion. It may be that the real grounds of hope for the future, for those who are of the House of Islam, lie in this latter tendency.[24]

Nabia Abbott introduces her book on Aisha the wife of the Prophet Muhammad thus:

> This, as far as I know, the first full-length biography of Aishah, was launched on its way partly by an urge to know and to make known more of the life of the First Lady of Islam and partly as a tribute to the new Moslem world. For progressive Moslems of today, be they Arab or Persian, Indian or Chinese, Mongol or Turk, not only are keenly interested in the problems of the current Moslem woman's movement but show a gratifying curiosity regarding the achievement of the historic women of Islam. Aishah, the most famous of this group, bids fair to be of special interest to the progressives of both East and West in a world so rapidly contracting.[25]

Ilse Lichtenstadter writes in 1935:

> There is one feature in the Arab woman, according to the *aiyam al-'arab,* that seems incompatible with European ideas of the female nature and disposition. This is her capacity not only for enduring the hardships incidental to unceasing tribal feuds, but even of taking an active part in the fight itself.[26]

It is doubtful if such an opinion would be expressed in a similar work in the 1990s.

Marx, Engels and Arab Socialism

Marxism, in general, and Engels' *The Origin of the Family, Private Property, and the State* (1884) have influenced the thought of Middle Eastern socialists, the policies of Arab socialist governments, and the scholarship of some Western scholars on gender relations.

In addressing the question of women in Islam and Middle Eastern history, Marxist, Socialist and Neo-Marxist thinkers project economic determinism onto the role of women. It is the economic system which determines the status of women and the changes which have occurred in the past or will occur in the future. In the Middle Eastern case, great emphasis has been placed on the transition from a bedouin nomad society where there was no immoveable private property to an agrarian-based empire, after the early Islamic conquests. Of course, no one today disputes the role of economics in moulding gender relations, but the relative role of economic factors as opposed to cultural and social influences is still open to debate.

Ideologists and scholars affiliated with the Left also emphasize that since the most outstanding characteristic of any society is its economic class structure, it is important not to generalize about women but to study and analyse differences in the situation of women according to their class. This approach, when accompanied by solid scholarship, has produced some excellent studies of Arab and Muslim women of various classes.[27] Another aspect of the class structure approach is to regard all women as constituting an exploited class in the sense that Fanon viewed all colonial societies. In the 1920s, Soviet theoreticians and decision-makers, for example, aiming to forward the revolution in the Islamic areas of the Soviet Union, regarded Muslim women as surrogates for the proletariat. This was the group who had been most exploited and had suffered most from the existing traditional regime, it was argued, and therefore, they had the greatest interest to mobilize for a deep social and economic revolution.[28] This experiment was abandoned after less than a decade.

Another theme that permeates the rhetoric of the Left is international or Western colonialism or imperialism as the central factor shaping the economy, politics, society and culture of the Middle East, and therefore, the status of women in the Middle East. Some writers argue that women have suffered more than men - economically, politically and socially - from colonialism and imperialism.

Arab socialist movements, such as the Ba'th party which eventually rose to power in Syria and Iraq, gave women's liberation high priority, on principle and for instrumental reasons similar to those of the nationalists. Participation of women in public affairs was deemed essential for the general goal of 'popular democratic participation'. Women's liberation is also necessary for their unique role in raising a new Arab generation.[29] The point of departure for most Arab socialists like their nationalist counterparts is not religious, but all except a few Marxists find the need to ground their ideas in new interpretations of the Quran and the *hadith*.

Arab socialist parties and governments take pride in their position on the advancement of women with some degree of justification. Syria and Iraq, for example, have made considerable progress in women's education.[30] The gap between platform and policy on women's issues as well as the very personal nature of family and gender relations dictate that the implementation of policies be verified and the actual influence on daily life be studied.

Western Feminism, Neo-Islamic Trends and Islamic Feminism

The renewed feminist movement began to influence Western academia in the late 1960s and early 1970s, reaching a peak in the UN Year of Woman in 1975. In the 1970s also a number of research centres on the subject of women were established in the Middle East: The Institute for Women's Studies in the Arab World in Beirut; The Women in Development Centre at al-Azhar Seminary in Cairo; The Centre for Research on Women in Khartoum, etc.

Initially, the focus of women's studies was exclusively the American and European woman. When interest was first aroused in women of other cultures, the trend was usually to include one chapter on 'Women in Islam' or women in a Middle Eastern country. In the latter half of the 1970s, the first studies and anthologies on Middle Eastern women generated by the feminist movement began to appear,[31] and the number of such works has increased enormously since then. At the same time, Middle East experts who amassed material on women as a by-product of their research on other subjects found that there was great interest in their work.[32]

The feminist movement that began in the 1960s influenced the literature on women in Islam and the Middle East in a number of ways. First, it sparked sharp (although not totally justified) criticism of the neglect, stereotypic writing and unfounded generalizations about women in Middle Eastern Studies.[33] Second, Western feminist theories changed the terms of reference by which the status of women in the Middle East was evaluated. One example, was the participation of women in warfare alluded to above. Another was the changing attitude to women's work within the family and outside the home which influenced the attitude toward Middle Eastern women's agricultural work. Third, the new analytical category of gender - implying a rejection of biological determinism; emphasizing cultural, social, political and economic factors which influence relations between men and women; regarding these relations as changing (in the past, and hopefully, in the future) rather than static; including the roles of men as well as those of women in the interplay between them[34] - entered the literature on women in Islam and the Middle East. (Ironically, it has proved difficult if not impossible to translate the term 'gender' into Middle Eastern languages.)

Another impact of the renewed feminist movement of the 1960s on the literature on women in Islam and the Middle East has been frank, sometimes controversial discussions about sexual matters. Sex was never a taboo subject in the Islamic Middle East as selection 15 and many other sources attest. Nevertheless, from the appearance of Nawal al-Sa'dawi's *Women and Sex* in 1972 (in Arabic), a number of works have appeared dealing with sexuality. Abdelwahab Bouhdiba's *Sexuality in Islam* originally appeared in 1975 in French and later in 1985 in English. In 1979, Fatima Mernissi wrote about the operations young Middle Eastern women undergo to restore their virginity before their marriage, and the negative effects of this on future married life as well as on the Arab male, which she terms 'the tragedy of the patriarchal man.'[35] A

Muslim woman writing under the pseudonym Fatna A. Sabbah analysed the images of woman and man in Arabic erotic and legal literature in *Woman in the Muslim Unconscious* (1984, first published in 1982 in French). Bassam Musallam studied the use of contraceptives in the pre-modern Islamic-Arab world (1983) challenging commonly-accepted demography theory in the process. Madelain Farah did the English-reading public a service in 1984 when she published *Marriage and Sexuality in Islam: A Translation of al-Ghazzali's Book on the Etiquette of Marriage from the Ihya'* (from which selection 15 is taken).

Another aspect of the influence of feminism on the literature about women in Islam and the Middle East is the new critical approach to various aspects of the subject of women and development. Until the late 1960s, the common wisdom was that development and modernization of the Third World according to the Western industrial model would solve many problems and bring people a better life. In the late 1960s and early 1970s, critics showed that industrialization and modernization do not necessarily bring the hoped-for results. A number of studies showed that women's situation in many Third World countries actually worsened in the wake of development policies. At first, these findings were explained by unequal access of women and men to new technologies. Since then, the debate on women and development has produced a number of approaches which relate not only to women's problems but to the impact of development in general.[36]

One outcome of the critical approach to the subject of women and development is an increased interest in the status of women in traditional Middle Eastern society prior to modernization in order to provide a basis of comparison for modern changes. In this manner, Aharon Layish has shown that changes legislated by the Israeli Knesset aiming to improve the situation of Muslim women did not always ameliorate the status of women and sometimes even brought about a worsening of their situation. In *Women in Nineteenth Century Egypt,* Judith Tucker documented the exclusion of women from the new field of European medicine because of Western prejudices about women's ability to become physicians despite the fact that Egyptian women had been medical practitioners for centuries. Earl Sullivan, writing about woman entrepreneurs in Egypt, pointed out that there is no obstacle in Islam to women owning property (see: selection 13 and 14).[37]

The neo-Islamic movements, usually referred to by the American Protestant term 'fundamentalism,' originate to a great extent from the ideology of Rashid Rida (1865-1935), one of Muhammad Abduh's disciples, who returned to the primary sources of Islam and fashioned a militant, revivalist view of Islam. The Arab-Israeli War of 1973 and the oil crisis which ensued were a turning point for the neo-Islamic trend, providing it with widespread popular support. For many Muslims, these events were viewed as military and economic victories reflecting the ascendancy of Islam. The establishment of the Islamic Republic in Iran by referendum in 1979 was obviously a watershed event.

Neo-Islamic movements aim to change their own societies, and sometimes their political regimes as well, in accord with Islamic norms (as they perceive them). They regard Islam as a superior, eternal and universal faith and way of life. Thus, the path to liberation of Islamic societies from cultural, social and political domination lies in the return of Muslims to the true values of Islam. Many of these movements have also revived the classical Islamic call to propagate and spread Islam throughout the world whether by persuasion or by belligerent means.

Although these movements have been the subject of much scholarly and popular interest in the West, relatively little attention has been paid to their views on subjects relating to women or on the roles they define for women in their new order (with the notable exception of Iran). Part of the reason for this is that although the neo-Islamic movements differ among themselves in theory and practice, similarity has obscured differences and strident rhetoric has hidden pragmatic practice.

Readers will have an opportunity to taste the internal conflicts on the subject of women in the ideology and organization of two neo-Islamic movements in selection 22 In general terms, these movements regard woman's role in society as biologically-determined (and sometimes psychologically and emotionally as well.) Thus, woman's primary roles are as mother and housewife. Nevertheless, women have a central and active role in guarding Islamic values and transmitting them to their children and other family members. On the ideological level, Islamic movements emphasize the need for female modesty, a degree of separation and limiting women's public roles. The Islamic approach on these issues are considered preferable to Western values which have resulted in promiscuity, pornography and the debasing of woman. In practice, however, women have played a significant role as activists within various Islamic movements. Also, Islamic leaders' attitudes toward women working outside the home, for example, differs in accordance with economic and national need much as in other societies. As a number of observers have noticed, women who have adopted full Islamic dress (as they understand it) are frequently active in politics, economics, culture, etc.

The reason that so many Muslims have abandoned the true Islam, according to the neo-Islamist thinkers, is Western cultural hegemony, specifically the ancient hatred of Western Christians for Islam. This 'Crusader mentality' has been expressed in colonial conquest, missionary activity, cultural colonialism, and Western support for Israel. Some authors refer to a Jewish-Christian plot to undermine Islam. Muslim women are a prime object of this onslaught and the Western (ized) feminist movement is part of this Zionist-Crusader plot. Feminists are 'man-haters' who advocate free sexual relations.[38]

Despite the antipathy of the neo-Islamic movements to Western-style feminism, there is no doubt that their views have been influenced by the debate with the feminist movement. True equality and respect for women may be found within Islam. The Quran, as we have seen, expresses women's equality and the Prophet did much to improve the status of women. The early female believers were actively involved in the struggles of the nascent Islamic community. They supported and aided the early Muslim men to adhere to their faith. In short, Islam does not debase woman (as Western society does) but rather respects her and regards her as different from but equal to man.

The debate between feminists and neo-Islamists has influenced Middle Eastern feminists as well and has produced the first signs of what I would term Islamic feminism. It would seem that Muslim women, some of whom live in the West but some live in the Middle East, have reached the conclusion that in order to improve the status of Middle Eastern women, and Muslim women in general, they must adopt Islamic discourse instead of Western feminist jargon. This is particularly true if they wish to break out of the limits of the Westernized elite and appeal to lower-class women.

Islamic feminism as I understand it is a return to the bedrock of Islam - the Quran, the *hadith* sayings of the Prophet, the biography of the Prophet and his female and male Companions - as well as the laws and customs which derive from them, in an attempt to highlight those traditions which promote women's equality and come to terms with problematic or outright misogynist primary sources. One method of dealing with these sources is by selective quotation. It is for this reason that Fatima Mernissi has established a research centre in Morocco to collect and disseminate Islamic materials supporting women's rights.[39]

More interesting are the attempts to re-interpret primary Islamic sources by feminist or neo-traditional methods. Several Muslim women have attempted feminist exegesis of the Quran, sometimes going so far as to re-interpret the meaning of a crucial word.[40] Feminist criticism of the normative *hadith* sayings of the Prophet has been suggested, and Mernissi has proven two misogynist sayings 'weak' by traditional critical methods.[41] A network of Women Living Under Muslim Laws shares information and supports individual causes. Typically, this group held a woman's study group of the Quran in 1990.[42] Although Islamic feminism is strongly influenced by ideological developments in various Western countries, it also responds to the challenge which indigenous neo-Islamic movements present. In this sense, it is no less an authentic Middle Eastern movement than its competitors.

From the advent of Islam to the neo-Islamic movements and Islamic feminism, in European travel literature and current popular books and films, a conflicting, sometimes confusing, variety of views of Muslim Middle Eastern women are projected. The best introduction to this fascinating subject is to read the primary source material with an open mind, and reread them in a search for alternative meanings. Hopefully, this collection of texts will whet the appetite of the readers and spur them to seek out other Islamic and Middle Eastern materials available in English.

Criteria of Selection, Translations and Format

The readings in this book are excerpts from a variety of genres providing information on various aspects of Muslim women's lives and reflecting differing attitudes from the advent of Islam to the present day. While every attempt has been made to encompass a wide range of sources and to place them in their proper context, the process of selection, consciously or subconsciously, may project certain messages. One criterion of selection was a conscious attempt to reflect the richness, multiple, even contradicting meanings and ambivalence of the Islamic and Middle Eastern sources relating to women. On the other hand, the texts are taken from the major literary tradition of the region, not obscure works or minority opinions. Only the poem which concludes the book is the product of a single, unknown voice.

Another problem in the process of selection is that the excerpts reflect to some extent the interests and areas of expertise of the compiler. Others who study Islam and Middle Eastern history have their own favourite woman, their preferred source, and most interesting of all, their most important question. Clearly, one volume cannot answer everyone's questions and meet all needs.

An additional criterion of selection was the availability of certain sources in English. The reason for this was not merely to reduce the work of translating but rather to enable the reader to proceed from the excerpt in this volume to the work from which it was taken. Also, a number of texts of particular interest to Israelis were available in Hebrew translations. Nevertheless, some texts were translated from the Arabic because of their importance to our subject.

The translations, therefore, were produced over a period from the nineteenth century to today, and for academic, governmental and popular audiences on at least three continents. One problem this entails is a lack of uniformity in the most basic tools of rendering Arabic, Turkish and Persian into English transliteration of names and terminology, and use of diacritical marks. 'A'isha, 'A'ishah, 'Ayisha, Ayse and Aisha - to take one prominent example - are all the same name. In this book, technical changes have been made in the original transliterations in order to maintain a degree of uniformity, and notes have been added to clarify the most important names and terms. In order not to burden the reader who is not familiar with Middle Eastern languages, a minimum of diacritical marks have been used (except in bibliographical references). The ' indicates the letter *'ayn* and the ' the hamza. The c in Turkish (pronounced ch, as opposed to the c pronounced j) has been retained, as has the s (pronounced sh).

On the issue of archaic language, little compromise has been made. Although this may burden the contemporary reader, it also conveys a sense of the times and subliminal messages as well. The classic example is the use of the term Mohammedan (with variant spellings) for believers in Islam which was prevalent until fairly recently. Although the term probably originates as a parallel to Christianity, the believers in Christ, it does not reflect the central beliefs of Islam and may be offensive to Muslims. Calling Muslims Muhammadans implies that they worship the Prophet, when in truth, any compromise of monotheism or the elevation of any individual to the level of partnership with Allah *(shirk)* is considered the most severe sin.

Non-Muslims have not infrequently quoted select Islamic sources to denigrate or mock Islam, or have reported certain details about Middle Eastern society to present it in a negative light (as we have seen). In reaction, some Westerners have projected their own Christian-oriented sensitivities onto Muslims, deciding that certain pieces of information maybe offensive to Muslims. Although certainly no offence was intended, this book aims to maintain a certain distance from the material (if not objectivity) and some Muslims may feel uncomfortable with some of the facts and opinions presented here. For this and other reasons, the selected texts are placed in their historical context and related to their literary genre.

Each text in this collection is preceded by an individual introduction. First the genre which the selection represents is described, and then, the specific source from which the selection was taken is outlined in some detail. In view of the controversial nature of the subject of women in Islam and Middle Eastern history, it is extremely important to place excerpts in their proper context. What proportion of a work deals with women and gender relations? Where is the information or opinions on women located in the format of the work as a whole? What subjects were dealt with immediately before the 'women's section' and immediately after? The answers to these questions often teach us a great deal about the attitudes authors bring to their subjects.

The introductions also contain whatever background information has been deemed necessary to prepare the reader to tackle texts which are surely not easy reading. Questions have been posed - some general, some specific - to guide the reader to some of the ambivalent and even contradictory passages. Clearly, every reading of material of this nature generates new questions. For this reason, the introductions include references to additional secondary material on each subject. More important, they refer the reader to other, similar primary sources available in English.

The order of the various selections is not strictly chronological. The first part deals with the bedrock material of Islam - the Quran, the biography of the Prophet Muhammad and the normative sayings of the Prophet. A dramatic rendition of the death of Fatima, daughter of the Prophet, although of fairly late date aims to reflect the oral tradition of Shi'i Islam.

Part two contains information on two royal women of the first two dynasties of Islamic history, the Umayyads and the Abbasids. These chapters on women in early Islamic history represent two ways that Muslim authors reported events in prominent women's lives - by biography or by interspersing the information in historical chronicles.

After the golden age of the Abbasid Empire, the sparsity of information on Middle Eastern Muslim women precludes linear historical description, dictating an approach more by subject than by date (although some sense of the flow of events and the chronological order of the authors has been retained). Islamic law, the subject of part three, takes pride of place in time and importance. An early legal compendium reflects women's role in the transmission and crystallization of Islamic jurisprudence. The content of this particular selection deals with the symbolic issue of ritual purity and the material subject of property ownership. A later legal guide addresses the circumstances in which women may be witnesses, a question related to their ability to be judges as well. Judges were government appointees, from the time of the early Islamic empires, and therefore, women's competence to be judges and viziers are both dealt with in the context of classical political theory.

Theorists and politicians used religious sources and historical precedent to exclude women not only from *de jure* positions of power but warned against *de facto* influence of women as well. This did not, however, prevent a small number of women from attaining the position of head of state in medieval Islamic polities, nor others from actually ruling from behind the throne. Part four is devoted to ambivalent theoretical stands on women's roles in medieval society and evidence of actual behaviour in politics, spiritual life, education, economics, sexuality and daily life of the common people.

Part five deals with twentieth-century vicissitudes which have impinged on women's lives. Statistical tables on women's education at the turn of the twentieth century and excerpts from the autobiographies of an Ottoman, Turkish feminist and nationalist bridge the traditional and twentieth-century worlds. A number of selections attempt to briefly reflect multiple, sometimes ambivalent, and often contradictory views on women in the Middle East and Islam in the twentieth century. The book concludes with a short poem which has a culture-specific format but a universal message.

Notes

1.   Shortly after the world-wide success of the Disney film *Aladdin* featuring Princess Jasmin, the paperback *Princess,* the story of an anonymous woman of the Saudi royal house, was on the *New York Times* best-seller list (October, 1993).

2.   33 *(al-Ahzab):35.*

3.   Amina Wadud-Muhsin, *Qur'an and Woman* (Kuala Lumpur: Penerbit Fajar Bakti SDN, BHD, 1992).

4.   Muhammad ibn Isma'il al-Bukhari, *The Translation of the Meanings of Sahih al-Bukhari: Arabic-English,* Al-Medina: Islamic University, 1973-76, 88 *(Kitab al-Fatn):18* cf. 59 *(al-Maghazi):82.*

5.   Fatima Mernissi, *The Veil and the Male Elite: A Feminist Interpretation of Women's Rights in Islam* trans. Mary Jo Lakeland (Reading, Mass.: Addison-Wesley, 1991); originally appeared in 1987 in French as *Le Harem politique.*

6.   Bukhari, 3 *(Kitab al-'Ilm):51.*

7.   Ruth Roded, *Women in Islamic Biographical Collections From Ibn Sa'd to Who's Who* (Boulder & London: Lynne Rienner, 1994), pp. 15-43 deals with the number and proportion of biographies of the female Companions of the Prophet and the rationales for their inclusion in the biographical dictionaries. Only the most prominent of these women have been the subject of in-depth study.

8.   Annemarie Schimmel, 'Women in Mystical Islam,' *Women's Studies International Forum* 5 (1982): 146-7.

9.   Margaret Smith, *Rabia the Mystic and Her Fellow Saints in Islam* (Cambridge: Cambridge University Press, 1984), pp. xxxii-xxxiii, 2,4.

10.   When Golda Meir served in David Ben Gurion's cabinet, a story circulated that he called her 'the only real man in my government.'

11.   G. H. A. Juynboll, 'Some *Isnad*-Analytical Methods Illustrated on the Basis of Several Woman-Demeaning Sayings from *Hadith* Literature,' *al-Qantara* 10 (1989):34-84; Leila Ahmed, *Women and Gender in Islam* (New Haven: Yale University Press, 1992).

12.   Norman Daniel, *Islam and the West: The Making of an Image* (Edinburgh: The University Press, 1960), pp. 141, 320. I am indebted to Professor B. Z. Kedar for bringing this material to my attention.

13.   Henry Harris Jessup, *The Women of the Arabs* (New York: Dodd & Mead, 1873), pp. 8-9.

14.   Mark Twain, *The Innocents Abroad* (London: Collins, 1869), pp. 226-7.

15.   Mary Eliza Rogers, *Domestic Life in Palestine* (London: Bell and Daldy, 1862), pp. 218-19; Cf. Isabel Burton, *The Inner Life of Syria, Palestine and the Holy Land* (London: King, 1875), pp. 148-50.

16.   Lucy M. J. Garnett, *The Women of Turkey and Their Folk-lore* (London: David Nutt, 1893), pp. 382-417. This book contains much valuable information which has since been verified from Ottoman sources.

17.   Edward Lane, *The Manners and Customs of the Modern Egyptians* (London: Dent, 1908), p. 166.

18.   Judy Mabro has published an anthology of selections relating to women from European travel books entitled *Veiled Half-Truths: Western Travellers' Perceptions of Middle Eastern Women* (London: Tauris, 1991). Billie Melman, *Women's Orients: English Women and the Middle East, 1718-1918* (Howdmills, Basingstoke: Macmillan, 1992).

19.   Qasim Amin, *Tahrir al-Mar'a*, pp. 131-2.

20.   Yvonne Haddad, 'Islam, Women and Revolution in Twentieth Century Arab Thought,' *The Muslim World* 74 (1984):145.

21.   Matiel Mogannam, *The Arab Woman and the Palestine Problem* (London: H. Joseph, 1937), p. 11.

22.   Mogannam, p. 25.

23.   Margaret Smith, *Rabi'a the Mystic and Her Fellow Saints in Islam* (Cambridge: Cambridge University Press, 1928); Ilse Lichtenstadter, *Women in the Aiyam al-'Arab: A Study of Female Life During Warfare in Pre-Islamic Arabia* (London: Royal Asiatic Society, 1935); Gertrude Stern, *Marriage in Early Islam* (London: Royal Asiatic Society, 1939); Nabia Abbott, *Aishah: The Beloved of Muhammad* (Chicago: Arno Press, 1942); *Two Queens of Baghdad: Mother and Wife of Harun al-Rashid* (Chicago: Chicago University Press, 1946).

24.   Smith, pp. 203-4, 204.

25.   Abbott, *Aishah*, p. ix.

26.   Lichtenstadter, p. 79.

27.   Judith E. Tucker, *Women in Nineteenth Century Egypt* (Cambridge: Cambridge University Press, 1985); Margaret L. Meriwhether, 'Women and Economic Change in Nineteenth-Century Syria: The Case of Aleppo,' *Arab Women: Old Boundaries, New Frontiers* ed. Judith E. Tucker (Bloomington and Indianapolis: Indiana University Press, 1993), pp. 65-83.

28.   Gregory J. Massell, *The Surrogate: Proletariat Moslem Women and Revolutionary Struggles in Soviet Central Asia, 1919-1929* (Princeton: Princeton University Press, 1974).

29.   Haddad, 'Islam, Women and Revolution,' p. 147.

30.   Valentine M. Moghadam, *Modernizing Women: Gender and Social Change in the Middle East* (Boulder, CO: Lynne Reinner, 1993), pp. 122,128.

31.   Among the first were: Elizabeth W. Fernea and B. Q. Bezirgan, eds. *Middle Eastern Muslim Women Speak* (Austin: University of Texas Press, 1977); Lois Beck and Nikki Keddie, eds, *Women in the Muslim World* (Cambridge: Harvard University Press, 1978).

32.   Ronald C. Jennings, 'Women in Early Seventeenth Century Ottoman Judicial Records - The Sharia Court of Anatolian Kayseri,' *Journal of the Economic and Social History of the Orient* 18 (1975):51-114; Haim Gerber, 'Social and Economic Position of Women in an Ottoman City, Bursa, 1600-1700,' *International Journal of Middle East Studies* 12 (1980):231-

44. Abraham Marcus and I revealed archival and quantitative data on women's economic activities in eighteenth and nineteenth century Aleppo as a by-product of other aspects of our research. Marcus, 'Piety and Profit: The Waqf in the Society and Economy of Eighteenth Century Aleppo' and Roded, 'The Waqf in Ottoman Aleppo: A Quantitative Analysis,' were both written simultaneously but independently of each other in 1978 and are scheduled to appear in *Social and Economic Aspects of the Muslim Waqf,* eds. Gabriel Baer and Gad Gilbar.

33. Nikki Keddie,' Problems in the Study of Middle Eastern Women,' *International Journal of Middle East Studies* 10 (1979): 225-40; Judith E. Tucker, 'Problems in the Historiography of Women in the Middle East: The Case of Nineteenth-Century Egypt,' *International Journal of Middle Eastern Studies* 15 (1983): 321-36.

34. Jill K. Conway, Susan C. Bourque and Joan W. Scott, 'Introduction: The Concept of Gender,' *Daedalus* 116 (1987):xxi-xxix.

35. 'Virginity and Patriarchy,' in *Women and Islam* ed. Azizah al-Hibri (Oxford: Pergamon Press, 1982), pp. 183-91 (from *Lamalif* 107 (1979).

36. See, for example: Susan C. Bourque and Kay B. Warren, 'Technology, Gender and Development,' *Daedalus* 116 (1987):173-97.

37. Aharon Layish, *Women and Islamic Law in a Non-Muslim State: A Study Based on Decisions of the Shari'a Courts in Israel* (New York and Toronto: John Wiley and Sons, 1975); Tucker, *Women in Nineteenth Century Egypt;* Earl L. Sullivan, *Women in Egyptian Public Life* (Syracuse: Syracuse University Press, 1986).

38. Haddad, 'Islam, Women and Revolution,' pp. 149-55.

39. Projet Promotion Femmes, Rabat, Maroc.

40. Aziza al-Hibri,'A Study of Islamic Herstory,' *Women's Studies International Forum* 5 (1982):217.

41. Fatima Mernissi, *The Veil and the Male Elite: A Feminist Interpretation of Women's Rights* trans. Mary Jo Lakeland (Reading, Mass.: Addison-Wesley, 1991), pp. 49-81.

42. A brief description of the origin, goals and projects of this women's network in a Muslim context may be found in: Marieme Helie-Lucas, 'The experience of networking at the international solidarity network Women Living Under Muslim Laws,' *International Documentation and Communication Centre: Women Voices Worldwide 2* (1994): 7-15. In July, 1990, thirty women activists and resource persons from ten different countries met to 'read for themselves the verses of the Qur'an related to women.'

PART ONE

THE FOUNDATIONS OF ISLAM

Muhammad received divine revelation and embarked on his mission as a prophet at a certain historical time and in a specific geographical and social setting. The founding materials of Islam thus reflect the situation of women in a seventh-century Middle Eastern society. These sources are also regarded as eternal truths by Muslims, shaping their attitudes and behaviour in a wide variety of fields, not the least of which is women's roles.

Over fifteen centuries, belief in Islam - the religion of Allah and His Prophet -has united a myriad of very different Islamic societies in vastly different geographical and cultural settings. The unique circumstances of each of these societies has impinged on the reading of the fundamental Islamic sources as well as the everyday reality of women's lives. The bedrock materials of Islam are the Quran, the word of Allah as revealed to Muhammad, amplified and complemented by the normative sayings and deeds *(hadith)* of the Prophet. The life story of the Prophet Muhammad provides models for proper behaviour, legal and customary precedents, and Quranic exegesis. The Shi'i sect has its own traditions in which martyrology plays a prominent role.

1

THE QURAN : DIFFERING INTERPRETATION OF
THE DIVINE WORD

[Marmaduke Pickthall, *The Meaning of the Glorious Koran* (New York: Dorset Press, n.d) *24(al-Nur):* 30-1; *33(al-Ahzab):* 32-3, 53, 59; 4(*al-Nisa'*):34-5.]

Much of the Quran is difficult to understand because of obscure references as well as the traditional arrangement of chapters and verses in which unrelated passages are interspersed. As a result, philological analysis and additional information obtained from the Prophet's Companions were utilized to explain and amplify the meaning of the revealed text. In theory, this imprecision should enable alternate readings of the legal and normative material in the Quran. In fact, classical exegetes created a mainstream Islamic interpretation of the Quran which was handed down from generation to generation. In the nineteenth and early twentieth century, Muslim scholars rejected the acquired wisdom as foreign and customary accretions and returned to the text of the Quran in search of true Islam. In recent years, there have been some modest attempts at feminist exegesis of certain passages of the Quran.

Only one woman is actually named in the Quran, but a large number of verses refer to women. These include exhortations addressed to 'the believing men and the believing women', revelations specific to women or to relations between men and women, and laws pertinent to marriage, divorce, inheritance, etc. According to one estimate, some 80 per cent of the legal material in the Quran refers to women.

It is interesting to note that according to Islamic tradition a number of women among the early believers had a role in the transmission of the text of the Quran. Aisha, the Prophet's favourite wife, heard passages of the Quran from the Prophet himself, ordered a full written copy to be prepared and corrected the scribe. Hafsa, daughter of the caliph Umar and widow of the Prophet, gave written pages of the Quran which she received from her father to the caliph Uthman. Uthman gathered the pages into a book and declared this text as the official version of the holy book. She also corrected a scribe who was writing a Quran. During the first four centuries of Islam, Uthman's text was only one of various versions of the Quran which were ascribed to Companions of the Prophet, the caliphs Umar and Ali, and widows of the Prophet -Aisha, Umm Salama and Hafsa. One of the Prophet's female Companions, Umm Waraqa, collected and recited the Quran and may have assisted Umar in assembling the text.

The first four excerpts below are the basis of the concept of *hijab* in the sense of the appropriate attire for Muslim women, their seclusion at home and the limitation of their contact with men who are not their kin. This subject has been and continues to be one of the central issues related to the status of women in Islamic Middle Eastern society.

Some specific questions arise from each of these verses. In The Light *(al-Nur):* 30-1, men and women are told to be modest. Is there a difference in the exhortations to the genders? What are women's adornment which should not be displayed? What sort of veils are referred to; what should they cover? Verses 32-3 and 53 of the chapter The Clans *(al-Ahzab)* refer to the wives of the Prophet. Should these regulations be inferred for all Muslim women? What is the definition of *hijab* in the context of the Quran? To whom is verse 59 addressed? What are the cloaks, also translated 'outer garments' *(jalabib, s.jilbab)?* Why should women 'draw them close round'?

The general questions which relate to all of the verses are: According to the text of the Quran, must a believing Muslim woman remain in her home? Must she be separated from men who are not her kin inside the house? What should she wear when she leaves the house? According to the Quran, what is Islamic dress? What should it cover? What may one reveal?

No less crucial are the classical, modernist and feminist interpretations of the opening phrase of verse 34, The Women, which the British Muslim Marmaduke Pickthall translated 'Men are in charge of women' *(al-rijal qawwamuna 'ala al-nisa').* Classical exegesis explained this phrase as referring to the superiority of men over women in a number of religious, political and intellectual fields, and it was frequently quoted to justify the exclusion of women from positions of authority over men (see selections 9 and 10). The modernist Muslim translator and commentator A. Yusuf Ali renders the phrase: 'Men are the protectors and maintainers of women.' The Muslim feminist Azizah al-Hibri takes the definition of *qawwamun* one step further to the concept of moral guidance and caring.

Another thorny issue is the seeming recommendation in the Quran to 'scourge' disobedient wives. Within the framework of the ethical message of Islam, classical Muslim scholars tried to protect women from undue violence from men but they did not question a man's right to use force to chastise his wife. Yusuf Ali builds on this tradition when he translates the verse: 'As to those women on whose part ye fear disloyalty and ill-conduct, admonish them (first), (next), refuse to share their beds, (and last) beat them (lightly);' If these three measures fail, Yusuf Ali adds, then a family council should be convened in accordance with the next verse (4:35) in order to work out the couples problems. Verse 35 of 'The Women' is usually quoted by Muslims to offset husbands' almost unilateral right to divorce their wives in a simple and informal procedure as defined in Islamic law.

From the voluminous bibliography on the *hijab,* a solid foundation may be found in *The Encyclopaedia of Islam* and Gertrude H. Stern, *Marriage in Early Islam* (London: Royal Asiatic Society, 1939). Alternative readings of these verses are given by: Mark N. Swanson, 'A Study of Twentieth-Century Commentary on Surat al-Nur (24):27-33,' *The Muslim World* 74 (1984): 187-203; Mostafa Hashem Sherif, 'What is *Hijab?' The Muslim World* 77 (1987): 151-63, and Fatima Mernissi, *The Veil and the Male Elite: A Feminist Interpretation ofWomen's Rights in Islam* trans. Mary Jo Lakeland (Reading, Mass.: Addison-Wesley, 1991) which originally appeared in French as *Le Harem politique* in 1987.

The implications of varying exegesis of a Quranic verse is also demonstrated in M. Hashim Kamali, 'Divorce and Women's Rights: Some Muslim Interpretations of S. 2:228,' *Muslim World* (1984). A careful reading of 4 (Women): 3 may reveal the modernist interpretation which concludes that in fact the Quran forbids polygamy.

A feminist exegesis of the Quran as a totality is Amina Wadud-Muhsin's *Qur'an and Woman* (Kuala Lumpur: Peberbit Fajar Bakti SDN. BHD., 1992).

The Quran

Surah XXIV Light

30. Tell the believing men to lower their gaze and be modest. That is purer for them. Lo! Allah is Aware of what they do.
31. And tell the believing women to lower their gaze and be modest, and to display of their adornment only that which is apparent, and to draw their veils over their bosoms, and not to reveal their adornment save to their own husbands or fathers or husbands' fathers, or their sons or their husbands' sons, or their

brothers or their brothers' sons or sisters' sons, or their women, or their slaves, or male attendants who lack vigour, or children who know naught of women's nakedness. And let them not stamp their feet so as to reveal what they hide of their adornment. And turn unto Allah together, O believers, in order that ye may succeed.

Surah XXXIII The Clans

32. O ye wives of the Prophet! Ye are not like any other women. If ye keep your duty (to Allah) then be not soft of speech, lest he in whose heart a disease aspire (to you), but utter customary speech.
33. And stay in your houses. Bedizen not yourselves with the bedizenment of the Time of Ignorance. Be regular in prayer, and pay the poor-due, and obey Allah and His messenger. Allah's wish is but to remove uncleanness far from you ...

53. O ye who believe! Enter not the dwellings of the Prophet for a meal without waiting for the proper time, unless permission be granted you. But if ye are invited, enter, and, when your meal is ended, then disperse. Linger not for conversation. Lo! that would cause annoyance to the Prophet, and he would be shy of (asking) you (to go); but Allah is not shy of the truth. And when ye ask of them (the wives of the Prophet) anything, ask it of them from behind a curtain [*min wara hijab* RR]. That is purer for your hearts and for their hearts. And it is not for you to cause annoyance to the messenger of Allah, nor that ye should ever marry his wives after him. Lo! that in Allah's sight would be an enormity.

59. O Prophet! Tell thy wives and thy daughters and the women of the believers to draw their cloaks [*jalabib, s.jilbab* RR] close round them (when they go abroad). That will be better, that so they may be recognized and not annoyed. Allah is ever Forgiving, Merciful.

Surah IV Women

34. Men are in charge [*qawwamuna* RR] of women, because Allah hath made the one of them to excel the other, and because they spend of their property (for the support of women). So good women are the obedient, guarding in secret that which Allah hath guarded. As for those whom ye fear rebellion, admonish them and banish them to beds apart, and scourge them. Then if they obey you, seek not a way against them. Lo! Allah is ever High Exalted,

Great.

35. And if ye fear a breach between them twain (the man and wife), appoint an arbiter from his folk and an arbiter from her folk. If they desire amendment Allah will make them one mind. Lo! Allah is ever Knower, Aware.

2

THE BIOGRAPHY OF THE PROPHET :

WOMEN IN BATTLE

[A. Guillaume, trans. *The Life of Muhammad: A Translation of lbn Ishaq's Sirat Rasul Allah* (Oxford: Oxford University Press, 1955), pp. 370-91, 755.]

The biography of the Prophet is one of the earliest types of historical writing produced in Arabic. This genre developed from stories about raids and campaigns *(maghazi)* undertaken by the early Muslims under Muhammad's leadership which paralleled tales of the military prowess of pre-Islamic Arabian tribes. As a result, much of the biography is devoted to descriptions of military forays, although other aspects of the Prophet's life are also dealt with.

The three most famous women in Islam are Khadija, Aisha and Fatima, wives and daughter of the Prophet. Khadija was a mature widow when she married the younger Muhammad and so long as she lived, he took no other wives. After the first divine revelation, she supported the Prophet both morally and materially. Muhammad had no sons who survived infancy, and information about his daughters is meagre. Nevertheless, Fatima, who was married to Ali, Muhammad's cousin and heir according to Shi'i beliefs, has been revered by Sunnis and Shi'is alike (see below selections 4 and 22).

Aisha, daughter of Muhammad's confidant Abu Bakr, is universally regarded as his favourite wife after Khadija. She was married to the Prophet while still a minor, the marriage was consummated several years later, and she was only eighteen years old at the time of his death. Nevertheless, her proximity to the Prophet (and perhaps her own talents) made her a crucial authority on Muhammad's words and deeds (see next chapter). She also appears prominently in Quranic exegesis, and in connection with legal and customary precedents. She did not, however, have much influence on the Prophet's political decisions until his dying days, which he spent in her room. She lived more than forty years after the Prophet's death, and played a symbolic and controversial role in the opposition to the third caliph Uthman and the rebellion against his successor Ali. This uprising, the first intra-Muslim conflict, ended in the Battle of the Camel - so named because Aisha's mount was deliberately disabled in the midst of the battlefield to motivate the warriors. This practice was a pre-Islamic custom which in essence challenged the men to fight to the death to protect the life of a noble woman.

Khadija, Fatima and Aisha are the most prominent women associated with the life of the Prophet Muhammad, but numerous other Muslim women of the first generation are memorialized in biographies and other sources, not all of whom were relatives of the Prophet. Over twelve hundred women who were in Muhammad's presence, were witnesses or actors in events connected to him, and related his sayings and actions appear in the Islamic sources. They represent roughly 10 to 15 per cent of the biographies of the Companions of the Prophet.

Ibn Ishaq (85-151/704-767) composed the earliest extant biography of the Prophet, based on earlier oral sources. He himself was of the third generation after the Prophet. The work has come down to us in the edited version of Ibn Hisham (died 218/833 or 213/828) whose notes explain or amplify the text. Women do not feature as prominently in Ibn Ishaq's work as in some other early Islamic sources because of the emphasis on Muhammad's military exploits rather than his legal judgements or normative behaviour.

The Battle of Uhud is one of the few military engagements in which women took an active role. Sometime after the flight of the early Muslims from Mecca to Medina *(hijra),* the conflict between Muhammad and his opponents took on a military dimension and a series of raids and battles ensued. In 624, Muhammad led an attack on the caravan to Mecca which culminated in a great political victory for the fledgling Muslim community- the Battle of Badr.

One year later, the Meccans marshalled a large army to avenge their losses at Badr. They were led by the Meccan tribe of Quraysh, the tribe of Muhammad, the Apostle of God. In the following selection, they are referred to as 'the unbelieving Quraysh,' in other words the pagans who did not accept Islam. The Meccan forces were commanded by Abu Sufyan son of Harb accompanied by his wife Hind daughter of Utba whose father, brother, uncle and oldest son had been killed at Badr. Hind later converted to Islam when the Muslims conquered Mecca, and her son Mu'awiya was the fifth successor to Muhammad as leader of the Islamic state and founder of the Umayyad dynasty. Although Hind was still a polytheist at the Battle of Uhud, the readers of Ibn Ishaq's work were well aware that she was Mu'awiya's mother. Before the Meccans went out to battle, a black slave named Wahshi was promised his freedom if he would kill Hamza, Muhammad's uncle, a hero of the Muslims who had killed many pagans at Badr.

The Quraysh camped on a hillside of a valley *(wadi)* near Mount Uhud outside Medina. After some deliberation, Muhammad and his supporters left the city to meet them. When the sides drew near, Hind led the Quraysh women in a battle-song. During the battle, Muhammad's uncle Hamza displayed his courage in the cause of Islam but Wahshi did manage to kill him. The situation was so desperate that it was believed that the Prophet himself had been killed. Sulafa, mother of warriors, and the wife of the hero Hanzala are referred to briefly and obliquely in Ibn Ishaq's narrative but their images provide us with another view of women and war. Then God sent help to the Muslims and the women of the enemy began to flee, but a woman named Amra raises the standard for Quraysh.

The tide again turns against the Muslims and man after man is killed trying to protect the Prophet. In the fray, Muhammad's tooth is broken and his face bloodied. Ibn Hisham notes the famous story of Nusayba daughter of Ka'b (also known as Umm Umara) who fought with sword and bow to protect the Prophet. The narrative focuses on Muhammad's fate and the exploits of various warriors but we are also informed inter alia of two old men who were sent up into the forts with the women and children.

As the polytheists retreat, Hind and the Quraysh women stop to mutilate the bodies of the fallen Muslims and she commits the act which earned Mu'awiya the epithet 'son of the liver eater'. As the battle draws to a close, the Muslims find the mutilated bodies of their dead comrades. Hamna daughter of Jahsh displays exemplary behaviour at the news of the death of her kin. Hamna's response also contains an important message about the relative importance to a woman of her brother, her maternal uncle and her husband. In this context, different views about women lamenting the dead are expressed. Muhammad's daughter Fatima makes a brief appearance. As the Muslim men go out in pursuit of the enemy, another attitude toward women during warfare is expressed when we learn that Jabir son of Abdallah was left behind to look after his sisters.

Ibn Ishaq's detailed description of the events is not easy reading but it is regarded by Muslims as a normative narrative to this day. In this work, the typically-Islamic method of oral transmission of information is utilized although not as rigorously as in other fields (see the next selection). Differing reports of events in the life of the Prophet Muhammad were transmitted from eye-witnesses and collected by learned traditionists. Muslim scholars, aware of human limitations, hesitated to judge the validity of crucial but sometimes contradictory fragments of information, so they tended to relate as many different versions as they heard, leaving the final judgement to a superior intellect (of Allah Himself). Ibn Ishaq did attempt to weave these fragments into a narrative but the results are still quite choppy. Moreover, the names of the eye-witnesses and traditionists who transmitted this material may be of little interest to the modern reader but was of crucial importance to Muslim scholars as the basis for evaluating the work. Women - such as Umm Sa'd daughter of Sa'd quoted in the following passage - were considered reliable informants about events in the Prophet's life.

Another characteristic of classical Arabic prose found in the following selection (and others) is the interspersion of poetry in the narrative. Verse is the foremost literary expression of the Arabs before and after the advent of Islam. It probably developed as a convenient medium to orally retain information as well as convey feelings in a non-literate society. The important social, political and even military roles of poets - male and female - are demonstrated in the description of the battle of Uhud.

Islam appeared in a tribal society in which tribes ascribed themselves to an eponymic ancestor and therefore were referred to as the Sons of Abdu Manat or in the Arabic original the Banu Kinana. Individuals were identified by a lineage which cited their father, grandfather and as many previous generations of forefathers as possible. Paternal lineage was more important but maternal descent was sometimes cited and could even be crucial. A man would normally be cited as Abu Sufyan son of Harb, or Muhammad son of Yahya son of Hibban but individual genealogies could stretch back for many generations. (For the sake of brevity, 'son of' or *ibn* in Arabic is usually noted as b.) Women, even after they were married, were usually ascribed to their father's patrilineage, such as Sulafa daughter of Sa'd son of Shuhayd. Another form of identification prevalent in Arab society, in the past and in the present, is an agnomen (*kunya*) which usually relates to the oldest son but can also refer to an outstanding characteristic or achievement. Thus, Abu Sufyan is the father of Sufyan and Umm Sa'd is the mother of Sa'd but Abu Dasma, the *kunya* of the black slave Wahshi, means father of darkness.

Ibn Ishaq's description of the battle of Uhud addresses a number of questions about women in warfare. What roles did women fulfil in the early Islamic battles? Under what circumstances did they actually fight? How are women generally viewed in the context of warfare? The arch-villain of this story, Hind, is magnificent in her fury, overshadowing the devout Muslim women. What explains Hind's vengeance against Hamza? Is her act regarded as a common practice or unusual? Is it accepted or condemned? Another issue which has been raised in recent years is the Prophet's reluctance to attack the Meccans. How can this reluctance be interpreted? In the course of the fighting, Hamza challenges Siba son of Abdu'l-Uzza. What can we learn from the form and content of Hamza's address? What is the message of Hamna's story; who is the most important man in a woman's life and why? Finally, why is lamentation a female specialization, and why is its permissibility debatable?

Background and comparative information on the role of women in the pre-Islamic nomadic environment may be found in Ilse Lichtenstadter, *Women in the Aiyam al-'Arab: A Study of Female Life during Warfare in Pre-Islamic Arabia* (London: Royal Asiatic Society, 1935).

Since Ibn Ishaq, innumerable Muslim authors have copied or composed biographies of the Prophet. Biographical collections and histories often opened with lengthy biographies of Muhammad. It is interesting to compare various depictions of the Prophet's life aimed at differing audiences. In response to Christian slanderers of Islam and some Western critical works on the Prophet, the modern Egyptian author Muhammad Husayn Haykal wrote *The Life of Muhammad* which was widely-published in Arabic from the 1930s and translated into English by Isma'il Ragi A. al-Faruqi (North American Trust Publications, 1976). The English edition also contains a bibliography of works in English on Muhammad's life. Two Muslim women, Leila Azzam and Aisha Gouverneur, have produced *The Life of the Prophet Muhammad* (Cambridge, England: The Islamic Texts Society, 1985) for youngsters. While remaining faithful to Ibn Ishaq's description of the battle of Uhud and the role of women, they also emphasize the Prophet's message of peace. A far more belligerent version of the battle of Uhud, in the form of audio-cassettes, is described and analysed in Audrey C.Shalinsky 'Women's Roles in the Afghanistan Jihad,' *International Journal of Middle East Studies* 25 (1993) 661-75. Arabic and English-language film biographies of the Prophet titled *'The Message (al-Risala)* were simultaneously produced by Muslim film-makers in 1976.

Ibn Ishaq's Biography of the Prophet

The Battle of Uhud

I have pieced together the following story about the battle of Uhud, from what I was told by Muhammad b. [=son of] Muslim al-Zuhri and Muhammad son of Yahya b. Hibban and Asim son of Umar b. Qatada and al-Husayn son of Abdu'l-Rahman b. Amr b. Sa'd b. Mu'adh and other learned traditionists. One or the other, or all of them, is responsible for the following narrative. When the unbelieving Quraysh met disaster at Badr and the survivors returned to Mecca and Abu Sufyan the son of Harb had returned with his caravan, Abdullah b. Abu Rabi'a and Ikrima b. Abu Jahl and Safwan b. Umayya walked with the

men whose fathers, sons, and brothers had been killed at Badr, and they spoke
to Abu Sufyan and those who had merchandise in that caravan, saying, 'Men
of Quraysh, Muhammad has wronged you and killed your best men, so help
us with this money to fight him, so that we may hope to get our revenge for
those we have lost,' and they did so ...

So Quraysh gathered together to fight the apostle when Abu Sufyan did
this, and the owners of the caravan, with their black troops, and such of the
tribes of Kinana as would obey them, and the people of the low country ...
Abu Azza [a poet] went through the low country calling the Banu Kinana [tribe]
and saying:

> Listen, Sons of Abdu Manat, the steadfast,
> You are stout warriors like your father,
> Do not promise me your help a year hence,
> Do not betray me, for betrayal is not right.

Musafi son of Abdu Manat b. Wahb b. Hudhafa b. Jumah went out to the Sons of
Malik b. Kinana [tribe] stirring them up and calling them to fight the
apostle, saying:

> O Malik, Malik, foremost in honour,
> I ask in the name of kindred and confederate,
> Those who are next-of-kin and those who are not,
> In the name of the alliance in the midst of the holy city,
> At the wall of the venerable Ka'ba.

Jubayr son of Mut'im summoned an Abyssinian slave of his called Wahshi, who
could throw a javelin as the Abyssinians do and seldom missed the mark.
He said, 'Go forth with the army, and if you kill Hamza, Muhammad's uncle,
in revenge for my uncle, Tu'ayma b. Adiy, you shall be free.' So Quraysh marched
forth with the flower of their army, and their black troops, and their adherents.
from the Banu Kinana [tribe], and the people of the lowland, and women in
howdahs went with them to stir up their anger and prevent their running away.
Abu Sufyan, who was in command, went out with Hind daughter of Utba [his
wife], and Ikrima son of Abu Jahl went with Umm Hakim daughter of
al-Harith son of Hisham b. al-Mughira; and al-Harith son of Hisham b.
al-Mughira went with Fatima daughter of al-Walid son of al-Mughira; and
Safwan went with Barza daughter of Mas'ud son of Amr b. Umayr the Thaqafite
who was the mother of Abdullah b. Safwan b. Umayya. [Ibn Hisham notes:
Others say her name was Ruqayya.] Amr son of al-As went with Rayta daughter
of Munabbih son of al-Hajjaj who was Umm [mother of] Abdullah b. Amr.

Talha b. Abdullah b. Abdu'1-Uzza b. Uthman b. Abdu'1-Dar went with Sulafa daughter of Sa'd son of Shuhayd al-Ansariya who was mother of the sons of Talha, Musafi, al- Julas and Kilab; they were killed with their father that day. Khunas daughter of Malik son al-Mudarrib, one of the women of the Banu Malik b. Hisl [tribe] went with her son Abu Aziz b. Umayr. She was the mother of Mus'ab b. Umayr. Amra daughter of Alqama, one of the women of the [tribe of] Banu al-Harith b. Abdu Manat b. Kinana went out. Whenever Hind passed Wahshi or he passed by her, she would say, 'Come on, you father of blackness, satisfy your vengeance and ours.' Wahshi had the title of Abu Dasma. They [the unbelieving Quraysh] went forward until they halted at Aynayn on a hill in the valley of al-Sabkha of Qanat by the side of the wadi opposite Medina.

When the apostle heard about them, he said to them, 'By God, I have seen (in a dream) something that augurs well. I saw cows, and I saw a dent in the blade of my sword, and I saw that I had thrust my hand into a strong coat of mail and I interpreted that to mean Medina. If you think it well to stay in Medina and leave them where they have encamped, for if they halt they will have halted in a bad position and if they try to enter the city, we can fight them therein, (that is a good plan).' Abdullah b. Ubayy b. Salul agreed with the apostle in this, and thought that they should not go out to fight them, and the apostle himself disliked the idea of leaving the city. Some men whom God honoured with martyrdom at Uhud and others who were not present at Badr said, 'O Apostle of God, lead us forth to our enemies, lest they think that we are too cowardly and too weak to fight them.' Abdullah said, 'O apostle of God, stay in Medina, do not go out to them. We have never gone out to fight an enemy but we have met disaster, and none has come in against us without being defeated, so leave them where they are. If they stay, they stay in an evil predicament, and if they come in, the men will fight them and the women and children will throw stones on them from the walls, and if they retreat they will retreat low-spirited as they came.' Those who wanted to fight Quraysh kept urging the apostle until he went into his house and put on his armour.

[The Prophet decides finally to lead the Muslims out of Medina to fight the Meccan Quraysh. They arrive at Uhud with an army of about 700 men including archers and cavalry. They faced a force of Quraysh consisting of about 3,000 men with 200 horses which they had led along with them. Before the battle, the Prophet gives his sword to Abu Dujana Simak b. Kharasha.]

Abu Sufyan had said to the standard-bearers of the Banu Abdu'1-Dar [tribe], inciting them to battle, 'O Banu Abdu'1-Dar, you had charge of our flag on the day of Badr - you saw what happened. Men are dependent on the fortunes of their flags, so either you must guard our standard efficiently or you must leave it to us and we will save you the trouble (of defending) it.' They pondered over the matter and threatened him, saying, Are we to surrender our flag to you? You will see tomorrow how we shall act when battle is joined' and that was just what Abu Sufyan wanted. When each side drew near to the other Hind daughter of Utba rose up with the women that were with her and took tambourines which they beat behind the men to incite them while Hind was saying:

> On ye Sons of Abdu'1-Dar,
> On protectors of our rear,
> Smite with every sharpened spear!

She also said:

> If you advance we hug you,
> Spread soft rugs beneath you;
> If you retreat we leave you,
> Leave and no more love you[1].

The people went on fighting until the battle grew hot, and Abu Dujana fought until he had advanced far into the enemy's ranks.

Whenever he met one of the enemy he killed him. Now among the pagans there was a man who dispatched every man of ours he wounded. These two men began to draw near one to the other, and I prayed God that He would make them meet. They did meet and exchanged blows, and the polytheist struck at Abu Dujana, who warded off the blow with his shield; his sword sank into the shield so that he could not withdraw it, and Abu Dujana struck him and killed him. Then I saw him as his sword hovered over the head of Hind daughter of Utba. Then he turned it aside from her. Al-Zubayr said, 'And I said, 'God and His apostle know best.'

Abu Dujana said, 'I saw a person inciting the enemy, shouting violently, and I made for him, and when I lifted my sword against him, he shrieked, and lo, it was a woman; I respected the apostle's sword too much to use it on a woman.'

Hamza fought until he killed Arta b. Abdu Shurahbil b. Hashim b. Abdu Manaf b. Abdu'1-Dar who was one of those who were carrying the standard. Then Siba b. Abdu'1-Uzza al-Ghubshani, who was known as Abu Niyar, passed by him, and Hamza said, 'Come here, you son of a female circumciser.' Now his mother was Umm Anmar, freedwoman of Shariq b. Amr b. Wahb al-Thaqafi, a female circumciser in Mecca. When they closed Hamza smote him and killed him.

Wahshi, the slave of Jubayr b. Mut'im, said, 'By God, I was looking at Hamza while he was killing men with his sword, sparing no one, like a huge camel, when Siba came up to him before me, and Hamza said, 'Come here, you son of a "female circumciser," and he struck him a blow so swiftly that it seemed to miss his head. I poised my javelin until I was sure that it would hit the mark, and launched it at him. It pierced the lower part of his body and came out between his legs. He came on towards me, but collapsed and fell. I left him there until he died, when I came and recovered my javelin. Then I went off to the camp, for I had no business with anyone but him.'

[When Wahshi returned to Mecca, he was freed as promised and when Muhammad eventually conquered Mecca, Wahshi quite naturally fled in fear of the Prophet's revenge. But later Wahshi was told that Muhammad does not kill anyone who becomes a Muslim, so he went to the Prophet and professed the faith. Muhammad does spare him but does not want to see Wahshi who recalls the memory of his uncle's death.]

Mus'ab b. Umayr fought in the defence of the apostle until he was killed. The one who killed him was Ibn Qami'a al-Laythi, who thought he was the apostle, so he returned to the Quraysh and said, 'I have killed Muhammad.' When Mus'ab was killed the apostle gave the standard to Ali, and Ali and the Muslims fought on.

Sa'd b. Abu Waqqas killed Abu Sa'd b. Abu Talba; Asim b. Thabit b. Abu'l-Aqlah fought and killed Musafi b. Talha and his brother al-Julas, shooting both of them with an arrow. Each came to his mother, Sulafa, and laid his head in her lap. She said, 'Who has hurt you my son?' and he replied, 'I heard a man saying as he shot me, "I am Ibn Abu'l-Aqla, take that!"' She swore an oath that if God ever let her get the head of Asim she would drink wine from it. It was Asim who had taken God to witness that he would never touch a polytheist or let one touch me ...

Hanzala b. Abu Amir, the washed one, and Abu Sufyan met in combat, and when Hanzala got the better of him, Shaddad b. al-Aswad, who was Ibn Sha'ub, saw that he had beaten Abu Sufyan, and so he struck him and killed him. The apostle said, 'Your companion, Hanzala, is being washed by the angels.' They asked his family about his condition, and when his wife was asked, she said that he had gone out to battle when he heard the cry while in a state of ritual impurity. [i.e. after having sexual relations.]

The apostle said, 'For this reason the angels washed him.'...

Then God sent down His help to the Muslims and fulfilled His promise. They slew the enemy with the sword until they cut them off from their camp and there was an obvious rout.

Yahya b. Abbad b. Abdullah b. al-Zubayr from his father from Abdullah b.

al-Zubyr from Zubayr said: I found myself looking at the anklets of Hind daughter of Utba and her companions, tucking up their garments as they fled. There was nothing at all to prevent anyone seizing them when the archers turned aside to the camp when the enemy had been cut off from it (Tabari[2] adds: making for the spoil). Thus they opened our rear to the cavalry and we were attacked from behind. Someone called out 'Ha, Muhammad has been killed.' We turned back and the enemy turned back on us after we had killed the standard-bearers so that none of the enemy could come near it.

A traditionist told me that the standard lay on the ground until Amra the Harithite daughter of Alqama took it up and raised it aloft for Quraysh so that they gathered round it. It had been with Su'ab, a slave of Banu Abu Talba, an Abyssinian. He was the last of them to take it. He fought until his hands were cut off; then he knelt upon it and held the flag between his breast and throat until he was killed over it, saying the while 'O God, have I done my duty?' He could not pronounce the *dhal*.

Hassan b. Thabit said about that:

> You boasted of your flag, the worst (ground for) boasting
> Is a flag handed over to Su'ab.
> You have made a slave your boast,
> The most miserable creature that walks the earth.
> You supposed (and only a fool so thinks,
> For it is anything but the truth)
> That fighting us the day we met
> Was like your selling red leather sacks in Mecca.
> It gladdened the eye to see his hands reddened,
> Though they were not reddened by dye.

Hassan also said about Amra and her raising the standard:

> When Adal were driven to us
> They were like fawns of Shirk
> With strongly marked eyebrows.
> We attacked them thrusting, slaying, chastising,
> Driving them before us with blows on every side.
> Had not the Harithite woman seized their standard
> They would have been sold in the markets like chattels.

The Muslims were put to flight and the enemy slew many of them. It was a day of trial and testing in which God honoured several with martyrdom, until the enemy got at the apostle who was hit with a stone so that he fell on his side and one of his teeth was smashed, his face scored, and his lip injured. The man who wounded him was Utba b. Abu Waqqas.

Humayd al-Tawil told me from Anas b. Malik: The prophet's incisor was broken on the day of Uhud and his face was scored. The blood began to run down his face and he began to wipe it away, saying the while, 'How can a people prosper who have stained their prophet's face with blood while he summoned them to their Lord?' So God revealed concerning that: 'It is not your affair whether He relents towards them or punishes them for they are wrongdoers' [Quran 3:123].

Hassan b. Thabit said of Utba:

> When God recompenses a people for their deeds
> And the Rahman punishes them
> May my Lord disgrace you, Utayba b. Malik,
> And bring you a deadly punishment before you die.
> You stretched out your hand with evil intent against the prophet,
> You blooded his mouth. May your hand be cut off!
> Did you forget God and the place you will go to
> When the final misfortune overtakes you!

(Ibn Hisham notes: We have omitted two obscene verses.)

According to what al-Husayn b. Abdu'l-Rabman b. Amr b. Sa'd b. Mu'adh told me on the authority of Mahmud b. Amr, when the enemy hemmed him in, the apostle said: 'Who will sell his life for us?' and Ziyad b. al-Sakan with five of the Ansar [Medinian supporters of Muhammad] arose. (Others say it was Umara son of Yazid b. al-Sakan.) They fought in defence of the apostle man after man, all being killed until only Ziyad (or Umara) was left fighting until he was disabled. At that point a number of the Muslims returned and drove the enemy away from him. The apostle ordered them to bring him to him and made his foot a support for his head and he died with his face on the apostle's foot.

(Ibn Hisham adds: Umara's mother, Nusayba daughter of Ka'bal-Maziniya, fought on the day of Uhud. Sa'id b. Abu Zayd al-Ansari said that Umm Sa'd daughter of Sa'd b. al-Rabi used to say: 'I went to see Umm Umara and said, "O aunt, tell me your story," and she answered: "I went out at the beginning of the day to see what the men were doing, carrying a skin with water in it, and I came up to the apostle who was with his companions while the battle was in their favour. When the Moslems were defeated, I betook myself to the apostle and stood up joining in the fight and protecting him with my sword and shooting with my bow until I suffered many wounds." Umm Sa'd said, "I saw on her shoulder a deep gash and asked who was responsible for it." She said, "Ibn Qami'a, God curse him!" When the men fell back from the apostle he came forward saying "Lead me to Muhammad; let me not survive if he does. Mus'ab b. Umayr and I and some men who held their ground with the apostle blocked his path. It was he who gave me this wound, but I struck him several times for that. However, the enemy of God was wearing two coats of mail".')

Abu Dujana made his body a shield for the apostle. Arrows were falling on his back as he leaned over him, until there were many stuck in it. Sa'd b. Abu Waqqas shot his arrows in defence of the apostle. He said, 'I have seen him banding me the arrows as he said "Shoot, may my father and my mother be your ransom" until he would even hand me an arrow that had no head, saying "Shoot with that".'

[*The word was being spread that the Prophet had been killed but in fact he was taken up to a glen where he washed his wounds.*]

The army had fled away from the apostle until some of them went as far as al-Munaqqa near al-A'was. Asim b. Umar b. Qatada from Mahmud b. Labid told me that when the apostle went out to Uhud Husayn b. Jabir, who was al-Yama Abu Hudhayfa b. al-Yaman, and Thabit b. Waqsh were sent up into the forts with the women and children. They were both old men and one said to the other, 'What are you waiting for, confound you? Neither of us will live much longer. We are certain to die today or tomorrow, so let us take our swords and join the apostle. Perhaps God will grant us martyrdom with him' So they took their swords and sallied out until they mingled with the army.

According to what Salih b. Kaysan told me, Hind daughter of Utba and the women with her stopped to mutilate the apostle's dead companions. They cut off their ears and noses and Hind made them into anklets and collars and gave her anklets and collars and pendants to Wahshi, the slave of Jubayr b. Mut'im. She cut out Hamza's liver and chewed it, but she was not able to swallow it and threw it away.[3] Then she mounted a high rock and shrieked at the top of her voice:

We have paid you back for Badr
And a war that follows a war is always violent.
I could not bear the loss of Utba
Nor my brother and his uncle and my first-born.
I have slaked my vengeance and fulfilled my vow.
You, O Wahshi, have assuaged the burning in my breast.
I shall thank Wahshi as long as I live
Until my bones rot in the grave.

Hind daughter of Uthatha son of Abbad b. al-Muttalib answered her:

> You were disgraced at Badr and after Badr,
> O daughter of a despicable man, great only in disbelief.
> God brought on you in the early dawn
> Tall and white-skinned men from Hashim,
> Everyone slashing with his sharp sword:
> Hamza my lion and Ali my falcon.
> When Shayba and your father planned to attack me
> They reddened their breasts with blood
> Your evil vow was the worst of vows.

Hind daughter of Utba also said:

> I slaked my vengeance on Hamza at Uhud.
> I split his belly to get at his liver.
> This took from me what I had felt
> Of burning sorrow and exceeding pain.
> War will hit you exceeding hard
> Coming upon you as lions advance.

Salih b. Kaisan told me that he was told that Umar said to Hassan, 'O Ibn al-Furay'a, I wish you had heard what Hind said and seen her arrogance as she stood upon a rock uttering her taunts against us, reminding us of what she had done to Hamza.' Hassan replied, 'I was looking at the lance as it fell, while I was on the top of Fari' - meaning his fort - 'and I realized that it was not one of the weapons of the Arabs. It seemed to me as though it was directed at Hamza, but I was not sure. But recite me some of her verse: I will rid you of her.' So Umar quoted some of what she said and Hassan said:

> The vile woman was insolent: her habits were vile;
> Seeing that disbelief accompanied her insolence.

Al-Hulays b. Zabban, brother of the Banu al-Harith b. Abdu Manat, who was then chief of the black troops, passed by Abu Sufyan as he was striking the side of Hamza's mouth with the point of his spear saying, 'Taste that, you rebel.' Hulays exclaimed, 'O Banu Kinana, is this the chief of Quraysh acting thus with his dead cousin as you see ?' He said, 'Confound you. Keep the matter quiet, for it was a slip.'

When Abu Sufyan wanted to leave he went to the top of the mountain and shouted loudly saying, 'You have done a fine work; victory in war goes by turns.

Today in exchange for the day (Tabari adds: of Badr). Show your superiority, Hubal, [a pre-Islamic, Meccan idol]' i.e. vindicate your religion. The apostle told Umar to get up and answer him and say, 'God is most high and most glorious. We are not equal. Our dead are in paradise; your dead in hell.' At this answer Abu Sufyan said to Umar, 'Come here to me.' The apostle told him to go and see what he was up to. When he came Abu Sufyan said, T adjure thee by God, Umar, have we killed Muhammad?' 'By God, you have not, he is listening to what you are saying now,' he replied. He said, 'I regard you as more truthful and reliable than Ibn Qami'a,' referring to the latter's claim that he had killed Muhammad.

Then Abu Sufyan called out, 'There are some mutilated bodies among your dead. By God, it gives me no satisfaction, and no anger. I neither prohibited nor ordered mutilation.' When Abu Sufyan and his companions went away he called out, 'Your meeting-place is Badr next year.' The apostle told one of his companions to say, 'Yes, it is an appointment between us.'

[Muhammad sends Ali to scout the enemy; the Muslims search for their dead.]

I have been told that the apostle went out seeking Hamza and found him at the bottom of the valley with his belly ripped up and his liver missing, and his nose and ears cut off. Muhammad b. Ja'far b. al-Zubayr told me that when he saw this the apostle said: 'Were it not that Safiya [Hamza's sister] would be miserable and it might become a custom after me I would leave him as he is, so that his body might find its way into the bellies of beasts and the crops of birds. If God gives me victory over Quraysh in the future I will mutilate 30 of their men.' Then the Muslims saw the apostle's grief and anger against those who had thus treated his uncle, they said, 'By God, if God gives us victory over them in the future we will mutilate them as no Arab has ever mutilated anyone'.

Burayda b. Sufyan b. Farwa al-Aslami from Muhammad b. Ka'b al-Qurazi, and a man I have no reason to suspect from Ibn Abbas told me that God sent down concerning the words of the apostle and his companions 'If you punish, then punish as you have been punished. If you endure patiently that is better for the patient. Endure thou patiently. Thy endurance is only in God. Grieve not for them, and be not in distress at what they plot.' [Quran 16:127.] So the apostle pardoned them and was patient and forbade mutilation. Humayd al-Tawil from al-Hasan from Samura b. Jundub told me: 'The apostle never stopped in a place and left it without enjoining on us alms-giving and forbidding mutilation.'

[Several episodes are related here which refer to the customary burial of Muslims who fall in battle.]

Then the apostle went back on his way to Medina and there met him Hamna daughter of Jahsh, so I have been told. As she met the army she was told of the death of her brother Abdullah and she exclaimed, 'We belong to God and to God we return,' and asked forgiveness for him. Then she was told of the death of her maternal uncle Hamza and uttered the same words. Then she was told of the death of her husband Mus'ab b. Umayr and she shrieked and wailed. The apostle said: 'The woman's husband holds a special place with her, as you can see from her self-control at the death of her brother and uncle and her shrieking over her husband.'

The apostle passed by one of the settlements of the Ansar of the Banu Abdu'l-Ashhal and Zafar and he heard the sound of weeping and wailing over the dead. The apostle's eyes filled with tears and he wept and said, 'But there are no weeping women for Hamza.' When Sa'd b. Mu'adh and Usayd b. Hudayr came back to the quarter, they ordered their women to gird themselves and go and weep for the apostle's uncle.

Hakim b. Hakim b. Abbad b. Hunayf from a man of the Banu Abdu'l-Ashhal told me: 'When the apostle heard their weeping over Hamza at the door of his mosque he said "Go home; may God have mercy on you; you have been a real help by your presence".'

(Ibn Hisham notes: On that day he forbade lamentation. Abu Ubayda told me that when the apostle heard their weeping he said: 'God have mercy on the Ansar; for it has long been their custom to provide consolation. Tell the women to go away.')

Abdu'l-Wahid b. Abu Aun from Isma'il b. Muhammad from Sa'd b. Abu Waqqas told me that the apostle passed by a woman of the Banu Dinar whose husband, brother, and father had been killed at Uhud, and when she was told of their death she asked what had happened to the apostle, and when they replied that thanks to God he was safe, she asked that she might see him for herself. When he was pointed out to her she said, 'Every misfortune now that you are safe is negligible.'

When the apostle rejoined his family he handed his sword to his daughter Fatima, saying, 'Wash the blood from this, daughter, for by God it has served me well today.' Ali also handed her his sword and said, 'This one too, wash the blood from it, for by God it has served me well today.' The apostle said, 'If you have fought well, Sahl b. Hunayf and Abu Dujana fought well with you'.

The battle was fought on the Sabbath in mid-Shawwal; and on the morning of Sunday the 16th of the month the apostle's crier called to the men to go in pursuit of the enemy and announced that none should go out with us unless he had been present at the battle on the preceding day. Jabir son of Abdullah b. Amr b. Haram said, 'O apostle of God, my father left me behind to look after my seven sisters, saying that it was not right for us both to leave the women without a man and that he was not one to give me the precedence in fighting with the apostle. So I stayed behind to look after them.' The apostle gave him permission to go and he went out with him. The apostle merely marched out as a demonstration against the enemy to let them know that he was pursuing them so that they might think he was in strength, and that their losses had not weakened them.

[Abu Sufyan wants to attack again and finish off the Muslims but he is told that Muhammad has come out with a strengthened and revitalized force. Abu Sufyan and his followers turn back to Mecca, but swear revenge.]

The day of Uhud was a day of trial, calamity, and heart-searching on which God tested the believers and put the hypocrites on trial, those who professed faith with their tongue and hid unbelief in their hearts; and a day in which God honoured with martyrdom those whom he willed.

Notes

1. Almost the same words were used by a woman of the Banu Ijl at the battle of Dhu Qar.

2. Muhammad ibn Jarir al-Tabari (225-310/839-923) is the author *The History of Prophets and Kings,* a history of the world from ancient times through the life of the Prophet and to the beginning of the tenth century. Selection 6 is taken from this massive work.

3. This seems to be a survival of prehistoric animism. By devouring an enemy's liver it was hoped to absorb his strength.

3

SAYINGS OF THE PROPHET : SELECTIVE

QUOTATION

[Muhammad ibn Ismail Bukhari, *The Translation of the Meanings of Sahih al-Bukhari: Arabic-English,* trans. Muhammad Muhsin Khan. al-Medina al-Munawwara: Islamic University, 1973-1976, 2nd revised edition, 1: nos 28, 97-A, 301, 347, 480, 552, 675, 823, 824, 825, 828, 829, 830, 832; 2:23, 326; 5:709; 9:219.]

The battle of the *hadiths,* selective quotation of sayings or traditions of the Prophet, is a prominent aspect of the ongoing debate about the role of women in Islam. This is because *hadiths* are the second most important source of Islamic law and normative behaviour after the Quran, consist of a much larger pool of (somewhat conflicting) material, and have been subject to traditional, modern and some neo-traditional criticism.

A *hadith* is actually a report of the words and deeds of the Prophet Muhammad passed on orally from one of his Companions through a chain of individual transmitters. Thus, a *hadith* consists of two parts: the chain of transmitters *(isnad)* and the content *(matn).* Within a few generations of the Prophet's death, the number of these reports escalated while their reliability became suspect. This process was exacerbated by the religious and political conflicts which plagued the Islamic community in its first century because each party wished to anchor its interpretation of Islam in the sayings and actions of the Prophet. Social, economic and cultural tensions within the early Islamic community may also be discerned in the differing thrust and varying versions of certain *hadiths.*

Early Muslim scholars were aware of the dangers inherent in the inflation of *hadiths* and devised methods for evaluating the authenticity of chains of transmission. *Hadith* criticism was based on the completeness of the chain, the reliability of the transmitters and the connections between the links'

Collections of sound traditions were compiled according to the original authority who was in contact with the Prophet *(musnad)* and later by subject. The most widely-recognized compilations of trustworthy *hadiths* (to this day) are the *Sahihs* of Bukhari (d. 256/870) and Muslim (d. 261/875). In the course of time, four other works of this type - produced by Abu Da'ud (d. 275/888), Tirmidhi (died 279/892), Ibn Maja (d. 283/896), and Nisa'i (d. 303/915) -were singled out and with Bukhari and Muslim were referred to as the six books. But innumerable collections of traditions were compiled and reorganized by different criteria, some of which comprised *hadiths* on specific subjects.

These collections in turn became primary sources and were transmitted from one scholar to another. The methodology of oral transmission dominated the study of *hadith* as well as other fields of Islamic learning even when compilations of traditions were written down. Centuries later, when printing was invented, traditional Muslim scholars were reluctant to print works in their domain. It seems that only in the twentieth century have printed collections of traditions become prevalent, and in the last decades some of these have been translated into English. Recently, the six books (along with some other primary Islamic works) have been rendered as computer-accessible data banks (on CD-ROM or diskettes), and some enterprising Muslim students have made Bukhari available on the computer Internet at gopher:// cwis.usc.edu//ll/Campus_Life/Student_Orgs/MSA/*Hadith*/Bukhari.

At least three aspects of the voluminous and extremely rich literature on *hadith* composed through the centuries relate to the role of women in Islam: women as transmitters, the image of women in the contents of traditions, and the use of alternative methods of criticism to determine the authenticity of reports on the words and deeds of the Prophet.

There is no question that women played a quantitatively and qualitatively significant role as primary transmitters of traditions of the Prophet. The archetype of these first-generation traditionists is Aisha, Muhammad's favourite wife, who related 1210 hadiths (228 of which are included in Bukhari's work and 242 in Muslim's). Some 1,000 other female Companions of the Prophet related traditions, 17 per cent of the trustworthy transmitters of the first generation by one count. Thus, the legitimacy of women as oral transmitters of this crucial Islamic material was established. The number and proportion of female transmitters drops dramatically from the second generation after the Prophet and only one or two appear among the teachers of the great compilers, all of whom were men. These scholars rigorously examined chains of transmission and authenticated only a minority of the traditions they had collected, but they seem to have weighed the reliability of traditions without regard to the gender of their transmitters, As collections of authenticated traditions authenticated traditions became prevalent, women were also prominent in transmitting these works, such as Bukhari's *Sahih* (as may be seen in the biography of Aisha the daughter of Muhammad b. Abd al-Hadi below).

Content analysis of this fundamental Islamic material has been hampered by its sheer volume. Instead, Muslims and non-Muslims have usually selected a number of sayings as evidence to prove a certain point. Several examples of this use of hadiths will be found in the subsequent readings. Seemingly minor differences in the wording of different versions of the same tradition may significantly change the meaning. G. H. A. Juynboll has shown how in-depth study of the misogynist saying 'I was shown the Hellfire and the majority of its dwellers were women ... ' can reveal the tension between two differing attitudes toward women, and even tentatively date the triumph of the negative view.

Hadith criticism was an important branch of Islamic learning up to the tenth century, but afterwards Muslim scholars concentrated on accurate transmission of the works of the great masters of the past. In the twentieth century, Western scholars began to examine hadiths and their transmitters unfettered by the bonds of faith. They questioned the authenticity of sound traditions based on analysis of their content, the existence of some of the transmitters, and attempted to reconstruct the history of Muslim traditions. Recently, Muslim feminists, recognizing the importance of *hadith* to Islamic law and custom, have suggested the use of feminist *hadith* criticism since they view the scholars of the past as men locked in a patriarchal society. Juynboll's methodology may provide tools for a feminist critique of the canon of the Prophet's words and deeds but such an approach will undoubtedly arouse opposition from traditional Muslim scholars. The Moroccan feminist Fatima Mernissi heads a project which aims among other things to collect and disseminate hadiths supporting women's rights. She has also used neo-traditional methods to undermine the authority of misogynist hadiths. Attempts by Muslims and non-Muslims to evaluate this fundamental source of Islamic law and culture without the mediation of traditional scholars have undoubtedly been facilitated by the publication, translation and dissemination of major *hadith* collections.

Muhammad ibn Isma'il Bukhari (died 256/870) began to learn hadiths by heart at the age of ten, travelled widely throughout the Islamic world in search of traditions and claimed to have heard them from over one thousand shaykhs. He evaluated the massive material he collected and selected 2,762 sound *(sahih)* traditions which he arranged according to subject. Bukhari cited each *hadith* under every possible subject alluded to in it, so the traditions in this comprehensive work actually number 7,397 when the repetitions are counted.

The *Sahih* of Bukhari comprises ninety-three books divided into chapters each of which has a subject title followed by the relevant tradition or traditions with their full chain of transmitters. Bukhari rarely added commentary or conclusions to the traditions. His intervention in the material was restricted to selection of hadiths based on their authenticity and presenting their contents according to categories determined by Islamic criteria. Bukhari begins with chapters on faith, knowledge, and the pillars of religious practice (prayer, charity, pilgrimage, fasting). These are followed by books relating to: property matters; *jihad;* the life of the Prophet and his Companions; Quran commentary; family matters (marriage, divorce, children); material culture; good manners; oaths and inheritance; Quranic injunctions and punishments *(hudud);* and a melange of subjects, ending with a book on the central Islamic concept of the unity or oneness of God *(tawhid).*

Muhammad Muhsin Khan's translation of the *Sahih al-Bukhari,* produced at the Islamic University of Medina, was published alongside the Arabic original 'for the use of Muslims who do not read Arabic.' It bears the written authorizations of several experts in the English language and Islamic law. In the translation, only the primary transmitters are cited but the Arabic has the full chain. This makes for easier reading for the lay person but precludes neo-traditional criticism of the transmitters. The book has been published in several revised editions and printings, sustaining (perhaps even enhancing) Bukhari's position as one of the most authoritative sources for Muslims to this day.

Every time Muslims mention the Prophet Muhammad, they append a eulogy - *Sala Allah 'alayhu wa-Salam* in Arabic, 'God bless him and grant him salvation,' -to his name. In the following excerpts, SAS an anglicized abbreviation of the Arabic is used. Other English-speaking Muslims prefer PBUH for 'Peace be upon him.' Still others use a rosette form of the Arabic letters or an asterisk. Names of Companions of the Prophet, the men and women who had direct contact with him are signified by the eulogy *Rada Allah 'Anhu/ha,* 'May God be pleased with him/ her.' This phrase is abbreviated below as RAA.

In selecting and presenting the excerpts below, an attempt has been made to retain as much of the original format as possible in order to convey Bukhari's methodology and line of thought. The selections are presented for the most part in the order in which they appear in the *Sahih.* Since the first reference to a *hadith* report is not always the most complete, sometimes a subsequent version has been preferred. Also, books and chapters whose entire contents relate to women (such as the book of menses, or the book of divorce) have not been reproduced in full. Each is worthy of separate consideration and study.

Among the first hadiths in Bukhari's work, in the book of Faith, is the problematic saying: 'I was shown the Hellfire and the majority of its dwellers were women ... 'By comparing the content and context to the version in the book of Menses (number 301), subtle differences may be discerned. It must be emphasized that Bukhari repeats this (and other) sayings a number of times, in different contexts and with differing degrees of abbreviation as required by the subjects under which he has catalogued it - in this case, faith, menses (and later fasting). He does not relate to the question of how negative the portrayal of women is in each version.

A large number of the hadiths quoted below refer to the question of whether women may attend communal prayer, and what limitations or gender-specific rules were set down for them. Why is the participation of women in congregational prayer important beyond the spiritual aspirations of devout Muslim women? Current practice regarding women's participation in communal prayer seems to be almost as variegated as Muslim women's dress.

Two *hadiths* from the book of Knowledge refer in rather picayune ways to teaching women and women learning. What attitude toward the education of women is reflected in these sayings? What is the implication for the development of women's education in the Islamic world? Similarly, a *hadith* cited by Bukhari in the books of Military Expeditions (Maghazi) and Afflictions *(Fitan, sing.:fitna)* has often been translated as 'A people who entrusts their affairs to a woman will not prosper.' In what context was it said by the Prophet and under what circumstances was it reported by Abu Bakra? Does it exclude women from positions of political authority? Does it necessarily imply that a woman may not be a head of state?

There is no religious constraint on translating *hadith* works, but the many archaic Arabic words as well as the religious and legal terminology are difficult to render in a form comprehensible to modern readers (particularly those who are not familiar with Arabic or the social milieu and material culture of the time of the Prophet). Any project of translation is open to the criticism that the true meaning has been lost and this is particularly true of this sensitive material. On the other hand, the English-reader may find some translations unwieldy at best. The main impetus for translating *hadith* works seems to be a growing demand among Muslims, a phenomenon which may have some interesting socio-religious ramifications. A by-product of these efforts is that more non-Muslims may also approach this primary source, and translators may also have this audience in mind. For all these reasons, the translations must be approached with caution, and those which appear alongside the original are undoubtedly preferable even for the beginning student of Arabic. Among the collections of *hadith* available in English are: A. H. Siddiqui, *Sahih Muslim,* four volumes; A. Hasan, *Sunan Abu Dawud,* three volumes; S. M. Abbasi, trans. [Abu Zakariya Yahya b. Sharaf] An-Nawawi, *Riyadh-us-Saliheen,* the two volume edition of which includes the Arabic original; four volumes of al-Khatib al-Tibrizi, *Mishkat al-Masabih,* translated by James Robson.

The second volume of Ignaz Goldziher's *Muslim Studies* (London: G. Allen and Unwin, 1967-71), generally considered the first milestone in Western *hadith* criticism, contains a short section devoted to women traditionists. Muhammad Zubayr Siddiqi's *Hadith Literature,* originally written in the 1930s, presents the orthodox Islamic viewpoint and relates to Western critical scholarship and the questions it raised. It also contains a section on women traditionists. Fatima Mernissi has questioned the authenticity of two misogynist sayings of the Prophet cited below using the tools of classical *hadith* criticism in *The Veil and the Male Elite:* 'Those who entrust their affairs to a woman,' and 'The dog, the ass and woman interrupt prayer.' Juynboll's 'Some *Isnad*-Analytical Methods Illustrated on the Basis of Several Woman-Demeaning Sayings from *Hadith* Literature' *Al-Qantara* 10 (1989) may be difficult reading for the novice but opens fascinating avenues for future *hadith* criticism. Roded's *Women in the Islamic Biographical Collections* contains several sections devoted to the numbers and proportions of women transmitters of traditions and *hadith* scholars through the centuries and the implications of this phenomen.

Bukhar's *Sahih*

II The Book of Faith

Chapter 21: To be ungrateful to one's husband.
Hadith No. 28. Narrated Ibn Abbas: The Prophet SAS said: 'I was shown the Hellfire and the majority of its dwellers were women who were ungrateful.' It was asked, 'Do they disbelieve in Allah?' (or are they ungrateful to Allah?) He replied, 'They are ungrateful to their husbands and are ungrateful for the favours and the good (charitable deeds) done to them. If you have always been good (benevolent) to one of them and then she *sees* something in you (not of her liking) she will say 'I have never received any good from you''

III The Book of Knowledge

Chapter 32: A man teaching (religion) to his woman-slave and his family.
97-A. Narrated Abu Burda's father RAA: Allah's Apostle SAS said: 'Three persons will have a double reward:
1. A person from the people of the scriptures who believed in his prophet (Jesus or Moses) and then believed in the Prophet Muhammad SAS (i.e. has embraced Islam).
2. A slave who discharges his duties to Allah and his master.

3. A master of a woman-slave who teaches her good manners and educates her in the best possible way (the religion) and manumits her and then marries her [cf. XLVI (Manumission of Slaves): 14.]

51: To be shy *(al-haya)* while learning (religious knowledge).

And Mujahid said, 'Neither a shy nor a proud person can learn the religious knowledge.' And Aisha RAA said, 'How excellent the women of the Ansar [supporters of Muhammad in Medina] are! They do not feel shy while learning sound knowledge in religion'.

VI The Book of Menses

Chapter 8: A menstruating woman should not fast.

301. Narrated Abu Sa'id al-Khudri RAA: Once Allah's Apostle SAS went out to the Musalla (to offer the prayer) of Id al-Adha or al-Fitr prayer. Then he passed by the women and said, 'O women! Give alms, as I have seen that the majority of the dwellers of Hellfire were you (women).' They asked, 'Why is it so, O Allah's Apostle SAS?' He replied, 'You curse frequently and are ungrateful to your husbands. I have not seen anyone more deficient in intelligence and religion than you. A cautious sensible man could be led astray by some of you/ The women asked, 'O Allah's Apostle SAS! What is deficient in our intelligence and religion?' He said, 'Is not the evidence of two women equal to the witness of one man?' They replied in the affirmative. He said, 'This is the deficiency in your intelligence. Isn't it true that a woman can neither pray nor fast during her menses? The women replied in the affirmative. He said, 'This is the deficiency in your religion; [cf. XXXI (Fasting): 41.]

VIII The Book of Salat (Prayers)

Chapter 2: It is obligatory to pray with the clothes on ...

347. Narrated Urn Atiya RAA: We were ordered to bring out our [unmarried mature virgins,] menstruating women and veiled women [or who stayed screened,] in the religious gatherings and invocations of Muslims on the two Id festivals. These menstruating women were to keep away from their Musalla. A woman asked, 'O Allah's Apostle SAS! What about one who does not have a veil *[jilbab]* ?' He said, 'Let her share the veil of her companion.' [cf. VI (Book of Menses):25; XV (Book of Two Ids):13-15; XXVI (Book of Hajj): 80.]

IX (The Book of) Chapter about the Sutra of Musalla (a symbolic barrier between praying person and others in front)

Chapter 13: A man facing of a man while praying.
490. Narrated Aisha RAA: The things which annul the prayers were mentioned before me. They said, 'Prayer is annulled by a dog, a donkey and a woman (if they pass in front of praying people).'I said, 'You have made us (i.e. women) dogs. I saw the Prophet SAS praying while I used to lie in my bed between him and the Qibla [direction of prayer]. Whenever I was in need of something, I would slip away, for I disliked to face him.'

X The Book of the Times of the Prayers

Chapter 27: Time of the Fajr (morning) prayer.
552. Narrated Aisha RAA: The believing women covered with their veiling sheets used to attend the Fajr with Allah's Apostle SAS, and after finishing the prayer would return to their homes and nobody could recognize them because of darkness.

XI The Book of the Adhan (The Call to Prayer)

Chapter 64: Whoever cuts short the prayer on hearing the cries of a child.
675. Narrated Abdullah ibn Abu Qatada: My father said, 'The Prophet SAS said, "When I stand for prayer, I intend to prolong it but on hearing the cries of a child, I cut it short, as I dislike to trouble the child's mother."

XII (The Book) Chapters on the Characteristics of Prayer

Chapter 80: Going of women to the mosques at night and in darkness.
823. Narrated Aisha RAA: Once Allah's Apostle SAS delayed the Isha prayer till Umar informed him that the women and children had slept. The Prophet SAS came out and said, 'None except you from amongst the dwellers of earth is waiting for this prayer.' In those days, there was no prayer except in Medina and they used to pray Isha prayer between the disappearance of the twilight and the first third of the night.
824. Narrated Ibn Umar RAA: The Prophet SAS said, 'If your women ask permission to go to the mosque at night, allow them.'

Chapter 81: The waiting of the people for the religious learned imam to stand up (after the prayer).

825. Narrated Um Salama RAA, the wife of the Prophet RAA: In the lifetime of Allah's Apostle SAS the women used to get up when they finished their compulsory prayers with Taslim.[1] The Prophet SAS and the men would stay on at their places as long as Allah will. When the Prophet SAS got up, the men would then get up.

828. Narrated Aisha RAA: Had Allah's Apostle SAS known what the women were doing, he would have forbidden them from going to the mosque as the women of Bani Israel [the Sons of Israel] had been forbidden.

829. Narrated Um Salama RAA: Whenever Allah's Apostle SAS completed the prayer with Taslim, the women used to get up immediately and Allah's Apostle SAS would remain at his place for someone before getting up. (The sub-narrator (al-Zuhri) said, 'We think, and Allah knows better, that he did so, so that the women might leave before men could get in touch with them).'

830. Narrated Anas RAA: The Prophet SAS prayed in the house of Urn Sulaim; and I, along with an orphan stood behind him while Urn Sulaim (stood) behind us.

Chapter 84: A woman should ask her husband's permission (on wishing) to go to the mosque.

832. Narrated Salim ibn Abdullah: My father said, 'The Prophet SAS said, "If the wife of any one of you asks permission (to go to the mosque) do not forbid her,"

XIII The Book of Jumu'a (Friday) Prayer

Chapter 11: Is the taking of a bath (on Friday) necessary for women, boys, and others who do not present themselves for the Jumu'a prayers?

23. Narrated Ibn Umar RAA: One of the wives of Umar (ibn al-Khattab) used to offer the Fajr and the Isha prayer in congregation in the Mosque. She was asked why she had come out for the prayer as she knew that Umar disliked it and he had great ghaira (self-respect). She replied, 'What prevents him from stopping me from this act?' The other replied, 'The statement of Allah's Apostle SAS: "Do not stop Allah's women slaves from going to Allah's mosques, prevents him."'

XXII *Chapters dealing with actions in Prayer (Irrelevant to Prayer)*

Chapter 27: Beckoning during the prayer (by a person in prayer).
326. Allah's Apostle SAS went forward and led the people in the prayer. When he completed the prayer he faced the people and said, 'O people! Why did you start clapping when something happened to you in prayer? Clapping is only for women. Say Subhan Allah.'[2] [cf. chapter 5, clapping is for women to catch men's attention.]

LIX *The Book of Military Expeditions*

Chapter 80: The letter of the Prophet SAS to Khosrau and Caesar.
709. Narrated Abu Bakra: During the days (of the battle) of al-Jamal, Allah benefited me with a word I had heard from Allah's Apostle SAS after I had been about to join the companions of al-Jamal (i.e. the camel) [led by Aisha] and fight along with them. When Allah's Apostle SAS was informed that the Persians had crowned the daughter of Khosrau as their ruler, he said, 'Such people as ruled by a lady will never be successful.' *[Lan yufliha qawm wallaw amrahum imra'a]*

LXXXVIII *The Book of Afflictions*

Chapter 18:
219. Narrated Abu Bakra: During the battle of al-Jamal Allah benefited me with a Word (I heard from the Prophet SAS): When the Prophet SAS heard the news that the people of the Persia had made the daughter of Khosrau their Queen (ruler), he said, 'Never will succeed such a nation as makes a woman their ruler.'

Notes

1. *Taslim* is a salutation ('Peace be upon you, and the mercy of God') which concludes the prayer.
2. *Subhan Allah* is a religious formula ('praise be to Allah') which serves as an exclamation.

4

SHI' I MARTYROLOGY :

THE DEATH OF FATIMA , DAUGHTER OF THE

PROPHET

[Colonel Sir Lewis Pelly, *The Miracle Play of Hasan and Husain, Collected From Oral Tradition* (London: Wm. H. Allen and Co., 1879), 1: 110-32.]

The Shi'a, or party of Ali, is generally defined in historical-political terms as those Muslims who believe that Ali, cousin and son-in-law of Muhammad, was the Prophet's chosen successor but was denied his proper place by some of the Companions (including Aisha).

Ali (fourth of the righteous caliphs by Sunni reckoning and first *imam* according to the Shi'is) was murdered in a mosque in Kufa in 40 A.H./661 A.D. by a member of the Khawarij separatist sect, and was buried five miles away at what became the city of Mashhad Ali or Najaf. His elder son Hasan, claimant to the leadership of the Muslim state, ceded in favour of Mu'awiya, governor of Syria, and was poisoned in 49/668, allegedly at Mu'awiya's instigation. Mu'awiya died in 60/680 and was succeeded by his son Yazid consolidating the Umayyad dynasty centred at Damascus. Shortly after Yazid's accession, events were set in motion which culminated in the massacre of Ali's second son (the third *imam)* Husayn with most of his family and followers on Thursday, 10 Muharram 61/10 October 680 at Karbala.

Husayn's sister Zaynab played an heroic role in the battle itself and during the subsequent humiliation of the defeated Alids. Her image was retained in the collective memory of Muslims to the extent that Benazir Bhutto (whose mother is a Shi'i) was compared to Zaynab, because her father was executed by Zia ul-Haqq and one of her brothers was killed under mysterious circumstances.

The Shi'is recognize a biological and spiritual line of leaders of the Muslim community (*imams*) descended from the Prophet through his daughter Fatima

58

and Ali. The last *imam* (according to most Shi'is) went into occultation *(ghayba)* in 260/874 and will reappear some day when God deems it appropriate.

The modern Shi'i scholar Muhammad Husayn Tabataba'i, in such works as *Shi'ite Islam* (1975) and *A Shi'ite Anthology* (1980), regards the theological and philosophical uniqueness of Shi'ism as more important than a mere historical struggle over succession. In the past, tensions between Sunnis and Shi'is ran high, to the point of bloodshed. In modern times, however, the call for rapprochement between the two major strands of Islam has grown and differences have been minimized. Nevertheless, certain practices unique to Shi'is are repugnant to Sunnis.

Legal experts cite the overall similarity between the major Islamic sects but focus on a number of differences that are related to women. The most outstanding is Shi'i recognition of a form of contractual, temporary marriage in which the woman receives remuneration *(mut'a)*, a practice regarded by Sunnis as illegal. The *Law of Desire: Temporary Marriage in Shi'i Iran* (1989) by an Iranian woman, Shahla Haeri, contains an analysis of the rules of *mut'a* marriage and fascinating case-studies of women and men involved in such arrangements. Shi'i law also restricts a husband's right to repudiate his wife *(talaq)* to a greater extent than Sunni law, and its rules of inheritance prefer male agnate relatives at the expense of female and cognate kin. At least one scholar, Wilferd Madelung, believes that these provisions which appear to reflect a more positive Shi'i attitude toward women actually derive from specifically Shi'i concerns such as the recognition of the rights of the Prophe's daughter and her descendants. This view is explicated in 'Shi'i Attitudes Toward Women as Reflected in Fiqh,' *Society and the Sexes in Medieval Islam* ed. Afaf Lutfi al-Sayyid Marsot (1979).

Shi'ism has also been viewed as an oppositional, popular and more emotional strain of Islam (akin to Sufi mysticism) as opposed to the legalist bent of Sunni scholars and the *raison d'état* (leaning to despotism) of Sunni rulers. The dramatic remembrance and representation of the martyrdom of the Imam Husayn and his family is the central Shi'i ritual in which the individual and the community identify with their suffering, death and eternal reward.

This ritual has its historical roots in the movement of penitents (61-65 AH) who chanted eulogies for the martyrs of Karbala to atone for their guilt of not having fought or died with Husayn. From a literary point of view, the origins of the *ta'ziya* passion play are in the pre-Islamic elegy and lamentation; linguistically, it is related to the comforting of relatives of the dead recommended to all Muslims. Mass processions commemorating the martyrdom of Karbala were recorded from the tenth century when the Shi'i Buyyid rulers took effective power from the Sunni Abbasid caliphs. Full-scale *ta'ziya* dramas have been dated to the sixteenth century when the Safavid dynasty established the Shi'a as the state religion in Persia. In a more profound sense, however, the *ta'ziya* is timeless. The martyrdom of Husayn is related backward in time to Abraham's willingness to sacrifice his son and to the death of the Prophet Muhammad. It is projected ahead to link up with contemporary political events.

The *ta'ziya* from which the following selection was taken was recorded by a Persian teacher and prompter of actors and translated into English during the course of several years at the request of Colonel Sir Lewis Pelly. Pelly had first been impressed by the emotional, popular appeal of the nightly dramas during the month of Muharram in India. Affiliated with the British legation in Persia 1859-1862, and serving as Persian Gulf Resident 1862-1873, he had further opportunity to witness the daily participation of Shi'i Muslims of all classes of society, men and women, in this daily, lengthy, intense drama. The play was published in thirty-seven of the original fifty-two scenes beginning from the story of Joseph and his brothers. Pelly, his editor and his publisher rendered this ta'ziya in the form of a formal script. The publicly-recited, chanted elegies, passion plays and mourning processions that form the core of Shi'i ritual from Karbala to Bombay, from Lebanon to the Persian Gulf, differ in detail not only from country to country but also from district to district.

Pelly's Persian *ta'ziya* begins with a scene about Joseph and his Brethren, followed by the death of Ibrahim, Muhammad's infant son; a parable of the disobedient son; Ali's offer to sacrifice his life; the Prophet's death, and the 'seizure of the caliphate' by Abu Bakr (the first caliph). Then the death of Fatima, Muhammad's daughter, is depicted as below. This scene is followed by the martyrdoms of Ali, Hasan, and some early Shi'is, climaxing in an extremely detailed, evocative drama of Husayn's martyrdom at Karbala.

Fatima, daughter of Muhammad and Khadija, was the wife of Ali son of Abu Talib, the Prophet's cousin and among the earliest believers in his prophecy, and the mother of Muhammad's beloved grandsons Hasan and Husayn. Their descendants were revered not only by the Shi'is but by all Muslims because of their blood tie to the Prophet.

There is relatively little information on Fatima in the early Islamic sources compared to other women directly connected with the Prophet. As a result, there are few facts about her life which may be considered authentic rather than later legends. On the basis of these few pieces of information, Fatima appears to have a marginal and even passive role in the great events of early Islam.

On the other hand, Fatima is the only one of the Prophet's daughters (his sons died in infancy) who achieved fame and glory. She is revered by all Muslims and is known as al-Zahra, the radiant, but the Shi'is in particular have glorified her. From the fourth/tenth century at least, Shi'i authors wrote of many miraculous events connected with Fatima, some of which appear in the drama below. The contrast between the 'historical' Fatima and the legendary Fatima prompted two famed orientalists Father Henri Lammens and Louis Massignon to draw diametrically-opposed portraits of her. Lammens, in a hypercritical monograph based primarily on the biography of the Prophet *Fatima et les filles de Mahomet* (1913), described her as not very beautiful, of average intelligence, sickly and constantly weeping. In general, he viewed her as a passive, even cowed woman. Massignon later portrayed Fatima as a woman who was not appreciated in her lifetime but had a very strong inner zeal for God as well as a large measure of mercy. The twentieth-century Iranian thinker, Ali Shari'ati, has produced still another depiction of Fatima as we will see below.

In the foreword to the following scene of Fatima's death, the editor interprets the Sun's shame to show his face while that of Zaynab is uncovered as a reference to female seclusion. Do you agree with this explanation? Can this metaphor be read in another fashion? What kind of woman does Fatima seem to be in this dramatic interpretation of her personality? What kind of role model would she be for Muslim women? What can we learn from the mundane details of washing Zaynab's hair and the children's clothes? What dramatic devices make this scene so popular?

A comparison of the appearance of the Prophet's tooth knocked out at the battle of Uhud in Fatima's death scene, to Ibn Ishaq's description of the event in his biography of Muhammad, illustrates varying treatment of the same basic Islamic materials.

A good starting-point to explore the image of Fatima is the entry in the *Encyclopaedia of Islam* on her name. *Ta'ziyeh: Ritual and Drama in Iran* (New York and Tehran, 1979), edited by Peter Chelkowski contains articles relating to historical, literary, dramatic and anthropological aspects of this ritual in various parts of the Muslim world. Chelkowski has written two excellent articles on 'Popular Shi'i Mourning Rituals' and the evolvement of the *ta'ziya* drama in *Alsarat: Papers from the Imam Husayn Conference* (London, 1984). Elizabeth Warnock Fernea's *Guests of the Sheik: An Ethnography of an Iraqi Village* (1965) has fascinating descriptions of a *ta'ziya* and other Shi'i rituals from women's perspective.

'The Miracle Play of Hasan and Husain',
Collected from Oral Tradition

Scene VII: The Death of Fatima, The Daughter of the Prophet Muhammad

Fatima, whose death is here recorded, was the daughter of Muhammad, whom she survived but a few months. She married Ali, and bore to him Hasan and Husayn, the martyr of Karbala. There is a tradition that the Prophet on one occasion said 'That among men there had been many perfect, but no more than four of the other sex had attained perfection; to wit Asia [sic], the wife of Pharaoh; Mary, the daughter of Imran; Khadija, the daughter of Khuwaylid (the Prophet's first wife); and Fatima, the daughter of Mohammad.'[1] This scene is noteworthy as indicating the abhorrence with which the people of the East regard any violation of the seclusion of the female sex.' The sun,' says the text, 'is ashamed to show his face while that of Zaynab is laid open to view; There is also an interesting enumeration of the souvenirs of Muhammad and his family most esteemed by the Shi'is.

Fatima: O holy Creator of all things, how long must I remain distressed and suffer grief owing to the loss of my father? I am dying; dying, indeed, from the pain caused by his departure. His sad memory has, as it were, poisoned my whole constitution; nay, it has already killed me with its venom. O Lord God, if it be possible, let me be honoured once more with the presence of that royal personage whose motto was, 'We have not known Thee, O Lord, but in part.'

Ali: O Thou whose holy nature is perfectly free from our imperfect qualities, whose essence is beyond the limit of our comprehension, Thou art He by whose universal cloud of mercy roses and lilies, as well as thorns and thistles, receive their existence and nourishment. It is from nearness to Thee that Haidar [=Ali] has become possessed of the glorious title of 'Were it not for thee I would not have created the heavens.'

Fatima (to her maid): O maid, kindly do me a service, and get me mourning dresses, that I may show my grief for my father. Darken my house of sorrow, and make it jet-black as night; and call all kind-hearted women of Hijaz to mourn together with me.

The Maid: O Lord, look upon me and see how my heart is bleeding from grief. O congregation of mourners, the hour of sorrow is come; yea, the time of perpetual anguish has arrived! Hoist up your flag of grief, and blacken your house of mourning. O Fatima, thou queen of the nymphs of Paradise, I have prepared the things belonging to the scene of affliction and sorrow.

Fatima: O father! thou sympathising king of thy nation, where art thou? O thou intercessor of the Day of Judgment, where art thou?

The Household: O father! thou sympathising king of thy nation, where art thou? O thou intercessor of the Day of Resurrection, where art thou?

Fatima: If thou comest, I will give thee my soul; if thou appearest not, grief will kill me. At any rate I die for thee, father, whether thou comest or not!

The Household: If thou comest, I will give thee my soul; if thou appearest not, grief will kill me. At any rate I die for thee, father, whether thou comest or not!

Fatima: Return, dear father, and put once more the turban on thy head, and let thy holy body be clothed with thy blessed cloak.[2]

The Household: Return, dear father, and put once more the turban on thy head, and let thy holy body be clothed with thy blessed cloak.

Fatima: Let Bilal, thy attendant, carry thy carpet for adoration to the mosque. Begin thou to sing the praises of God, and hold the rod in thy hand, O father! *The Household:* Let Bilal, thy attendant, carry thy carpet for adoration to the mosque. Begin thou to sing the praises of God, and hold the rod in thy hand, O father!

Fatima: After thee, O father, the Hand of God [Ali] will not set his feet on the pulpit. The mosque, the pulpit, and the altar respectively derived their lustre from thee when thou wast on earth.

The People of Madina: O ye inhabitants of Madina, both small and great, be it known unto all of you, that the Prophet's daughter is disturbing us not a little by her continuous lamentation. Let us go soon to her husband, Ali, the Lion of God, and state the matter fully unto him; peradventure he may prevail upon her to keep quiet.

(*Addressing Ali*) O prince of believers, we have come to our last breath on account of Zahra's continual weeping and wailing. Forbid her, we pray thee, from crying day and night. Tell her to be quiet either at night or in the day-time, that we may, too, have a period of rest.

Ali: Alas! the fire of these your sad words has consumed my heart; the arrow of your petition has bent my back like a bow. You have made me very distressed by your request. How can Fatima cease from weeping since her mother and father are both dead?

Fatima: Alas! alas! again Ali's groanings are heard. Wherefore has Ali the deliverer arisen and come forth from the mosque? Why is Abu Turab [Ali] shedding twilight on the moon? Why does he let fall stars on the sun?

Ali: My sun-like face, O Fatima, has become a pale moon through thee; my sighs and groans are on account of thy weeping and impatience. Multitudes of men and women are complaining of anguish through thy sad cryings. Have pity on these poor people; they are Muslims after all.

Fatima: O Ali, how long wilt thou prohibit a sorrowful creature like me from crying? Dost thou not know that my dear father is dead, and so I mourn for him? Alas! woe unto me! why should it be thought a shame for one in my condition to weep? Is this city so small and limited that a miserable person like me cannot be left alone? O Ali, I am in deep distress; it is, indeed, a mighty evil to be an orphan! O Ali, I am greatly despised; desolation is most truly unbearable.

Ali: How long wilt thou complain of being an orphan, and thus sadly bewail? Who dares say thou art despised, seeing thou art the dearest of the age? But the people are simply complaining of thy piercing cries, and they beg thee, most respectfully, to forbear if possible.

Fatima: O Ali! if the people of Madina are tired of my crying – if they are weary of my lamentation and wailing, it is an easy thing for me to leave the city. I offer Madina a present to its inhabitants; I will go to the sepulchre of the Prophet, and dwell there. Let Madina be an offering to the followers of the Prophet. *(Turning towards the tomb.)* O thou chief of the creation of God, who art His true Messenger, peace be on thee! Hear my grievous complaints of thy followers, O God's Apostle! I have come in thy presence, father, with uncovered head, to express how sadly I am vexed with thy people; for they are truly tired of me. Better take me to thyself in the grave, so that thy people may thereby find themselves happy!

Ali: O thou Venus of the Heavens, who art the sun surrounded by two moons and one star! O thou whose eyebrows are the new moon of the world, look at me and pity me! O Fatima, cease thy crying and weeping; how long wilt thou shed tears from thine eyes?

Fatima: O thou who art higher than the highest heavens, the very floor of whose residence is above the divine throne! thou knowest that since the death of my father, the king of Time, my soul has experienced nothing but oppression and cruelty. My soul lives between fire and water. Even Bilal, my father's crier, is cruel; why does he not make proclamation for prayers, and seek to pacify my heart thereby?

Ali: Since thy father's death, O Fatima, poor Bilal has been himself, too, between fire and water. Still, however, O watchful black-fortuned Bilal, in whose book of fate there shall be no entry on the Day of Judgment (for nothing shall be written against thee in the volume of thy actions), get up, according to the request of Fatima, the queen of the morn of resurrection, and cry out for prayers.

Bilal (the crier): A mosque wherein no Messenger of the two worlds can be found, what sort of a mosque can that be? and what proclamation, what pulpit, and what cleanliness can it have? How can I go to the top of the minaret to sing out my proclamations like a nightingale, seeing thorns of affliction have filled my soul with blood, like as it were a rosebud? No heart has remained for

Bilal after the decease of the Apostle of God. What can he do? How can he cry for prayer?

(*He proclaims*)

'God is greater than all! God is greater than all!'

Fatima: The nightingale of Muhammad's garden is pouring forth its song. He ravishes the heart and disables it with his melodious notes, depriving it of patience and understanding. Sing on, O ye nightingale, if thou meanest to help me, for I am shedding blood, not tears, from my eyes, on account of my father's absence.

Bilal: I bear witness that there is no other God but God! I bear witness that there is no other God but God!

Fatima: O Hasan, my son, take thou the Quran of my poor father; and thou, O Husayn, carry the carpet of thy grandfather, the Messenger of the two worlds. Take them to the mosque, and tell the people to be ready, for the Prophet of God will shortly come to pray. And, O Bilal, go on with your proclamation, and untie the knot of sorrow that is in our heart.

Bilal: I testify that Muhammad is the Messenger of God. I testify that Muhammad is the Messenger of God.

Fatima (faintly): Alas! O Muhammad, my crowned father, father! Alas! O Muhammad, my magnified moon!

Hasan and Husayn (together): For God's sake, O crier, have pity on us, and cry no more; for Zahra, the daughter of the Prophet, is already dead. O disturbed mother, wherefore shouldst thou so long lament and weep? Why dost thou not speak to us, and why art so restless?

Fatima: May Zahra be a sacrifice for your elegant bodies, dear sons! May she be an offering for your shining faces, beloved children! (*Turning to her maid.*) Come, O thou grievously afflicted damsel, O thou fellow-companion of my daughter Zaynab, come to me.

The Maid: O thou, my tear-shedding mistress! O thou rest of my wounded heart! May I be a sacrifice for thy pair of tearful eyes! May all thy pains come to the soul of this thy maiden! What is thy command, O thou who art grievously troubled, that I may obey it with my whole soul and heart?

Fatima: Get me ready, O damsel, a hand-mill, to grind.

The Maid: What art thou going to grind in this state of poverty?

Fatima: I wish to grind some barley.

The Maid: Leave this toil to me, mistress.

Fatima: Yesterday it was thy turn, and thou didst perform it.

The Maid: Why should I get rest from labour at all?

Fatima: My father has so enjoined, and I must carry out his wishes.

The Maid: What were the terms of his command, I pray?

Fatima: He said, 'Have a regard for thy maid, poor girl.'

The Maid: Why? Handmaids are kept for service only.

Fatima: Get me some clay, wherewith to rub the head.

The Maid :For what is the clay? May my head be offered for thine!

Fatima: I want to wash Zaynab's head therewith.

The Maid: Oh! my heart has come into my mouth by this saying of thine!

Fatima: Bring me a basin, O afflicted maiden!

The Maid: What dost thou want to do with the basin, sad lady?

Fatima: I want to wash my children's clothes in it.

The Maid: Oh! I am extremely troubled in my mind at these thy words.

Fatima: Whether I be well or unwell, I have always to work for my children.

Pour water, O damsel, though it be from the fountain of thy eyes, that I may wash my husband's and my children's clothes. This very turban, which is now tinged with blood, though its fabric was spun by the beautiful nymphs of Paradise, shall be saturated with the blood of Ali's head, in the arched niche of the altar for prayer, through [Abd al-Rahman] the son of Muljam's cruel sword. Let me smell this shirt, which has the scent of the rose in it; let me cleanse it well, for it belongs to Hasan, my elder son. He shall put on this very shirt, and hold it close to his heart when suffering the pangs of deadly poison. Let my sighs and groans reach the heavens! I am rinsing the clothes of my younger son, Husayn, O friends! This very shirt, woe to me! shall be pierced through, in innumerable places, by the sharp arrows of the daring enemy. This very shirt, which I have washed clean, like snow, shall stick like mud to the horse-shoes of the enemy! O Lord God, Thou alone art aware of the state of my suffering heart, as I am washing now the head-dress of Zaynab, my dear daughter. I must clean this rose-leaf, this beautiful head-dress, to be a handkerchief in future for Shimar,[3] the unbeliever. This head-dress, which I have washed and arranged, shall be pulled off from Zaynab's head, and flung away on the ground. She shall ride with uncovered head, on a camel, and be carried from Karbala to Sham[4] with music and drumming, to her shame and my grievance!

The Maid: O my distressed lady, look upon my bleeding heart, and allow me, O dear mistress, to turn this mill for thee.

Zaynab: O mother, do not lament and bewail any more, nor so oft shed blood from thine eyes. Oh, let me, for Husayn's sake, turn the millstone for thee!

Hasan and Husayn together: O our afflicted mother, who art so solicitous about a whole family's welfare, let us, without any further ado, turn the mill for thee.

Fatima: O Hasan, I adjure thee by Husayn's soul, leave me for awhile; and I implore thee, O Husayn, by the soul of Hasan, hearken to my voice. Thee also, O maid, I beg, by the soul of Zaynab, go away for awhile; and thee, O Zaynab, by the soul of Fatima, stop thy importunity: for, by the breath of Ali do I swear,

I have some secret with the Lord. I want to talk a little with the millstone.

O millstone, thou companion of every afflicted spirit! O millstone, thou friend of my chamber! seeing millstones are generally turned by water, I have furnished thee always with the same from the head-fountain of my eyes! Thou art my witness, O millstone, that I have never stained my hands with henna to make them look red, but always with the heart's blood. Thou art my witness that day and night I have been in want of food and rest, in order simply to support Hasan and Husain, my children. O millstone, if thou wilt not bear witness in my favour in the Day of Judgment, when I shall have to render to God an account of all my actions, they will stop me in the scorching heat of the sun in that day. Oh! how difficult to bear the heat of that day's sun. Oh! my heart is quite faint within me, through feebleness, and the severity of the grief arising from my dear father's death. Oh! alas! alas! all my strength has left me at once. (*Falls into a swoon.*)

Angels in Paradise (one of whom comes forward): O ye assembly of nymphs inhabiting the celestial garden of Paradise, descend from your delightful abodes to the house of Zahra, the daughter of Muhammad; for she has fainted owing to excessive grief and distress. You must diligently employ yourselves in her service, and attend on her as slaves on their mistress.

Fatima: O ye singing birds of the plantations of heaven!

The Angel: Yes, thou queen of the throne and palace of heaven, what is thy order?

Fatima: Who are these that are thus weeping for me?

The Angel: They are all thy slaves, the nymphs of Paradise.

Fatima: Why have they come here all at once?

The Angel: They are summoned here to attend on thee as servants.

Fatima: Do these nymphs act at the bidding of anyone, or of their own accord?

The Angel: Yes; they belong to the illustrious companions of the Prophet.

Fatima: Whose is this bright-faced moon-like creature?

The Angel: It is Salina; and she belongs to Salman.[5]

Fatima: To whom belongs yonder sad angel?

The Angel: That is Makduda; and she belongs to Mikdad, another companion of the Prophet.

Fatima: Tell me whose is that sprightly sun-like nymph?

The Angel: That is called Izar, and belongs to Abazar.[6]

Fatima: I have a question which must be answered fairly.

The Angel: May we know what is the question of thy highness?

Fatima: Are there better nymphs in Paradise than these?

The Angel: Certainly, O lady of the Day of Judgment.

Fatima: Tell me, to whom do they generally belong?

The Angel: Know thou that they belong chiefly to the sympathisers with Husayn.

Fatima: On whom else will God bestow such nymphs?

The Angel: To those who truly weep for Husayn.

Fatima: Dost thou know anything about the Prophet?

The Angel: Yes; I saw him sitting sadly at the corner of al-Kauzar[7] [in Paradise].

Fatima: Has he been ill-treated there by his foolish people?

The Angel: His sadness was chiefly on thy account.

Fatima: Did he not say when Zahra will be delivered from her sorrows?

The Angel: Yes; tomorrow thou shalt be with him in Paradise.

Fatima: Thanks be to God my Creator, that He thus permits me to go to Paradise to see the face of my dear father! O my poor maid, who art sick with fever of sorrow, O thou incarnate night of affliction and grief, come hither; for my heart is overflowing with unusual sadness, as I intend to wash Zaynab's hair. Go thou, O ill-fated, black-starred creature, and get some rose-water and a comb for me.

The Maid: O hand of death, come forth and comb with the comb of destruction the curls of my life! May I be offered for thy weeping eyes! Here is some rose-water and also a comb; take them from thy handmaid.

Fatima: Come, Zaynab; may I be offered for thy hair! Come, let me smell thy musky locks. O heaven, order thy stars to shut their eyes, for Zaynab is going to uncover her head that it may be washed. And thou, O sun, remain hidden under the earth, that thou mayest not see Zaynab's hair uncovered. And thou, O day, be buried in the dark night for ever, for Zaynab's face and hair are about to be divested of their usual covering!

The People of Madinah: O thou lion of the thicket of almighty power! O Ali, bring out the hand of Godhead from thy sleeves, and save us! Why should the day be buried in perpetual night? Why does not the sun, the ruler of the day, put on his crown of light and reign? Has Zahra concealed her face from the world, that the sun should, out of shame, remain enveloped in the clouds?

Ali (conversing with Bilal): O Bilal, seeing that the bright day is thus turned into a dark night, and the sun has totally hidden himself from view, one might suppose that Zaynab my daughter has unveiled her face, or that they are going to wash her head.

An Angel: O Ali, the Lion of God! king of the great empire of faith! central force of the divine system of might and power! thus saith the Lord: 'Be pleased to order that Zaynab's head should be covered; otherwise the sun will not come out from his dark retreat for ever.'

Ali: O Zahra, about what art thou so busy?

Fatima: O Ali, I am combing my daughter's hair.

Ali: Put a veil on her face, that day and night may continue their regular courses.

Fatima: I have nothing to do, man, with day and night.

Ali: The sun is ashamed to show his face while that of Zaynab is laid open to view.

Fatima: But, alas! this same Zaynab's hair shall become full of blood.

Ali: Oh! shall Zaynab indeed become acquainted with grief?

Fatima: Yes; and this her head shall be broken by the wood of the litter, when led away as a captive.

Ali: Will the band of cruelty be stretched against her?

Fatima: Yes; in Kufa[8] they will cast stones at her.

Ali: Oh! shall she be deprived of the pleasures of life?

Fatima: Ah! she shall be spurned by the daughters of Sham.

Ali: Will she, truly, be subject to contempt at the hands of her enemies?

Fatima: Yes; they will pass her through the bazars with uncovered head, and so disgrace her.

Ali: From whom hast thou heard these predictions?

Fatima: From the holy mouth of the Prophet himself.

Ali: O Fatima! thou worthy companion of mine! thou peace of my troubled spirit! thou hapless, friendless sufferer, the whole of whose body looks sickly, like the eye itself! Thou from every eyelash of whom a flood of tears continually runs down; tell me, dear wife, what kind of fruit dost thou like most?

Fatima: O Lion of God, and the high priest of His people, my father, the Prophet of God, has charged me not to drink water when I am parched, though my heart should burn with thirst. Since my body is seized with a very hot fever, I should like to quench its flames with a little piece of some pomegranates.

Ali (addressing the people of Madina): O God, for the merit of the sigh of the needy, put me not to shame before Zahra, the daughter of Muhammad. O afflicted companions of God's Messenger, the virgin Fatima has requested pomegranates from her poor husband Ali.

The Inhabitants of Madina: May our heads be strewn under thy sacred feet! May our parents be offered as ransoms for thy soul! None has got pomegranates with him in this town save Simeon the Jew.

Ali: Necessity, O merciful Lord, has obliged the king of faith to go to an unbelieving Jew. Ali, notwithstanding his natural abilities, is reduced to great difficulties today; so that he must go to an infidel. Yes, the mirror may be in want of ashes sometimes. Come out, O Simeon, from thy house; for Ali, the hand of God Almighty, needs thee!

Simeon: Peace be on thee, O king of the throne of judgment! O solar orb of the heaven of justice! what has made thee, O tribunal of justice and faith, cast thine eyes so bashfully on the ground? O majestic Ali, tell me, what is thy request?

Ali: The sun has condescended to shine upon an insignificant atom.

Simeon: Why is the face of thy wishes wrapped in a veil?

Ali: A certain sick person has requested a thing from me.

Simeon: What may that request be, and who is the sick person?

Ali: Fatima is the invalid, and a pomegranate the request.

Simeon: Pomegranates are not to be had at this season.

Ali: It is not good to keep her waiting longer.

Simeon: O thou, who art the only tree of generosity in the garden of creation! they brought me some pomegranates lately from Taif, but I sold the whole, since people were eager to buy them. I do not sew bags in which to preserve pomegranates.

Ali: O Jew, go and make diligent search. Thou hast got still two loads of pomegranates left thee; get me one pomegranate therefrom, please.

Simeon: O Ali, God knoweth that thou art aware of all things. Thou hast well spoken, indeed, and uttered what is true. I confess with shame that I said falsely; so I penitently ask thy pardon. But the pomegranates thou mentionest had been stolen, and stored up somewhere by my wife against my knowledge; and so I am partly right, O thou collyrium of mine eye. Be it as it may, thou mayest take this pomegranate from me, and carry it as a present to Zahra thy wife.

Ali: Praise be unto God, the sole Creator of all things, who would not suffer me to be put to shame before Zahra.

[*At this point, there is a scene in which a sick, blind man approaches Ali, reminding him of the suffering of the martyrs at Karbala. Ali offers the blind young man solace, and when he asks for pomegranates, Ali gives him the fruit meant for Fatima. The blind man's suffering also reminds Ali (and the audience) of the fate of the fourth imam Zayn al-Abidin who was sent to Damascus with his aunt Zaynab as one of the prisoners of Karbala.*]

Angels bringing pomegranates for Fatima: O Lord God, angels' hearts are broken in consequence of excessive grief! How long shall Zahra suffer pain in expecting Ali's return? Come along, ye large-eyed, beautiful nymphs of Paradise, with salvers on your heads bearing pomegranates to your mistress Fatima, the mother of Husayn. O ye servants of the court of him whom the angels serve with joy [Ali], let one of your number come behind the door and open it for us!

Fatima (to her maid): O damsel, I heard a voice at the door; hasten and see if it be not Ali, Zahra's husband.

The Maid: Who is he that knocks outside at the door? What is his name? Why does he so, and what may be the news?

The Angel: I am a porter of this court, a home-born slave of God's defender

[Ali]; and have come from him with pomegranates for Zahra his wife. Be thou pleased to take them from his servant.

The Maid (to Fatima): Dear Lady, may my soul be offered for thy head! Thy husband has sent thee pomegranates.

Fatima: O damsel, since my lord and husband is not present to partake of the same with me, the pomegranates do not seem agreeable to my palate.

Ali: O Fatima, thou matron of Muhammad's family! thou queen of the palace of Arabia's divine king, good news! thy companion is come; but tell me, whence didst thou get these pomegranates?

Fatima: O Ali, this very moment, when I was in the midst of hope and despair, there came some one and knocked at the door, saying, 'Take these pomegranates, sent by Zahra's husband, Ali the most high.'

Ali: Rest awhile, O most faithful Zahra, and do not make sighs and lamentations any more; for that was Gabriel, the sweet angel of revelation, who came and knocked; and these pomegranates are from the garden of Paradise.

Fatima (to her maid): Come, O damsel, take this plate of pomegranates to keep for my poor children, who are soon about to become orphans. And thou, O Ali, go to the mosque, there to pray for us, and to think awhile about our painful state of mind.

Ali: How can I voluntarily go away from thy happy presence, or how can I leave thee alone in the house? O Lord God, for the merit of Hasan and the soul of Husayn, forgive thou the sins of the followers of the latter.

Fatima: Come to me, poor Zaynab, apart from the others.

Zaynab: What is thy object in thus speaking, O sorrowful mother?

Fatima: Hold my arms and help me to get up, child.

Zaynab: Oh! may God put an end to the days of my life!

Fatima: Carry me, and leave me near that box, girl.

Zaynab: Mother, thou turnest my bright day into dark night.

Fatima: See that Husayn be not about, either far nor near.

Zaynab: His moon does not shine in the room, which is consequently dark.

Fatima: Take this key from me, and unlock the box.

Zaynab: I have done it; what are thy further orders?

Fatima: Take this casket, but keep it carefully.

Zaynab: What can there be in it, good mother?

Fatima: There is in it the Prophet's tooth, which was knocked out in the battle of Uhud.

Zaynab: Let me kiss it; for fresh blood still gushes therefrom.

Fatima: Hold this casket also in thy hand.

Zaynab: What is in this again, mother? for my eyes begin to shed blood as soon as I hold it in my hands.

Fatima: In it is the evidence of Husayn's blood.

Zaynab: What evidence, O thou brightness of the two worlds, is this?

Fatima: It is an evidence with which I shall succeed in the last day in making intercession for the sins of our people.

Zaynab: Oh, how happy such a people; how blessed!

Fatima: Take out the third casket, daughter.

Zaynab: What can be in that, dear mother?

Fatima: Nothing but the ring that was on King Solomon's finger.

Zaynab: Why hast thou hid it here in a casket?

Fatima: Because my dear grandson Ali Akbar will suck water out of it when thirsty in Karbala.[9]

Zaynab: Oh, may I die! for my soul has become restless.

Fatima: Husayn shall wear this ring on his finger.

Zaynab: Will anybody take it from off his finger?

Fatima: Yes; a camel-driver shall cut Husayn's finger, and take off the ring.

Zaynab: Yes; see how his friends weep on this sad occasion.

Fatima: Take out that bundle of clothes from the box.

Zaynab: My heart overflows with blood at the sight of this bundle.

Fatima: Look at this shirt, torn into pieces.

Zaynab: Let it be a burial shroud for Zaynab.

Fatima: This is the shirt of Husayn my son.

Zaynab: O Lord! see the sad state of my Husayn.

Fatima: When my Husayn shall prepare himself for the field of battle –

Zaynab: Oh, tell me what to do at that time, mother.

Fatima: Kiss his dear throat, and remember me.

Zaynab: Oh! mother, kill me at once, that I may not see such a thing.

Fatima: Come and open for me the other box, girl.

Zaynab: What is this one, O dear mother?

Fatima: Take out the three bottles filled with camphor.

Zaynab: I have done it; but for what dost thou intend them?

Fatima: When I die thou must sprinkle one over my body.

Zaynab: What shall I do with the remaining two?

Fatima: One of the two belongs to Haidar, thy father.

Zaynab: Say, whose is the third, dear mother?

Fatima: That is for Hasan, thy elder brother, dear.

Zaynab: Where is Husayn, my helpless brother's, share?

Fatima: Husayn's body shall receive no washing, no lotus leaves' powder, and no camphor when he dies.

Zaynab: But why, dear mother? What is his fault?

Fatima: His camphor shall be the dust of Karbala.

Zaynab: O ye Muslims, weep on for him.

Fatima: Go away, dear daughter, and let my maid come to me now.

Zaynab: Come, thou suffering, broken-hearted damsel, Fatima, my mother, the best among women, wanteth thee.

The Maid: What dost thou desire, O crown of my head? Declare it to me.

Fatima: Look at me, and prepare for me camphor and funeral garments. There is a shroud of mine in that closet, with some camphor of paradise placed on it. Run quickly, my poor damsel, and bring it at once to me.

The Maid: Alas! woe unto me, from the injustice of time! My mistress is going away from us for ever. My Hasan will be in great affliction and sorrow, and my Husayn will have no one to take care of him. Dear lady, may my head be given a ransom for thee! Here is the winding-sheet and the camphor; take them.

Fatima: O heaven, thou hast at length begun thy torments! Thou hast thrown me suddenly from a close union to distant separation! Thou takest away Hasan from me, and buildest up a wall of partition between me and Husayn! O dear Hasan, may I be made a ransom for thy soul; a sacrifice for thee and thy tearful eyes! And, O Husayn, may I be offered for thy head, and be made an oblation for thee and thy throat! What is thy sin, child, that it should happen to thee to be deprived of all, and fall naked before the hot sun in the plain of Karbala? O great God, I leave this world never to see it again, having experienced no pleasures in my short life, which consists only of eighteen years; and am going cheerfully to the Messenger of God, my father in heaven. Therefore do I bear witness that there is no real God besides the true One.

Notes

1. Sale's *Koran,* 1734, p. 458.

2. The Prophet wrapped his cloak around himself, his daughter, his son-in-law and his two grandsons.

3. Shimar was one of Yazid's generals who slew Husain on the plain of Karbala in 680 AD.

4. Syria.

5. Salman the Persian, a Companion of the Prophet, is one of the most popular figures of Muslim legend. He is particularly venerated by Shi'is and is the source of *hadiths* honouring Ali and his family.

6. One of Muhammad's four closest friends.

7. One of the rivers of Paradise which supplies the Pond of the Prophet.

8. Kufa, south of Baghdad, was one of the important centres of early Islam.

9. Ali Akbar, son of Husayn the Martyr, was slain on the plain of Karbala 680 AD.

PART TWO

EARLY ISLAMIC HISTORY

The history of the first four successors to Muhammad's leadership of the Islamic state, the righteous caliphs, is shrouded in a twilight zone between religious—legal precedents and military-political chronicles. Ambivalent messages on women's activities drawn from this period are a case in point.

Islamic history in the true sense of the word begins with the Umayyad dynasty (41-132/661-750) whose capital was Damascus, overthrown by the Abbasids based in Iraq. During this formative period, up to the acme of the Abbasid Empire (in the third/ninth century), canonical religious and legal works established what would be regarded as orthodox Islam. As we learn more about the prominent women of this period, we may gain insight into the molding of Muslim scholars' attitudes to woman.

At the same time, Muslim historians collected biographical information about women as well as men, and referred to women in their chronicles. The format and content of these two genres reveal the place of women in these authors' world-view.

5

HISTORICAL BIOGRAPHIES:

A ROYAL WOMAN OF THE UMAYYAD DYNASTY

['Ali b. al-Hasan Ibn 'Asakir, *Tarikh madinat Dimashq: Tarajim al-nisa'*. ed. Sukayna al-Shihabi (Damascus, 1982), no. 60.]

The biographical dictionary, comprising entries for anywhere from about 70 to 12,000 individuals, is a unique Islamic literary genre. Hundreds, if not thousands, of works of this type were compiled from the early centuries of Islam to this day. Some of the biographical collections are retrospective and/or historical in orientation while others deal with the authors' contemporaries or near-contemporaries.

The proportion of women included in the biographical collections ranges from less that 1 per cent to 23 per cent for the period from the advent of Islam to the fifteenth century (ninth Islamic century), and drops drastically in the subsequent centuries. The classical compendia may have only a handful of biographies of women or as many as 1,500.

The History of Damascus of Ibn Asakir (died 571/1176) is actually a collection of some 13,500 biographies of individuals connected with the city from the age of the Prophet to the author's time. The format of the biographies reflects certain aspects of Islamic scholarship and Arabic prose which appeared in the biography of the Prophet and Bukhari's compilation of the Prophet's sayings. After a brief introduction describing the subject of the biography, a series of discrete pieces of information and stories are presented with little attempt to link one to another. As in Bukhari's work, each item is preceded by a detailed list of the informants and scholars who are the sources and transmitters of the information (which have been abbreviated below for the convenience of the reader). This methodology, developed to verify the

77

authenticity of crucial normative religious material, was applied to mundane historical (and cultural) information. Also, stories which appear to have originated as exegesis on popular verse, are turned into historic episodes. One can imagine such unstated questions as 'which woman threatened warriors in verse with denial of sexual favours;' and 'who did the poet describe as the griefstricken wife trying to prevent her husband from going out to war.' One cannot but be impressed by the diligent scholarship of the classical Islamic biographers who compiled scraps of information and preserved them with minimal critical comment. The kind of information included in these biographies as well as the format of presentation reflect the biographers attitude toward different areas of human endeavour. At the end of Ibn Asakir's work, after over 13,000 biographies of men, 200 women appear. A large number of these are royal women of the Umayyad dynasty whose capital was Damascus.

The question of succession to the Prophet became the subject of dispute at an early stage in Islamic history, as we have seen, but the first four righteous caliphs (Abu Bakr, Umar, Uthman and Ali) are revered by all Muslims despite some of their shortcomings. The Ummayyad dynasty (41-132/661-750), however, is often depicted in a negative light, particularly since most of the sources on the Umayyads date from the time of the Abbasids who overthrew them. The early Umayyad caliphs were descendants of Abu Sufyan thus their epithet Sufyanids. The Marwanid branch of the family came to power from the time of Marwan son of al-Hakam (64/685).

The accompanying genealogical chart of the Umayyad rulers may be useful in identifying the main characters who appear in the following biography.

Atika daughter of Yazid is titled mother of sons *(umm al-banin)* to identify her as a free-born woman. Concubines who bore their masters children were styled *umm walad* and were usually emancipated. As the Muslim community was transformed into a vast and wealthy empire, concubines began to play a greater role in the life of the ruling classes.

Why did Ibn Asakir include Atika daughter of Yazid in his *History of Damascus?* What does the author regard as her most outstanding achievements? Is Hind, daughter of Utba, founding mother of the Umayyad dynasty, mentioned among the many Umayyad kin? Why? Are other female relatives of the Umayyad rulers cited? How does woman's relationship to warfare in a vast, institutionalized empire differ from that in the early Islamic community? Which branch of the Umayyad family did Atika support - her own clan or that of her husband? Why? What aspects of Atika's character emerge from this biography? Whose response to the death of a son is deemed more appropriate by the author: Atika's or Abd al-Malik's? Does this story have implications about women's character?

For another perspective on Atika's historical role, see: *The History of al-Tabari*, vol. 23 'The Zenith of the Marwanid House: The Last Years of 'Abd al-Malik and the Caliphate of Al-Walid' trans. Martin Hinds. A portrait of Atika drawn from a number of biographies may be found in Ruth Roded, *Women in the Islamic Biographical Collections* (Boulder, CO: Lynne Reinner, 1993). Nabia Abbott's 'Women and the State in Early Islam: The Umayyads.' *Journal of Near Eastern Studies* 1 (1942): 341-68, is a survey of the role of women at this time.

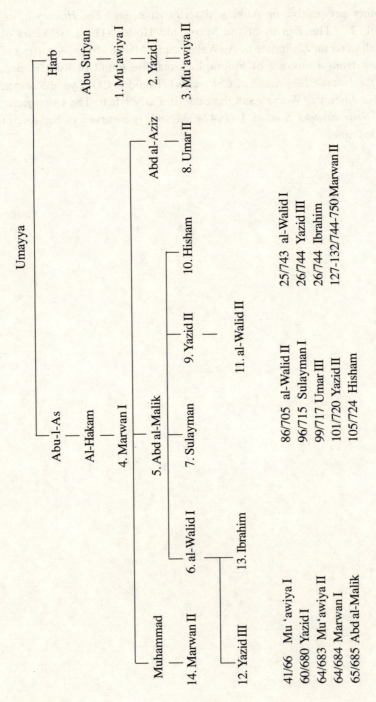

Umayya

Harb

Abu Sufyan

Abu-l-As

Al-Hakam

1. Mu'awiya I

2. Yazid I

3. Mu'awiya II

Abd al-Aziz

8. Umar II

4. Marwan I

5. Abd al-Malik

7. Sulayman

10. Hisham

9. Yazid II

11. al-Walid II

Muhammad

Marwan II

6. al-Walid I

13. Ibrahim

14. Marwan II

12. Yazid III

41/66	Mu'awiya I
60/680	Yazid I
64/683	Mu'awiya II
64/684	Marwan I
65/685	Abd al-Malik
86/705	al-Walid II
96/715	Sulayman I
99/717	Umar III
101/720	Yazid II
105/724	Hisham
25/743	al-Walid I
26/744	Yazid III
26/744	Ibrahim
127-132/744-750	Marwan II

The Umayyad Caliphs

Source : *A Middle East Studies Handbook, ed. Jere L. Bachrach, Cambridge: Cambridge University Press, 1984, p. 18.*

Ibn 'Asakir's, History of Damascus: Women's Biographies

60-Atika daughter of Yazid, son of Mu'awiya, son of Abu Sufyan son of Harb son of Umayya, *umm al-banin* the Umayyad.

Her mother [was] Umm Kulthum daughter of Abdallah son of Amir ibn Kurayz. She was the wife of Abd al-Malik son of Marwan, and the mother of Yazid son of Abd al-Malik. The Atika area outside the Jabiya gate is ascribed to her. She had a palace there where Abd al-Malik son of Marwan died.

Muhajir the father of Amr ibn Muhajir al-Ansari related [traditions] from her.

Abu al-Husayn b. al-Fara' told us ...

Among the names of the children of Yazid son of Mu'awiya are: Abdallah ibn Yazid who was called al-Uswar and Atika who gave birth to Marwan and Yazid the sons of Abd al- Malik.

Umar ibn Abu Bakr al-Mawsili transmitted to me ...

When Abd al-Malik was about to go out to battle against Mus'ab b. al-Zubayr, his wife Atika daughter of Yazid grabbed him and cried. Her slave-girls cried with her. He sat down and said: [the poet] Ibn Abu Jum'a [better known as Kuthayyir Azza] hit the mark when he said: (in verse)

A woman, adorned by a pearl necklace, who prizes her honor,
will not restrain a man from embarking on a military expedition;
She forbade him, and when she saw that the ban did not hinder him, she cried, and
her servants cried as well because of her.

Then he left. The mother of the two [Atika and Mus'ab] was Umm Kulthum daughter of Abdallah son of Amir b. Kurayz b. Habib b. Abd al-Shams.

Abu Muhammad b. al-Akfani told us ...

Among the women who related [traditions] in Syria: Atika daughter of Yazid son of Mu'awiya. Muhajir al-Ansari told from her.

Abu Ghalib and Abu Abdallah the sons of al-Banna related to us ...

I heard Mahmud say that in the third generation[1] [of traditionists was] Atika daughter of Yazid son of Mu'awiya; and al-Kilabi added that she was a Damascene.

Abu al-Faraj Ghayth b. Ali informed us ...

Atika daughter of Yazid son of Mu'awiya used to take off her veil in the presence of twelve caliphs all of whom were in a degree of consanguity to her precluding marriage *(mahram):* her father Yazid son of Mu'awiya, her brother

Mu'awiya son of Yazid, her grandfather Mu'awiya son of Abu Sufyan, her husband, Abd al-Malik son of Marwan, her husband's father Marwan son of al-Hakam, her son Yazid son of Abd al-Malik, her husband's sons al-Walid and Sulayman and Hisham, her grandson al-Walid son of Yazid, her husband's grandson Yazid son of al-Walid son of Abd al-Malik, and Ibrahim son of al-Walid who was forced to abdicate who was also her husband's grandson. Abu Muhammad b. al-Akfani told us ...

Abd al-Malik son of Marwan said to Atika daughter of Yazid: ' [What do you think about] making a witnessed bequest of your property to your children.' She said: 'Send some reliable relatives in to me so that they can act as witnesses.' He sent a number of them to her and with them he sent Rawh b. Zinba. Rawh gave her Abd al-Malik's message. She said: 'O Rawh, my children do not need my property because of their father and their status vis-à-vis the caliphate. But I would like you to witness my endowment *(waqf)* of all of my property to the family of Abu Sufyan. They need it more because their situation has been changed [since they are no longer caliphs].' Rawh blanched as he left and Abd al-Malik said to him: 'What happened to you?' He said: 'You sent me to 'Mu'awiya sitting in his robes!' [i.e. Atika]', and then he told him the whole story.

From Wazira ...

The daughter of Yazid son of Mu'awiya asked Abd al-Malik son of Marwan for permission to go on the pilgrimage, and he gave her permission. He said: 'Give me a list of what you need and leave me.' [Meanwhile,] Aisha daughter of Talha[2] went on the pilgrimage. 'I would prefer it if you remained,' [he said], but she refused. She gave him a list and made preparations, and provisioned her. When she was between Mecca and Medina, a group of riders approached, upset her and dispersed her caravan. They said: ' [It is] Aisha daughter of Talha, with one of her slave-girls.' Then, a similar retinue came by and they said: ' [It is] her hairdresser.' Then, a procession appeared which was larger than that one by three hundred camels. Atika said: 'What God preserves for me is better.' Abu Bakr Wajih b. Tahir told us ...

Abd al-Malik summoned me with some Damascene Quran-reciters. When we went in to him, his wife Atika daughter of Yazid son of Mu'awiya was sitting there and her young son was sick. We began to pray and he began to pray to God saying: 'By virtue of my rank where You placed me.' He did not move until the boy died. He had mourned more than the child's mother, but when the boy died he bore it with patience and fortitude. I said: 'O Commander of the Faithful,[3] previously you mourned more than she did, and now she is mourning more than you are!' He said: 'We are sad about troubles so long as they do not occur, but once they happen, we bear them with patience and fortitude.'

I heard that Atika daughter of Yazid lived until her grandson, al-Walid son of Yazid son of Abd al-Malik, was killed.

Notes

1.   A generation *(tabaqa)* in the reckoning of traditionists is not strictly chronological but refers to the distance from the original source.

2.   Aisha daughter of Talha was an infamous woman of the second generation after the Prophet, known for her worldliness and arrogance. Abd al-Malik provided her with sixty royal mules for her entourage on the pilgrimage. For more details about this fascinating woman, see: Roded, *Women in Islamic Biographical Collections,* pp. 50-3.

3.   Commander of the Faithful was one of the titles of the caliph.

CHRONICLES: MOTHER OF ABBASID CALIPHS

[The History of al-Tabari: Volume XXX *The 'Abbasid Caliphate in Equilibrium,* trans. C. E. Bosworth. Albany: State University of New York Press, 1989) pp. 42-5, 91-2, 98-9, 102, 107.]

In the historical biographies, information collected from a number of sources was brought together to sketch portraits of prominent women. These biographies give us a sense of the kinds of women who could achieve prominence in Middle Eastern history and culture. They also concentrate on the woman who is the subject of the biography, detaching her to some extent from the flow of events surrounding her life. The short, infrequent and scattered references to women in historical chronicles, on the other hand, place these women's activities in the context of political, social and religious history deemed important by the great Muslim chroniclers.

The historical chronicle - a description of a series of dated historical events - appeared in the Islamic world in the middle of the third/ninth century. Works of this type grew out of the biographies of the Prophet, biographical dictionaries and monographs of rulers which had appeared previously. They were also influenced by the classical Graeco-Roman historiographical tradition as well as the Persian books of kings. Most of these works took the form of universal histories, aiming to encompass all events from ancient times to the lifetime of the author (with a geographic element as well). The compilation of historical material on the classical periods of Islam reached its culmination in the work of Muhammad ibn Jarir al-Tabari (225-310/839-923). Subsequent Muslim historians usually relied on Tabari's *History* for materials on the early centuries of Islam, and continued his annalistic descriptions of events to their time.

Like most traditional Muslim scholars, Tabari was first and foremost a traditionist and his commentary on the Quran is considered a summation of the early development of Quranic exegesis. To complement this monumental work, Tabari composed *The History of Prophets and Kings* - a wide-ranging history of the world from an Islamic perspective. Beginning from ancient times, Tabari traces the life of the Prophet, the rise of Islam and annual events in the Islamic world to the year 915. The methodology of *hadith* transmission, which was adapted to biographical collections, is evident in Tabari's chronicle as well, but in a much less rigorous form (more akin to Ibn Ishaq's biography of the Prophet). The entire work is now being translated into English by an international team of scholars headed by Ehsan Yarshater as *The History of al-Tabari,* a thirty-eight volume project of the State University of New York series in Near Eastern Studies.

Volume thirty of *The History of al-Tabari,* covering the very brief caliphate of Musa al-Hadi and the twenty-three year reign of Harun al-Rashid, has been subtitled *The 'Abbasid Caliphate in Equilibrium.* During these years, the Abbasid empire faced two external enemies, Christian Byzantium and the Turkish peoples of Inner Eurasia who threatened the north-eastern frontiers of the Caucasus and Central Asia. Internally, Shi'ite and radical, egalitarian Kharijite uprisings challenged the caliphate but did not pose serious political threats.

Khayzuran was a concubine of the third Abbasid caliph Muhammad al-Mahdi (ruled 775-785) who bore him two sons, Musa and Harun. She was noted for her beauty and proficiency in poetry and song. When Muhammad became caliph, he emancipated her and took her as a second wife (in addition to his cousin Rayta). Muslim historians write that Khayzuran had great influence during her husband's reign, but the specific cases cited are not connected to crucial political matters nor do they show her in a positive light. In one story, for example, her agent is pitted against an honest judge who refuses to bow to her power and wealth. Khayzuran's political influence was expressed primarily in the struggle for succession between her two sons, particularly after her husband's death, and during their reigns. Al-Mahdi had initially named Musa as his heir but later changed his mind and wanted to designate Harun to succeed him. Musa refused to accept this decision and revolted against his father. On a campaign against his rebellious son, al-Mahdi suddenly died, leading to the allegation that he had been poisoned by his son's agents. There were rumors that Khayzuran, who had remained in the capital, would engineer the succession of her favourite Harun, but he decided to respect his father's dying wishes and give the oath of allegiance to Musa al-Hadi as caliph.

The following selections are references to Khayzuran found in Tabari's description of the events of the reigns of Musa al-Hadi and Harun al-Rashid. Although the caliphs had many wives, concubines, sisters and other female relatives, Khayzuran is one of the few women dealt with at any length in the historical chronicle. In what contexts does Tabari mention this royal woman? How important are the events cited compared to those that precede or follow them? What impression do we get of Khayzuran?

Further information on Islamic histories may be found in the entry 'Ta'rikh, Ilm al-' in *The Encyclopaedia of Islam,* and in Franz Rosenthal's *A History of Muslim Historiography* (Leiden: E. J. Brill, 1952). A scholarly biography of Khayzuran based on a variety of sources forms half of Nabia Abbott's *Two Queens of Baghdad: Mother and Wife of Harun al-Rashid* (Chicago, 1946). For a description of the material culture and social life of this period based on a wide variety of sources, see: Muhammad Manazir Ahsan's *Social Life Under the Abbasids, 170-289/786-902* (London and New York: Longman, 1979).

Tabari's History

The Caliphate of Musa al-Hadi: The Events of the Year 170

The Reason Why al-Khayzuran Had Ordered the Slave Girls to Kill al-Hadi

Yahya b. al-Hasan has mentioned that when al-Hadi became caliph, he became openly hostile towards and quarreled with his mother. Khalisa (i.e., al-Khayzuran's slave girl) came to him one day and told him, 'Your mother seeks a gift of clothing from you,' so he ordered a storehouse full of clothing to be given to her. He related: There were found in al-Khayzuran's house (after her death) among her possessions eighteen thousand sleeveless robes of figured silk. He related: At the opening of Musa's caliphate, al-Khayzuran used to exercise her authority over him in all his affairs without consulting him at all, and she used to behave in regard to him, by assuming sole control over matters of ordaining and forbidding, just as she had done previously with his father (i.e., al-Mahdi). Hence, al-Hadi sent a message to her, 'Do not step beyond the boundaries of a woman's traditional modest position into demeaning yourself by being careless with your honor. It is not dignified for women that they should involve themselves in affairs of state. Instead, stick to your perfomance of the worship, to recounting God's praises, and to devoting yourself to pious works for God. Then after that, be conformable to the female role which is incumbent upon you.' He related: During Musa's caliphate, al-Khayzuran used frequently to bombard him with requests for favors, and he used to grant whatever she asked. This went on for four months of his caliphate, and people thronged round her, seeking her aid, and processions of people used to resort to her door.

He related: One day, al-Khayzuran spoke to him about a matter concerning which he saw no way to satisfy her. He made an appropriate excuse, but she exclaimed, 'You must satisfy my request without fail!' He replied, 'I won't do it!' She expostulated, 'But I've already promised this unreservedly to Abdallah b. Malik.' He related: Musa became enraged and said, 'Woe upon the son of a whore! I have already realized that he is the person behind this request, but by God, I won't grant you it!' She retorted, 'In that case, by God, I'll never ask anything of you again!' He said, 'By God, in that case, I don't care a bit!' and he grew hot and enraged. Al-Khayzuran got up to go, equally angry, but he ordered her, 'Stay where you are, and take good note of my words! (I swear) by God, on pain of forfeiting my status as a kinsman of the Messenger of God[1] if I do not fulfill this oath, that if ever I hear about any of my commanders or any of my close courtiers or servants standing at your door, I shall certainly have their heads chopped off and their possessions confiscated. Let whoever will, follow that course! What are all these processions of suppliants which come each day, by morning and evening, to your door? Have you no spindle to keep you busy, or copy of the Quran to remind you (of God) or house to keep you safe (from the public gaze)? Beware, and again beware, lest you open your door, whether to any Muslim or to any Dhimmi [non-Muslim]!' So she went off, hardly conscious where she was stepping; and after this, she never again uttered in his presence a single word (literally, either a sweet or a bitter word).

Yahya b. al-Hasan related that his father transmitted the information to him, saying: I heard Khalisa telling al-Abbas b. al-Fadl b. al-Rabi' that Musa sent to his mother al-Khayzuran a dish of rice, saying, 'I found this tasty and accordingly ate some of it; so you have some too!' Khalisa related: But I said to her, 'Don't touch it until you investigate further, for I am afraid that it might contain something to your detriment.' So they brought in a dog; it ate some and fell down dead. Musa sent to al-Khayzuran afterwards and said, 'How did you like the dish of rice?' She replied, 'I enjoyed it very much.' He said, 'You can't have eaten it, because if you had, I would have been rid of you. When was any Caliph ever happy who had a mother (still alive)?'

He related: A certain man of the Hashimites[2] transmitted the information to me that the cause of al-Hadi's death was that when the latter directed his efforts at depriving Harun (of his succession rights as next heir) and at having allegiance done to his own son Ja'far (as heir instead of Harun), and when al-Khayzuran became fearful for Harun's safety at al-Hadi's hands, she secretly despatched at the time of al-Hadi's illness some of her slave girls to kill him by covering over (his mouth and nose) and sitting on his face (i.e., thus suffocating him). She sent to Yahya b. Khalid the message that 'The man has died, so act decisively in what you have to do and don't fall short in the appropriate measures!'

Muhammad b. Abd al-Rahman b. Bashshar has mentioned that al-Fadl b. Sa'id transmitted the information to him from his father, saying: Musa kept receiving information about his commanders' resorting to his mother al-Khayzuran, these persons hoping by speaking with her thereby to have their various requests fulfilled by the Caliph. He related: She, for her part, was aiming at securing an ascendancy over his affairs just as she had enjoyed over al-Mahdi's affairs. Ali-Hadi kept barring her from achieving this and would say, 'What have women to do with the discussing of men's affairs?' When he began to find excessive the number of his commanders who were resorting to his mother, he gathered the commanders together one day and said to them, 'Who is better, I or you!' They replied, 'Certainly, you are, O Commander of the Faithful!' He said, 'Who then is better, my mother or your mothers?' They replied, 'Assuredly, your mother, O Commander of the Faithful!' He continued,

'Which then of you would like to have men talking about his mother's affairs, saying'So-and-so's mother did this, and so-and-so's mother acted in this way, And so-and-so's mother said this?" They replied, 'None of us would like that.' He said, 'So what do you think about the men who keep coming to my mother and who subsequently make her affairs the subject of their conversations?' When they heard this, they ceased their visits to her completely. Al-Khayzuran was deeply mortified by that; she kept away from him and swore that she would never speak to him again. Thereafter, she never entered his presence until death came upon him.

The Events of the Year 170 (cont'd July 3,786-June 21,787)

Harun s Assumption of the Caliphate on Musa al-Hadi's Death
Allegiance was given to al-Rashid Harun son of Muhammad son of Abdallah son of al-Abbas as caliph on the night of the Friday during which his brother Musa al-Hadi died. On that day when he assumed power he was twenty-two years old. It is also said that on the day when allegiance was given to him as caliph he was twenty-one years old. His mother was a slave wife from Jurash in the Yemen called Khayzuran, and he himself was born at al-Rayy on the twenty-sixth of Dhu al-Hijjah 145 (March 17, 763) during al-Mansur's caliphate. In regard to the Barmakis,[3] according to what has been mentioned, they assert that al-Rashid was born on the first of al-Muharram 149 (February 16, 766) and that al-Fadl son of Yahya [al-Barmaki] was born seven days before him, al-Fadl's day of birth being the twenty-second of Dhu al-Hijjah 148 (February 8, 766). Al-Fadl's mother, Zaynab daughter of Munir, was appointed a wet nurse to al-Rashid. Thus, she gave milk to al-Rashid from the suckling of al-Fadl, and al-Khayzuran gave milk to al-Fadl from the suckling of al-Rashid.[4]

In this year [170], al-Rashid appointed Yahya son of Khalid [al-Barmaki] as his vizier and told him, 'I have invested you with responsibility for the subjects' affairs and have transferred the burden from myself to you. So exercise authority in this with what you consider to be sound judgement; appoint as your subordinate governors whom you think fit; and conduct affairs as you consider best.'At the same time, he handed his seal ring over to him. Concerning this event, Ibrahim al-Mawsili recited,

Have you not seen that the sun was sickly,
but when Harun assumed power, its light gleamed forth.
Through the auspicious effects of the trusted one of God, Harun,
the munificent one?

For Harun is its ruler, and Yahya its vizier.

Al-Khayzuran was the one who had the oversight of affairs; Yahya used to lay matters before her and do things on her advice.

In this year, Harun gave orders concerning the share of the Prophet's kindred (i.e., the share from the poor-tax), and it was divided out among the Hashimites in equal portions.

In this year, he gave a guarantee of safe-conduct to those who had fled or who had gone into concealment, with the exception of a group of the dualist infidels ...

In this year, al-Rashid detached the whole of the Byzantine marches from al-Jazira and Qinnasrin, and made them into a single (administrative) region called 'the frontier strongholds.'

In this year [171], Harun had Abu Hurayra Muhammad b. Farrukh, who was governor of al-Jazira, executed. Harun sent Abu Hanifa Harb b. Qays to him, who brought Abu Hurayra back to the caliph at the City of Peace; he was then decapitated in the Khuld Palace ... Al-Fadl b. Sa'id al-Haruri rebelled, but Abu Khalid al-Marwarrudhi killed him.

In this year, Rawh b. Hatim (al-Muhallabi) arrived in Ifriqiya.

In this year, al-Khayzuran set out in the month of Ramadan for Mecca, and she stayed there until the time for the Pilgrimage, and then she performed it.

The Events of the Year 173

... In this year, al-Khayzuran, mother of Harun al-Rashid and Musa al-Hadi, died.

The Time of al-Khayzuran's Death and Her Burial

Yahya b. al-Hasan has mentioned that his father transmitted the information to him, saying: I saw al-Rashid on the day when al-Khayzuran died - this being in the year 173 - wearing a Sa'idi robe and a patched and ragged *taylasan* [long cap with train] which was tied around his waist, gripping the framework of the funeral bier and walking barefoot through the mud until he reached the cemetery of Quraysh. He washed his feet and then called for a pair of boots, prayed over her corpse and went down into her grave. When he came away from the cemetery, a stool was set down for him, and he sat down on it. He summoned al-Fadl b. al-Rabi' and said to him, 'By the right of al-Mahdi!'- and he never used to swear such an oath except when he was expressing himself forcefully - 'For some time now, I have been intending to confer on you some administrative charge or similar responsibility, but my mother has (hitherto) been restraining me and I have accordingly been obedient to her command; but now, take over the seal ring from Ja'far (son of Yahya al-Barmaki).'

Notes

1. The Abbasids claimed descent from Abbas, uncle of the Prophet.
2. The Hashimites are descendants of Hashim, great-grandfather of the Prophet.
3. The Barmakis were a prominent family several of whom were viziers to the Abbasid caliphs of this period.
4. Suckling created a kinship-like relationship, so al-Fadl, son of the powerful vizier Yahya the Barmaki, would be Harun's brother. No less important, Khayzuran would be mother to al-Fadl, sealing her alliance with the Barmaki family.

PART THREE

WOMEN AS SOURCES, ACTORS AND SUBJECTS
OF ISLAMIC LAW

Islam is a legalistic religion — all facets of life are regulated by a body of highly-developed law which has been the official legal code of Islamic empires and states up to modern times. In practice, legal theory was mitigated by local custom and by the extent of popular knowledge of the law.

Islamic law crystallized from the time of the Prophet up to the third/ninth century, a process in which women had a limited role. After this formative period, judges and jurisconsults - most but not all of whom were male - continued to adapt theoretical precepts to daily life within parameters set by classical jurisprudence. Although legal scholars tried to limit the Quranically-rooted right of women to serve as witnesses, women appeared as litigants in suits relating to social and economic issues (some of which are demonstrated in part four).

Despite attempts to reform Islamic law dating to the nineteenth century, it is still relevant to a greater or lesser extent in many Muslim countries, particularly in family matters. Moreover, 'Restore the Shari'a!' has today become a leading slogan of all neo-Islamic movements, and countered by feminists and their allies.

7

AN EARLE LEGAL COMPENDIUM: PURITY, LEGAL

COMPETENCE AND PROPERTY OWNERSHIP

[Malik ibn Anas, *al-Muwatta,* trans. Aisha Abdurrahman Bewley (London: Kegan Paul International, 1989), 16-7, 20-2, 252, 353.]

The primary source of Muslim law is, of course, the Quran. The Quran contains detailed instructions on some matters relating to women, such as inheritance; guidelines on other subjects, such as marriage and divorce; and principles or very specific ordinances on other matters, such as the evidence of women. The second source of Islamic law is the normative sayings and actions *(sunna)* of the Prophet which were transmitted by his Companions to later generations through a chain of transmitters. Another source was the consensus of the legal authorities of the Islamic community *(ijma').* The fourth pillar of Islamic law is analogy *(qiyas)* based on the Quran or the sunna. From the eighth century, legal scholars in various parts of the Islamic empire developed the law employing the sources and independent reasoning to varying degrees. By the tenth century, four recognized and equally valid schools of law emerged named for their dominant scholars: Hanafi, Maliki, Shafi'i and Hanbali.

Malik ibn Anas (died 795) composed the earliest surviving Muslim law-book, the *Muwatta.* In relating to each subject, Malik first brings several versions of relevant sayings of the Prophet or other precedents. He then gives his own opinion and/or the consensus of the scholars of Medina.

The first chapters of the work are devoted to the pillars of Islam – prayer, alms, fasting, *hajj, and jihad-* which comprise almost half of the book. Among the many chapters about prayer, the subject of purification is dealt with in detail. The rest of the work is devoted to legal issues in modern terms, such as fixed shares of inheritance, marriage, divorce, business transactions punishments for crimes, etc. Other matters of religious or moral import and customs connected with food and dress are also dealt with.

The first two excerpts are taken from the chapter on purity. The question of when *ghusl*, full ritual washing of the body, is required would not normally be of interest to anyone but an observant Muslim. The Prophet's saying on the 'two circumcised parts,' however, is relevant to the question of whether female circumcision is required or condoned by Islamic law.

Since menstruation is an ultimate reflection of womanhood, the attitude of Islam to this mundane, biological phenomenon to some extent symbolizes its view of woman. Islam adheres to the almost universal view that a menstruating woman (as well as a woman after childbirth) is unclean. The degree of severity with which the issue of woman's impurity is dealt with in Islamic tradition may, however, be compared to similar restrictions in other cultures. In some African societies, for example, impure women are completely separated from the community for a prescribed period of time. In extreme orthodox Iudaism, a woman's impurity contaminates objects she touches. Moreover, to be on the safe side, all mature women are assumed to be unclean. How rigid are the regulations for a menstruating woman (and her husband) specified below? What are the implications of these rules for women, for men and for the image of women?

Hudud are limits or punishments of certain acts set down by Allah in the Quran, including unlawful intercourse (*zina*), false accusation of unlawful intercourse, theft and others. Despite the strong tendency in Islamic jurisprudence to restrict the application of these punishments, implementation of *hudud* has been viewed as a particular threat to women. In Malik's chapter on *hudud* punishments, Amra daughter of Abd al-Rahman, a prominent female transmitter of traditions of the second generation after the Prophet is quoted. Here the legitimacy of a woman not only as a transmitter of crucial Islamic material but also in making legal judgements is illustrated. Moreover, the issue involved is not one in which a woman should have special expertise. This precedent should be born in mind in reading subsequent selections relating to women's competence as witnesses and judges.

Another story about Amra, from the chapter on business transactions, refers obliquely to female property ownership.

A good summary of some of the major aspects of Islamic law relating to women is Iohn L. Esposito, *Women in Muslim Family Law* (Syracuse: Syracuse University Press, 1982).

In the last decade-and-a-half, a growing number of books and articles have dealt with the practice of female circumcision, primarily in African Muslim countries. The Egyptian writer, physician and feminist, Nawal El-Saadawi, broke the taboo on this subject in her shocking book *The Hidden Face of Eve* (published in English in 1980 by Zed Press). *Khul Khaal: Five Egyptian Women Tell Their Stories* by Nayra Atiya (London: Virago Press, 1988) contains some different perspectives on this controversial issue. Some historical perspective on the subject may be found in Jonathan Berkey, 'Circumcision Circumscribed, Female Excision and Cultural Accommodation in the Medieval Near East,' *The International Journal of Middle East Studies* 28 (1996): 19-38.

The subject of menstruation and purity in Islam has received less attention although all classical and modern works of *hadith* and law contain chapters devoted to it. For comparative purposes, Mary Douglas, *Purity and Danger: An Analysis of Concepts of Pollution and Taboo* (London: Routledge and K. Paul, 1966); lanice Delaney, Mary Jane Lupton, and Emily Toth, *The Curse: A Cultural History of Menstruation* (New York: E. P. Dutton, 1976) and Thomas Buckley and Alma Gottleib, eds *Blood Magic: The Anthropology of Menstruation* (Berkeley: University of California Press, 1988) may prove useful.

Malik's *al-Muwatta*
Chapter II. Purity

2.17 How to do Ghusl for Major Ritual Impurity ...
Hadith No 69. Yahya related to me from Malik from Hisham ibn Urwa from his father from Aisha, *Umm al-Muminin* [Mother of the Believers][1], that whenever the Messenger of Allah, may Allah bless him and grant him peace, did *ghusl* for major ritual impurity, he would begin by washing his hands, and then do *wudu'* [ritual washing] as for prayer. He would then put his fingers in the water and rub the roots of his hair with them. Then he would pour as much water as two hands can hold on to his head three times, and over the entire surface of his skin.

70. Yahya related to me from Malik from ibn Shihab from Urwa ibn al-Zubayr from Aisha, *Umm al-Muminin,* that the Messenger of Allah, may Allah bless him and grant him peace, used to do *ghusl* for major ritual impurity from a vessel which contained *a faraq* [pot].[2]

71. Yahya related to me from Malik from Nafí' that when Abdullah ibn Umar used to do *ghusl* for major ritual impurity he would begin by pouring water on his right hand and washing it. Then, in order, he would wash his genitals, rinse his mouth, snuff water in and out of his nose, wash his face and splash his eyes with water. Then he would wash his right arm and then his left, and after that he would wash his head. He would finish by having a complete wash and

pouring water all over himself.

72. Yahya related to me from Malik that he heard that Aisha was asked about how a woman should do *ghusl* for major ritual impurity. She said, 'She should scoop water over her head with both hands three times and rub the roots of her hair with her hands.'

2.18 Ghusl from the Two 'Circumcised Parts' Meeting

73. Yahya related to me from Malik from ibn Shihab from Sa'id ibn al-Musayyab that Umar ibn al-Khattab and Uthman ibn Affan and Aisha, the wife of the Prophet, may Allah bless him and grant him peace, used to say, 'When the circumcised part touches the circumcised part, *ghusl* is obligatory.'

74. Yahya related to me from Malik from Abu al-Nadr, the *mawla* [freed slave] of Umar ibn Abdullah that Abu Salama ibn Abd al-Rahman ibn Awf related that he had asked Aisha, the wife of the Prophet, may Allah bless him and grant him peace, what made *ghusl* obligatory. She said, 'Do you know what you are like, Abu Salama? You are like a chick when it hears the cocks crowing and so crows with them. When the circumcised part passes the circumcised part, *ghusl* is obligatory.'

75. Yahya related to me from Malik from Yahya ibn Sa'id from Sa'id ibn al-Musayyab that Abu Musa al-Ash'ari come to Aisha, the wife of the Prophet, may Allah bless him and grant him peace, and said to her, 'The disagreement of the companions about a matter which I hate to bring before you has distressed me.' She said, 'What is that? You did not ask your mother about it, so ask me.' He said, 'A man penetrates his wife, but becomes listless and does not ejaculate.' She said, 'When the circumcised part passes the circumcised part *ghusl* is obligatory.' Abu Musa added, 'I shall never ask anyone about this after you.'

76. Yahya related to me from Malik from Yahya ibn Sa'id from Abdullah ibn Ka'b, the *mawla* [freed slave] of Uthman ibn Affan, that Mahmud ibn Labid al-Ansari asked Zayd ibn Thabit about a man who penetrated his wife but became listless and did not ejaculate. Zayd ibn Thabit said, 'He does *ghusl;* Mahmud said to him, 'Ubayy ibn Ka'b used not to think that *ghusl* was necessary,' but Zayd ibn Thabit said, 'Ubayy ibn Ka'b drew away from that position before he died.'

77. Yahya related to me from Malik from Nafi' that Abdullah ibn Umar used to say, 'When the circumcised part passes the circumcised part, *ghusl* is obligatory.'

2.26 What is Permitted to a Man from his Wife when she is Menstruating

95. Yahya related to me from Malik from Zayd ibn Aslam that a man questioned the Messenger of Allah, may Allah bless him and grant him peace, saying,

'What is permitted to me from my wife when she is menstruating?' The Messenger of Allah, may Allah bless him and grant him peace, said, 'Let her wrap her waist-wrapper round herself tightly, and then what is above that is your concern.'

96. Yahya related to me from Malik from Rabi'a ibn Abu Abd al-Rahman that on one occasion Aisha, the wife of the Prophet, may Allah bless him and grant him peace, was sleeping with the Messenger of Allah, may Allah bless him and grant him peace, in one garment, when suddenly she jumped up sharply. The Messenger of Allah, may Allah bless him and grant him peace, said to her, 'What's the matter with you? Are you losing blood?' meaning menstruating. She said, 'Yes.' He said, 'Wrap your waist-wrapper tightly about you, and return to your sleeping-place.'

97. Yahya related to me from Malik from Nafi' that Ubaydullah ibn Abdullah ibn Umar sent a question to Aisha asking her, 'May a man fondle his wife when she is menstruating?' She replied, 'Let her wrap her waist-wrapper around her lower part and then he may fondle her if he wishes.'

98. Yahya related to me from Malik that he had heard that Salim ibn Abdullah and Sulayman ibn Yasar were asked whether the husband of a menstruating woman could have sexual intercourse with her when she saw that she was pure but before she had had a *ghusl*. They said, 'No, not until she has had a *ghusl*'.

2.27 The Purity of a Woman after Menstruation

99. Yahya related to me from Malik from Alqama ibn Abu Alqama that his mother, the *mawla* [freed slave] of Aisha, *Umm al-Muminin,* said, 'Women used to send little boxes to Aisha, *Umm al-Muminin,* with a piece of cotton cloth in each one of which was yellowness from menstrual blood, asking her about the prayer. She said to them, 'Do not be hasty until you see a white discharge.' By that she meant purity from menses.

100. Yahya related to me from Malik from Abdullah ibn Abu Bakr from his paternal aunt from the daughter of Zayd son of Thabit that she had heard that women used to ask for lamps in the middle of the night to check their purity. She would criticise them for this saying, 'Women never used to do this,' i.e. in the time of the Companions.

101. Malik was asked whether a woman whose period had finished could do *tayammum* [purification without water] to purify herself if she could not find water and he said, 'Yes, because she is like some one in a state of major ritual impurity, who, if he cannot find water, does *tayammum;*

2.28 Menstruation in General

102. Yahya related to me from Malik that he had heard that Aisha, the wife of the Prophet, may Allah bless him and grant him peace, said that a pregnant woman who noticed bleeding left off from prayer.

103. Yahya related to me from Malik that he asked Ibn Shihab about a pregnant woman who noticed bleeding. Ibn Shihab replied, 'She refrains from prayer.'

Yahya said that Malik said, 'That is what is done in our community.'

104. Yahya related to me from Malik from Hisham ibn Urwa from his father that Aisha, the wife of the Prophet, may Allah bless him and grant him peace, said, 'I used to comb the head of the Messenger of Allah, may Allah bless him and grant him peace, while I was menstruating.'

105. Yahya related to me from Malik from Hisham ibn Urwa from his father from Fatima daughter of al-Mundhir son of al-Zubayr that Asma daughter of Abu Bakr al-Siddiq said, 'A woman questioned the Messenger of Allah, may Allah bless him and grant him peace, saying, "If menstrual blood gets onto our clothes how do you think we should deal with it?" The Messenger of Allah, may Allah bless him and grant him peace, said, "If menstrual blood gets onto your clothes you should wash them, and sprinkle them with water before you pray in them."'

2.29 Bleeding as if Menstruating

106. Yahya related to me from Malik from Hisham ibn Urwa from his father that Aisha, the wife of the Prophet, may Allah bless him and grant him peace, said, 'Fatima daughter of Abu Hubaysh said, "Messenger of Allah, I never become pure - am I permitted to pray?" The Messenger of Allah, may Allah bless him and grant him peace, said, "That is a vein, not menstruation. So when your period approaches, leave off from the prayer, and when its grip leaves, wash the blood from yourself and pray."'

107. Yahya related to me from Malik from Nafi' from Sulayman ibn Yasar from Umm Salama, the wife of the Prophet, may Allah bless him and grant him peace, that a certain woman in the time of the Messenger of Allah, may Allah bless him and grant him peace, used to bleed profusely, so Umm Salama consulted the Messenger of Allah, may Allah bless him and grant him peace, for her, and he said, 'She should calculate the number of nights and days a month that she used to menstruate before it started happening, and she should leave off from prayer for that much of the month. When she has completed that she should do *ghusl*, bind her private parts with a cloth, and then pray.'

108. Yahya related to me from Malik from Hisham ibn Urwa from his father from Zaynab daughter of Abu Salama that she saw Zaynab daughter of Jahsh,

the wife of Abd al-Rahman ibn Awf, and she used to bleed as if menstruating. She would do *ghusl* and pray.

109. Yahya related to me from Malik from Sumayy, the *mawla* [freed slave] of Abu Bakr ibn Abd al-Rahman that al-Qa'qa ibn Hakim and Zayd ibn Aslam sent him to Sa'id ibn al-Musayyab to ask how a woman who was bleeding as if menstruating should do *ghusl*. Sa'id said, 'She does a glusl to cover from the end of one period to the end of the next, and does wudu' for every prayer, and if bleeding overtakes her she bind up her private parts.'

110. Yahya related to me from Malik from Hisham ibn Urwa that his father said, 'A woman who bleeds as if menstruating only has to do one *ghusl*, and then after that she does *wudu* for each prayer.'

Yahya said that Malik said, 'The position with us is that when a woman who bleeds as if menstruating starts to do prayer again, her husband can have sexual intercourse with her. Similarly, if a woman who has given birth sees blood after she has reached the fullest extent that bleeding normally restrains women, her husband can have sexual intercourse with her and she is in the same position as a woman who bleeds as if menstruating.'

Yahya said that Malik said, 'The position with us concerning a woman who bleeds as if menstruating is founded on the *hadith* of Hisham ibn Urwa from his father, and it is what I prefer the most of what I have heard about the matter.'

31 Business Transactions ...

31.11 *Keeping Back a Portion of the Fruit*

17. Yahya related to me from Malik from Rabi'a son of Abd al-Rahman that al-Qasim son of Muhammad would sell produce from his orchard and keep some of it aside.

18. Yahya related to me from Malik from Abdullah ibn Abu Bakr that his grandfather, Muhammad ibn Amr ibn Hazm sold the fruit of an orchard of his called al-Afraq for 4000 dirham [silver coins],[3] and he kept aside 800 dirhams worth of dry dates.

19. Yahya related to me from Malik from Abu al-Rijal Muhammad son of Abd al-Rahman son of Haritha that his mother, Amra daughter of Abd al-Rahman, used to sell her fruit and keep some of it aside.

Malik said, 'The generally agreed-upon way of doing things among us is that when a man sells the fruit of his orchard, he can keep aside up to a third of the fruit, but that is not to be exceeded. There is no harm in what is less than a third.'

Malik added that he thought there was no harm for a man to sell the fruit of his orchard and keep aside only the fruit of a certain palm-tree or palm-trees which he had chosen and whose number he had specified, because the owner was only keeping aside certain fruit of his own orchard and everything else he sold.

41 *Hudud* [Transgressions] ...

41:11 *Things for Which the Hand is Not Cut Off*
35. Yahya related to me from Malik that Yahya son of Sa'id said that Abu Bakr son of Muhammad son of Amr son of Hazm informed him that he had taken a Nabatean who had stolen some iron rings and jailed him in order to cut off his hand. Amra daughter of Abd al-Rahman sent a girl *mawla* [freed slave] called Umayya to him. Abu Bakr said that she had come to him while he was among the people and said that his aunt, Amra, sent word to him saying, 'Nephew! You have taken a Nabatean for something insignificant which was mentioned to me. Do you mean to cut off his hand?' He had replied, 'Yes.' She said, 'Amra tells you not to cut off the hand except for a quarter of a dinar [gold coin] or more.'
Abu Bakr added, 'So I let the Nabatean go.'

Notes

1. Mothers of the Believers is a title for the Prophet's wives.

2. A *faraq* is a kind of pot containing three measures of water.

3. The precise value of the *dirham* silver coin and the gold *dinar* at the time the sale took place and when Malik compiled his law-book is extremely difficult to ascertain. The relationships rather than the absolute values are more important for subsequent generations of Muslims.

8

THE EVIDENCE OF WOMEN; EQUALITY IN
MARRIAGE: A LEGAL GUIDE

['Ali ibn Abi Bakr al-Marghinani, *The Hedaya or Guide: A Commentary on the Mussulman Laws,* trans. Charles Hamilton. Lahore, 1963, pp. 353-5, 39-41.]

Unlike the *Muwatta'* of Malik, no original, written works of Abu Hanifa (died 150/767), the eponym of the Hanafi school of Islamic law, exist and adherents of this school rely on the works of their Imam's two disciples, Abu Yusuf (died 182/798) and in particular al-Shaybani (died 189/805). Shaybani's writings are the oldest surviving texts which embody Hanafi law, and some regard him as the true founder of this school. Through the centuries, scholars interpreted, elaborated, excerpted and summarized branches of Islamic law according to the outlines drawn by the great jurists of the eighth and ninth centuries. The roots or sources of the law were not re-evaluated, and, therefore, no fundamental changes were made. Islamic law could, however, be adapted to changing circumstances by the judgements *(fatwas)* of jurisconsults.

Ali ibn Abu Bakr al-Marghinani (died 593/1197) is best-known as the author of a concise legal commentary which served as a guide to later Hanafi jurists. Hamilton's English edition was translated from a Persian version of the original Arabic prepared for the Indian Anglo-Muhammadan legal system. The English is rather archaic but this highlights the cultural, historical and linguistic distance of the original.

The overall organization of the *Hedaya* is similar to that of the works of Malik, Bukhari and the Muslim jurists who followed them. Within each book or chapter, however, we do not find a collection of sayings of the Prophet with

their attribution to chains of traditionists. Occasionally, a Companion of the
Prophet who related sayings of Muhammad, such as Zuhri, is cited. Also, legal
opinions are sometimes ascribed to renowned authorities such as Shafi'i and
Imam Muhammad al-Shaybani. On the whole, however, the *Guide* provides
concise summaries of the Hanafi position on various legal issues.

Although the Book of Evidence is twenty-first according to the traditional
Islamic arrangement of legal material, the issue of women's testimony in court
is fundamental to an understanding of their status in Islamic law and,
therefore, precedes the substantive subject below. The Book of Evidence opens with
a section emphasizing the duty of every Muslim to testify if called upon to do
so. This duty is mitigated, however, by a reluctance to malign a fellow Muslim
and a desire to prevent corporal punishment. In cases involving property, the
rights of the owner require a witness to come forth with his evidence. Against
this background, evidence required in cases of different degrees of severity is
discussed, beginning with fornication *(zina')*. Illicit sexual relations are
extremely difficult to prove in Islamic law because the Quran requires four
witnesses to the act. Moreover, a person who falsely accuses another of
fornication is severely punished.

The issue of women's testimony is based on a verse of the Quran dealing
with contracting a debt:

> And call to witness, from among your men, two witnesses.
> And if two men be not (at hand) then a man and two women,
> of such as ye approve as witnesses, so that if one [of the
> women RR] erreth (through forgetfulness) the other will
> remember. [*2(al-Baqara):* 282]

In theory, Muslim legalists could have interpreted this Quranic
prescription in a broader or more narrow fashion. The selection from the Book of
Evidence reproduced below provides some insights into the jurists line of
thought on this issue. Why is the evidence of women accepted in an Islamic court of
law? What limitations are placed on women's testimony and what are
the reasons for these limitations? When is the evidence of women essential?

Of the many legal issues relating to women, the concept of equality in
marriage *(kafa'a)*, dealt with in the second selection, is perhaps not the most
important (and in fact is unique to the Hanafi school of law). The discussion
of *kafa'a* reveals a theoretical approach to power relations in marriage which
translates, in practice, into conflicts between a woman and her legal guardian.
Attempts by legal guardians to nullify marriages contracted independently by
a mature woman on grounds of the groom's inequality were recorded in Egypt up to
the 1940s at least, and in Sudan in 1973. One early twentieth-century

Muhammad, went to court to annul the marriage of his daughter to a well-known journalist. The father claimed that the groom lacked noble descent, was not financially equal to the woman's family, and was engaged in a demeaning profession.

The selection below indicates that tribal genealogical attribution was still considered relevant centuries after the Arab conquering tribes had dispersed throughout the vast, heterogeneous Islamic empires. The pre-Islamic concept of noble lineage was also translated into reverence for the descendants of the Prophet Muhammad *(sharifs)*, his extended family (Hashimites) and other clans of his tribe Quraysh. Hanafi jurists also deal with the tension between ascription and Islamic religious achievement. In the twentieth century, it has been argued that educational equality between a couple is more important than lineage, a view that can be grounded in Islamic attitudes towards learning.

In reading the rules of *kafa'a,* the following questions should be addressed. Why is equality necessary in marriage? Which two parties to a marriage must be equal? What does the equality of these two parties imply about the economic and social position of women? What dimensions of equality are enumerated in the selection? What can we learn about Islamic society from this list?

Further information on *kafa'a* may be found in Farhat Ziadeh, 'Equality in the Muslim Law of Marriage,' *American Journal of Comparative Law* 6 (1957) 503-17. The suit of the head of the Egyptian Sadat family against the marriage of his daughter to a journalist is discussed in Beth Baron, 'The Making and Breaking of Marital Bonds in Modern Egypt,' in *Women in Middle Eastern History,* Nikki R. Keddie and Beth Baron eds (New Haven: Yale University Press, 1991). Abbas Kelidar views the episode against the background of the groom's biography and regards the marriage to the daughter of a prominent *sharif as* calculated social climbing ('Shaykh 'Ali Yusuf: Egyptian Journalist and Islamic Nationalist,' *Intellectual Life in the Arab East, 1890–1939* Marwan R. Buheiry ed. Beirut: American University of Beirut, 1981).

Marghinani's Legal Guide

Introduction ...

The evidence required in fornication is that of four men. Evidence is of several kinds. The evidence required in a case of fornication [*zina'*] is that of four men as has been ordained in the Quran, and the testimony of a woman in such case is not admitted, because Zuhri says, 'in the time of the Prophet and his two immediate successors it was an invariable rule to exclude the evidence of women in all cases inducing punishment or retaliation;' and also, because the testimony of women involves a degree of doubt, as it is merely a substitute for evidence, being accepted only where the testimony of men cannot be had; and therefore it is not admitted in any matter liable to drop from the existence of a doubt.

In other criminal cases, two men. The evidence required in other criminal cases is that of two men, according to the text of the Quran, and the testimony of women is not admitted, on the strength of the tradition of Zuhri above quoted.

And in all other matters, two men, or one man and two women. In all other cases the evidence required is that of two men, or of one man and two women, whether the case relate to property or to other rights such as marriage, divorce, agency, executorship, or the like. Shafi'i has said that the evidence of one man and two women cannot be admitted excepting in cases that relate to property, or its dependencies such as hire, bail, and so forth because the evidence of women is originally inadmissible on account of their defect of understanding, their want of memory and incapacity of governing, whence it is that their evidence is not admitted in criminal cases.

Objection: Since, according to Shafi'i, the evidence of women is originally invalid, it would follow that their evidence alone is not admissible even in a case of property; whereas the evidence of four women alone is, in his opinion, admissible in such case.

Reply: The evidence of four alone is necessarily admissible in cases of property because of their frequent occurrence, contrary to the mode of proceeding with respect to marriage (for instance), which being a matter of greater importance and more rare occurrence than mere matters of property, cannot therefore be classed with them.

The reasoning of our doctors [of law] is that the evidence of women is originally valid because evidence is founded upon three circumstances: namely, sight, memory, and a capability of communication; for by means of the first the witness acquires knowledge; by means of the second he retains such knowledge; and by means of the third he is enabled to impart it to the Qadi; and all these three circumstances exist in a woman (whence it is that her communication of a tradition or of a message is valid); and with respect to their want of memory, it is capable of remedy by the junction of another; that is, by substituting two women in the room of one man; and the defect of memory being thus supplied, there remains only the doubt of substitution; whence it is that their evidence is not admitted in any matter liable to drop from the existence of a doubt, namely, retaliation or punishment: in opposition to marriage, and so forth, as those may be proved notwithstanding a doubt; whence the evidence of women is admitted in those instances.

Objection: As the evidence of two women is admitted in the room of that of one man, it would follow that the evidence of four women alone ought to be admitted in cases of property and other rights; whereas it is otherwise.

Reply: Such is the suggestion of analogy. The evidence of four women alone, however, is not accepted (contrary to what analogy would suggest), because if it were, there would be frequent occasions for their appearance in public in order to give evidence; whereas their privacy is the most laudable.

The evidence of women alone suffices concerning matters which do not admit the inspection of men. The evidence of one woman is admitted in cases of birth (as where one woman, for instance, declares that 'a certain woman brought forth a certain child'). In the same manner also the evidence of one woman is sufficient with respect to virginity, or with respect to the defect of that part of a woman which is concealed from man. The principle of the law in these cases is derived from a traditional saying of the Prophet: 'The evidence of women is valid with respect to such things as it is not fitting for man to behold.' Shafi'i holds the evidence of four women to be a necessary condition in such cases. The foregoing tradition, however, is a proof against him. And another proof against him is that in the cases in question the necessity of male evidence is remitted and female evidence credited because the ocular examination of a woman in these cases is less indecent than that of a man. And hence also as the sight of two or three persons is more indecent than that of one, the evidence of more than one woman is not insisted on as a condition in those instances. It is to be remarked, however, that if two or three women give evidence in such cases, it is a commendable caution because the evidence may be of an obligatory tendency. The law with respect to the evidence of women in cases of birth has been fully set forth in the book of divorce, treating of the establishment of parentage, where it is said that 'if a man marry a woman, and she bring forth a child at a period of six months, or more, after her marriage, and the husband deny the parentage, in that case the evidence of one woman is sufficient to establish it,' and there are also other examples recited to the same effect. The law with respect to the evidence of a woman in cases of virginity is that if a woman complain of the impotency of her husband and assert that her virginity still exists, and another woman bear evidence of the same, in that case one year must be suffered to elapse and then a separation must be effected between the husband and wife. (That is provided he show no proof of virility in the interim.) Because virginity is a real entity, and the existence of it has here been attested by evidence. The same rule also holds where a person purchases a female slave on condition of her being a virgin and afterwards desires to return her because of her being a woman. For if, in that case, another woman should examine into her condition and then declare her to be a virgin, her evidence must be credited, as virginity is an entity and the existence of it is here proven by evidence; or if, on the contrary, she declare her to be a [sexually experienced] woman, her sexual maturity (which is a defect) is established in virtue of such declaration and the plea of the purchaser holds good whence the seller is required to take an oath that such defect did not exist when he sold her, which, if he refuse to do, he is bound to receive her back.

It is not admitted to prove that a child was live-born further than relates to the rites of burial. The evidence of a woman with respect to a stillborn child[1] or the noise made by a child at its birth is not admissible in the opinion of Hanifa so far as relates to the establishment of the right of heritage in the child, because this noise is of a nature to be known or discovered by men, but is admissible so far as relates to the necessity of reading funeral prayers over the child, because these prayers are merely a matter of religion. In consequence of her evidence, therefore, the funeral prayers are to be repeated over it. The two disciples [of Abu Hanifa] maintain that the evidence of a woman is sufficient to establish the right of heritage also because the noise in question being made at birth, none but women can be supposed to be present when it is made. The evidence of a woman, therefore, to this noise is the same as her evidence to a living birth, and as the evidence of women in the one case is admissible so also is it in the other.

The Book of Marriage

Of Equality
Definition of Kafa'a. Kafa'a, in its literal sense, means equality. In the language of the law it signifies the equality of a man with a woman in the several particulars which shall be immediately specified.

Equality necessary in marriage. In marriage, regard is had to equality because the Prophet has commanded, saying, Take ye care that none contract women in marriage but their proper guardians and that they be not so contracted but with their equals;' and also, because the desirable ends of marriage such as cohabitation, society, and friendship, cannot be completely enjoyed excepting by persons who are each other's equals (according to the customary estimation of equality), as a woman of high rank and family would abhor society and cohabitation with a mean man. It is requisite, therefore, that regard be had to equality with respect to the husband; that is to say, that the husband be the equal of his wife. But it is not necessary that the wife be the equal of the husband since men are not degraded by cohabitation with women who are their inferiors. It is proper to observe, in this place, that one reason for attending to equality in marriage is that regard is had to that circumstance in confirming a marriage and establishing its validity. For if a woman should match herself to a man who is her inferior, her guardians have a right to separate them so as to remove the dishonour they might otherwise sustain by it.

In point of tribe or family. Equality is regarded with respect to lineage this being a source of distinction among mankind. Thus it is said, 'a Quraysh is the equal of a Quraysh throughout all their tribes,' that is to say, there is no pre-eminence among them between Hashimites and Niflis, Taymis or Adawis.[2] And in like manner they say, 'an Arab is the equal of an Arab.' This sentiment originates in a precept of the Prophet to this effect, and hence it is evident that there is no pre-eminence considered among the Quraysh tribes. And with respect to what Imam Mohammed [al-Shaybani] has advanced that 'pre-eminence is not regarded among the Quraysh tribes or families excepting where the same is famous, such as the house of the caliphs,' his intention in this exception was merely to show that regard should be had to pre-eminence in that particular house out of respect to the caliphate and in order to suppress rebellion or disaffection, and not to say that an original equality does not exist throughout...

The Banu Ballala tribe are not the equals of Arabs of any other description whatsoever, they being notorious throughout Arabia for every species of vice. And none of those before mentioned esteem them as upon an equality with themselves.

In point of religion. Mawalis [non-Arab clients of Arab tribes], that is to say, Ajims [non-Arabs, Persians], who are neither Qurayshis nor Arabs, are the equals of each other throughout, regard not being had among them to lineage, but to Islam. Thus an Ajim whose family have been Muslims for two or more generations is the equal of one descended of Muslim ancestors. But one who has himself embraced the faith, or he and his father only, is not the equal of an Ajim whose father and grandfather were Muslims because a family is not established under any particular denomination (such as Muslim, for instance) by a retrospect short of the grandfather. This is the doctrine of Hanifa and

Mohammed [al-Shaybani]. Abu Yusuf says that an Ajim whose father is a Muslim is the equal of a woman whose father and grandfather are Muslims.

An Ajim who is the first of his family professing the faith is not the equal of a woman whose father is a Muslim.

In the point of freedom. Equality in point of freedom is the same as in point of Islam in all the circumstances above recited, because bondage is an effect of infidelity and the properties of meanness and depravity are therein found.

In point of character. Regard is to be had to equality in piety and virtue, according to Hanifa and Abu Yusuf. And this is approved because virtue is one of the first principles of superiority and a woman derives a degree of scandal and shame from the profligacy of her husband beyond what she sustains even from that of her kindred. Mohammed [al-Shaybani] alleges that positive equality in point of virtue is not to be regarded as that is connected with religion, to which rules regarding mere worldly matters do not apply, excepting where the party, by any base or degrading misconduct (such as a man exposing himself naked and intoxicated in the public street, and so forth), may have incurred derision and contempt.

In point of fortune. Equality is to be regarded with respect to property, by which is understood a man being possessed of a sufficiency to discharge the dower and provide maintenance; because if he is unable to do both, or either of these, he is not the equal of any woman; as the dower is a consideration for the carnal use of the woman, the payment of which is necessary of course; and upon the provision of a support to the wife depends the permanency of the matrimonial connection; and this is therefore indispensable a fortiori. This, according to some, is found in the ability to support a wife for one month only, but others say for a year. By a man possessing sufficient to enable him to discharge the dower is understood his ability to pay down that proportion of it which it is customary to give immediately upon the marriage and which is termed *mu'ajjal,* or prompt; the remainder, termed the *mu'ajjal,* or deferred, it is not unusual to pay until a future season. And hence it is that the ability to pay that part of the dower is not made a condition. Abu Yusuf teaches that regard is to be had only to the man's ability to support his wife, and not to the discharge of the dower because the latter is of a nature to admit of delay in the payment but not the former. And a man is supposed to be sufficiently enabled to pay the dower when his father is in good circumstances. According to the doctrine of Hanifa and Mohammed, however, the fortune of the man is to be considered in general (without regard to any particular ability) insomuch that a man who may even be qualified both to pay the dower and to provide subsistence, yet may not be held the equal of a woman possessed of a large property, since men consider wealth as conferring superiority and poverty as inducing contempt. Abu Yusuf, on the other hand, maintains that wealth is not to be regarded in this respect since it is not a thing of a stable or permanent nature, as property may be acquired in the morning and lost before night.

And in point of profession. Equality is to be regarded in trade or profession, according to Abu Yusuf and Mohammed. There are two opinions recorded of Hanifa upon this point, and there is also an opinion related of Abu Yusuf, that the profession is not to be regarded, unless where it is of such a degrading nature as to oppose an insurmountable objection, such, for instance, as barbers, weavers, tanners, or other workers in leather, and scavengers, who are not the equals of merchants, perfumers, druggists, or bankers. The principle upon which regard is to be had to trade or profession is that men assume to themselves a certain consequence from the respectability of their callings whereas a degree of contempt is annexed to them on account of the meanness thereof. But a reason, on the other hand, why trade or profession should not be regarded is that these are not absolute upon a man since he is at liberty to leave a mean profession for one of a more honourable nature.

Notes

1. If a child dies immediately on its birth, without making a noise, it is then considered in law to have been brought forth dead, and it neither succeeds to a portion of its father's estate, nor are funeral prayers read over it. If, however, it make the smallest noise it is then held to die possessed of its portion, and funeral prayers are read over it. Thus if a person should die, leaving his wife pregnant, the division of his estate is in that case suspended till the birth of the child: if it proves a dead child (that is, one that appeared dead immediately at the birth and made no noise), the estate is divided as if no such child had been born; but if it have made a noise, its share is in that case allotted and divided amongst its heirs. The determination of the heirs, and consequently the nature of the division of the estate, must often rest upon this circumstance. For instance, if a person die without children, leaving a brother, and his wife who is at that time pregnant, and the child at its birth make a noise, and immediately after die, it is held to be an heir, and the mother; in exclusion of the uncle, succeeds to the whole; but if it make no noise before its death, the uncle is then considered to be an heir, and no share is allowed to the child. The law is the same in the case of a grandson, whose father had before died, being left under such circumstances.

2. Hashimites, scions of Hashim ibn Abd Manaf, are the most prestigious family among the Quraysh and the family of the Prophet, the Shi'i *imams* and the Abbasid caliphs. Niflis are descendants of Nawfal ibn Abd Manaf (Hashim's brother). Taymis, trace their descent to Taym ibn Murra, are a more distant clan of Quraysh and count among their number the first caliph Abu Bakr and his daughter Aisha wife of the Prophet. Adis, from Adi ibn Ka'b, are a still more distant branch of Quraysh.

9

THEORY OF GOVERNMENT : MUST VIZIERS AND

JUDGES BE MEN?

[Abu al-Hasan 'Ali ibn Muhammad al-Mawardi, *al-Ahkam al-sultaniyya*. pp. 26, 61–2.]

The early Islamic community was a simple, tribal society and neither the Quran nor the deeds and sayings of the Prophet contain a political theory or detailed rules of public administration appropriate to a large, complex state. According to Sunni Islamic tradition, the first four righteous caliphs (particularly Umar) developed principles and institutions of government in response to the needs of the growing Islamic empire. Modern Western historians have usually cited foreign, Graeco-Roman or Sassanian Persian, concepts and institutions as the sources of Islamic government. In the eighth century, the first books of advice to rulers appeared in Arabic, and at the same time, Muslim legal experts wrote treatises on some aspects of public law (such as taxation) at the request of their sovereigns. These apparently were the precursors of the first comprehensive work of Islamic political theory which appeared in the eleventh century.

As a scholar and judge who undertook various posts in government service, Mawardi (364–450/974-1058) was uniquely placed to compose a classic work of Islamic public law. His point of departure is the Islamic state, its leader, and institutions (in contrast to most religious, legal scholars who gave precedence to the Muslims' religious obligations and dealt with the political aspects of Islam secondarily if at all.) Nevertheless, Mawardi's approach is that of a Muslim scholar and his rules of public administration are derived from the Quran, the *hadith* and the opinions of legal experts; followed by precedents from the first four righteous caliphs, the Umayyad and the Abbasid rulers, in that order.

Two related issues concerning women are raised in the first six chapters of the book. These chapters deal with the head of the Islamic state (called *imam* here); viziers *(wazirs);* governors of provinces; commanders in the holy war; leaders of wars of public utility; and judges.

In the chapter dealing with viziers, this post is divided into two basic types: viziers who exercise delegated authority and can make independent judgements; and viziers whose powers are limited to executing the decisions of the ruler. The former must have almost all of the requirements of the ruler himself (except lineage), and he must be a free male possessing wisdom. The latter, executive vizier, need not necessarily be a free male because he has no independent authority; he does not necessarily have to be wise because he merely transmits information to and from the ruler. The seven qualities required of the executive vizier are: (1) loyalty; (2) freedom in expressing his views; (3) freedom from influences; (4) lack of rancour toward those he deals with; (5) a good memory so he can transmit information to and from the ruler; (6) subtlety and wisdom; and (7) dispassion. If this kind of vizier participates in deliberations, he requires an eighth quality - worldly wisdom gained through experience.

At this point, Mawardi briefly addresses the question of whether a woman can hold this office. Why might one assume that a woman could be an executive vizier? Why does Mawardi reach the conclusion that women in fact should be barred from this post? Why may non-Muslims act as executive viziers while Muslim women may not?

The chapter on the judiciary opens with seven qualifications required of judges, the very first of which is maleness. The six other requirements are: intelligence, freedom (as opposed to slavery), belief in Islam, honour, good hearing and sight, and legal knowledge.

Did all the classical Muslim jurists bar women from being judges? Why might they permit a woman to serve as a judge? In what kinds of cases could she do so? Why does Mawardi conclude that women may not be judges?

Mawardi's *Rules of Government*

Chapter 2: On Appointment to the Post of Minister

A woman may not undertake this position, even though information she transmits is acceptable, because of the implication of the [sovereign] powers it involves which the Prophet (SAS) declared to be foreign to women, saying: 'A people who entrusts[1] their affairs to a woman will not prosper.' Moreover, the exercise of these powers requires independent reasoning and strength of determination for which women are too frail; and also appearing prominently or in public to manage affairs [of state] which is forbidden or restricted for them.

The executive vizier may be one of the Protected People *(ahl al-dhimma)*[2]

.....

Chapter 6: On Administering the Judiciary

Anyone appointed to the judiciary must perfectly fulfil conditions that make him suitable to be appointed and that make his decisions legally valid. There are seven conditions:

1. The person must be a man, which combines two properties - legal majority and maleness. As for majority, a minor is not responsible for his actions; a judgement against him may not depend on his statement, and more important, a judgement against someone else may not depend on his statement. As for women, although they are deficient for certain positions, judgements may depend on their statements. Abu Hanifa said: women are permitted to act as judges in matters in which their testimony is admissible but they are not permitted to act as judges in matters in which their testimony is not admissible. Ibn Jarir al-Tabari alone permits them to act as judges in all cases; but one should not learn from an opinion that is opposed by the Consensus[3] and the word of Allah the Almighty: 'Men are in charge of women, because Allah hath made the one of them to excel the other ...' [4 (Women): 34], that is, in intelligence and independent reasoning. Thus, they may not be in charge of men.

Notes

1. In this version of the *hadith,* the verb *asnadu* is used which also means to base a tradition on someone as its first authority.

2. A free, non-Muslim subject living in a Muslim country, generally a Christian or a Jew.

3. *Al-ijma',* one of the four foundations of Islamic law, has been interpreted as the consensus of the scholars of a certain region or period, or the consensus of all of the Muslims.

PART FOUR

WOMEN'S ROLES IN MEDIEVAL SOCIETY

Women's public roles in traditional Islamic societies were determined by an interplay of legal, theoretical rules and social reality. In principle, women were severely limited in the political arena, but could achieve prominence through spiritual endeavour, learning and by exploiting their relatively liberal property rights.

The strategies used and the limitations imposed in the interplay of theory and practice provide us with an insight into actual behaviour of some traditional women (as recorded by men). The scope of individual phenomena reflected in the following selections has been documented, in some cases, by quantitative studies.

Islamic views of male and female sexuality have been expressed far more frankly than those of the Christian West, leading to misunderstanding, fascination and disdain by non-Muslims. Perceived as a public as well as a private matter, sexual relations were discussed in various literary genres, providing primary sources on this subject.

One of the historian's most challenging tasks is to reconstruct the lives of the common people. Folk tales reflect popular attitudes on women and may even provide information on private, family life as well.

10

RULES FOR KINGS REGARDING THEIR WIVES:

DANGEROUS PRECEDENTS

[Nizam al-Mulk, *The Book of Government or Rules for Kings: The Siyasat-nama or Siyar al-Muluk* trans. Hubert Darke (London: Routledge & Kegan Paul, 1960), pp. 185–92.]

Counsels for rulers are one of the earliest forms of writing and have been found for all ancient cultures. The genre was assimilated into Arabic in the eighth century, and Islamic Persian and Turkish works of this kind were written from the eleventh century.

Nizam al-Mulk (1018-92) was the chief vizier for over thirty years of the Seljuk sultans, a Turkish dynasty which ruled Central Asia, Persia and Iraq. After the accession of the eighteen-year-old Malikshah (1072), he was the virtual ruler of the empire, although naturally various individuals and groups tried to challenge his position. Among these was one of the sultan's wives, Terken Khatun. She used her influence over the sultan to press for the formal designation of her infant son as heir, while Nizam favoured the ruler's eldest son by another wife.

The *Siyasat-name* or *Book of Government* was written in 1091 towards the end of Nizam's long, influential political career. The sultan specifically requested his vizier to prepare an analysis of the internal problems of the state and suggest reforms. This book of rules for kings is, therefore, both an ideal model of government and a product of practical political experience. The fifty-chapter work begins with the duty of the king, who has been chosen by God, to dispense justice personally to his subjects. Next, the various agents of government (tax-collectors, viziers, judges, inspectors, etc.) are discussed and the need to regulate and investigate their activities is emphasized. Then, aspects of the royal

117

court are addressed, with the bulk of the work devoted to the behaviour of the ruler and his relations with those who surround him. At the end of this lengthy section, 'those who wear the veil' and underlings in general are dealt with. The book concludes with a number of chapters on specific enemies of the state.

Throughout his work, Nizam al-Mulk relies on precedents not only from the classic Islamic Arabic sources but also from legends handed down from the ancient Greeks and Persians that were assimilated into Arabic and Persian literature. Several characters that appear in the following selection were familiar to educated Muslims of Nizam's time, but may require elucidation for the English-language reader.

Kai Kavus is a mythical king of ancient, pre-Islamic Persia whose stories originate in semi-historical, secular works of the Zoroastrian, old Persian (Pahlavi) literature. These legends were translated into Arabic after the conquest of Persia by the Muslim Arabs in the seventh century. The bare outline of the tale of Kai Kavus's wife Saudaba's treachery appears in short in Tabari's *History of the Prophets and the Kings* in the section devoted to the ancient Persian kings. This story and similar legends were also preserved in Islamicized, Persian-language versions from which the great fourth/tenth century poet Firdawsi wove his powerful epic poem, the *Shah-nama (The Book of Kings)*. The attempted seduction of Prince Siyavosh by his stepmother and its repercussions are dramatically related in detail by Firdawsi who places the scheming wife (who resorts to sorcery) in apposition to the pure-hearted young hero. Rustam who is briefly mentioned in this passage from Nizam al-Mulk is the most famous herculean hero of Firdawsi's epic, and Siyavosh's tutor. The story is reminiscent of the tale of Joseph and Potiphar's wife in the Bible which was very familiar to Muslims since it appears prominently in the Quran as well as popular collections of tales of the prophets.

Some tales of Alexander the Great were apparently known to the Arabs from early times and certain passages of the Quran refer to him and his legendary deeds. Tabari, in his history, is mainly concerned with the defeat of Alexander (Iskandar in Arabic) of the Persian king Darius (or Dara). He also mentions Alexander's marriage to Darius's daughter, at the king's dying request, to perpetuate Persian nobility and glory through their progeny. Firdawsi depicts the adventures of Sikandar as one chapter in a long series of tales of heroic rulers. The Persian king's death-bed scene serves to reinforce the chivalrous image of the Greek conqueror, and the proposed marriage to the Persian princess is one of the measures to protect the safety of the defeated royal house. When Alexander ascends the throne of Persia, he amasses a large and varied harem from among the conquered population of Persia. Nizam al-Mulk has chosen, however, to highlight another aspect of the character of Alexander, a legendary hero noted for his wisdom.

The Khusrau referred to is one of the last Sasanid kings of Persia, Khusrau II Parvis (ruled 590-628), before the Muslim Arab conquest. Shirin (the sweet) was his favourite wife and maintained great influence over him throughout his reign. Khusrau's son by another wife assassinated his father, ascended the throne and put the son of Khusrau and Shirin to death. On this historical frame, legends were woven about the great love of Khusrau and Shirin, Shirin's poisoning of her rival co-wife, and Shirin's suicide over the body of Khusrau rather than accept the proposal of marriage by his murderer and successor. A sub-plot on the love affair of Shirin and Farhad developed which was resolved when the king sent his rival away and caused his death. Interestingly, even in the more dramatic versions of the romance of Farhad and Shirin, King Khusrau and Shirin are reconciled and the tale ends with her great devotion to him.

Buzurjmihr was the vizier of the Persian, Sasanian King Khusrau I Anushirwan (ruled 531-79). Anecdotes and witty sayings attributed to him appear in Arabic and Persian literature.

Aisha, favourite wife of the Prophet Muhammad and daughter of his confidant and successor Abu Bakr, is undoubtedly the most famous woman in Islamic history. Despite Muhammad's devotion to her and the fact that he spent more time with her than any of his other wives, there is little evidence that she influenced any of his political decisions. When Muhammad became deathly ill, he asked to be moved to her room and there he spent his final days surrounded by his wives. As a result, various stories are told about attempts by Aisha (and sometimes Hafsa, daughter of Umar, as well) to promote the causes of their male kin in the conflict over the succession. In one of these stories, the Prophet requests that Abu Bakr lead the prayer in his place (a sign that he regards him as his successor) but his wives Aisha and Hafsa try to dissuade him from this choice. Muhammad insists on his decision and is angered at his wives' interference, calling them 'friends of Yusuf'. The reference is to the Egyptian women in the Quranic story of Joseph and Potiphar's wife who inadvertently cut their own fingers when they were dazed by Joseph's beauty. In the version below, Joseph the son of Jacob, also known as Israel, is transformed into Yusuf 'one of The Sons of Israel'. This serves Nizam as a convenient transition to the next illustration of the dire consequences of heeding a wife's advice.

The story of Yusuf and Kirsuf is apparently one variation on the universal folk theme of the granting of three wishes. The version in the passage below is Islamicized in several details. No less interesting, however, is the moral which Nizam al-Mulk emphasizes compared to the usual point of the tale.

The caliph al-Ma'mun, son of Harun al-Rashid, ruled the Abbasid empire during the years 813-33. He was a witness to the successful efforts of Zubayda, Harun's wife, to have her son Muhammad, his younger brother, designated heir at the age of five and eventually to accede to the caliphate (in 809). When the civil war that broke out between the brothers after their father's death turned against her son Muhammad al-Amin, Zubayda cultivated her ties to his rival al-Ma'mun. After the murder of her son al-Amin (in 813), she refused to participate in an attempt to avenge him. Instead, she deftly switched loyalties and made her peace with al-Ma'mun, claiming he was her foster son (since she had helped raise him after the death of his biological mother in childbirth). Thus, al-Ma'mun was speaking from personal experience when he rails against the involvement of women in affairs of state.

Umar ibn al-Khattab, the second caliph (ruled 634–44), seems to have a reputation as a misogynist in Islamic sources, and various attempts to limit women's activities are attributed to him.

Denise Spellberg has analysed parts of this selection in detail in 'Nizam al-Mulk's Manipulation of Tradition: Aisha and the Role of Women in the Islamic Government,' *Muslim World78* (1988): 111-7. She has also treated the earliest example of a Muslim woman attaining political influence - Aisha's involvement in the movement to avenge the murder of the caliph Uthman opposing the caliphate of Ali - in 'Political Action and Public Example: 'A'isha and the Battle of the Camel,' in *Women in Middle Eastern History: Shifting Boundaries in Sex and Gender,* eds Nikki R. Keddie and Beth Baron. (New Haven: Yale University Press, 1991), 45-57. Her book *Politics, Gender, and the Islamic Past: The Legacy of 'A'isha bint Ahi Bahr* (New York: Columbia University Press, 1994) is a broader treatment of the subject.

In the story of Adam and Eve in the Quran, the first wife is not portrayed as tempting her husband to defy Allah's command as Eve does in the Bible. As Smith and Haddad have shown in their 'Eve: Islamic Image of Woman,' which appeared in *Women's Studies International Forum* in 1982, Eve's culpability first appears in traditional Islamic sources in commentaries on the Quran and in tales of the prophets. It is from this later material that Nizam al-Mulk took his earliest example of the dire consequences of undue influence of wives on their husbands. Modern Islamic authors have chosen the original Quranic version or the later traditional view of Eve in line with their approach to the broader issue of woman's role in society.

More extensive and dramatic treatments of the stories of Saudaba and Siyavosh and the adventures of Sekandar may be found in *The Epic of the Kings: Shah-Nama the National Epic of Persia by Ferdowsi* translated by Reuben Levy (London: Routledge and Kegan Paul, 1967).

Some works on Muslim women of the past who were *de jure* or *de facto* rulers: Nabia Abbott, *Two Queens of Baghdad: Mother and Wife of Harun al– Rashid* (Chicago: Chicago University Press, 1946); Bahriye Uçok, *Femmes turques souveraines et regentes dans les états Islamiques,* trans. Ayse Çakmakli. (n.p.: Basari Matbaacilik, n.d.); the chapter on women in Islamic history in Weibke Walter's, *Women in Islam* (1981); Leslie Penn Peirce, *The Imperial Harem: Women and Sovereignty in the Ottoman Empire* (New York: Oxford University Press, 1993). One modern example of a woman attaining political influence through her husband is described in Earl L. Sullivan, *Women in Egyptian Public Life* (Syracuse: Syracuse University Press, 1986).

A fairly large number of advice to Muslim rulers and similar books on principles of government from the eighth to the twentieth centuries have been translated into English. The reader may wish to examine some of these to determine how prevalent Nizam al-Mulk's attitude was.

Nizam al-Mulk, The Book of Government

On the subject of those who wear the veil, and keeping underlings in their place

The king's underlings must not be allowed to assume power, for this causes the utmost harm and destroys the king's splendour and majesty. This particularly applies to women, for they are wearers of the veil and have not complete intelligence. Their purpose is the continuation of the lineage of the race, so the more noble their blood the better, and the more chaste their bearing the more admirable and acceptable they are. But when the king's wives begin to assume the part of rulers, they base their orders on what interested parties tell them, because they are not able to see things with their own eyes in the way that men constantly look at the affairs of the outside world. They give orders following what they are told by those who work amongst them such as chamberlains and servants. Naturally their commands are the opposite of what is right, and mischief ensues; the king's dignity suffers and the people are afflicted with trouble; ruin comes to the state and the religion; men's wealth is dissipated and the ruling class are put to vexation. In all ages nothing but disgrace, infamy, discord and corruption have resulted when kings have been dominated by their wives. Let us discuss a little of this subject in the hope that much will be made clear.

The first man who suffered loss and underwent pain and trouble for obeying a woman was Adam (upon him be peace)[1] who did the bidding of Eve and ate the wheat [in Islamic tradition rather than an apple], with the result that he was expelled from paradise, and wept for two hundred years until God had mercy on him and accepted his repentance.

The story of Saudaba, wife of Kai Kavus and her domination over him

When Kai Kavus sent messengers to Rustam asking for the return of Siyavush because he longed to see him - Siyavush was his son and Rustam had fostered him until he reached the age of manhood - Rustam sent Siyavush to him. Now Siyavush was exceedingly handsome. Saudaba saw him from behind the curtain and was enamoured of him. She said to Kai Kavus, 'Tell Siyavush to come into the women's apartments so that his sisters may see him.' Kai Kavus said to Siyavush, 'Go into the women's apartments for your sisters to see you.' Siyavush said, 'It is my lord's command, nevertheless it were better that they be in their apartments and I in the hall.' When he went into the night-quarters, Saudaba assaulted him and drew him to herself with mischievous intent. Siyavush became angry and wresting himself from her embrace, he left the women's apartments and went to his own house. Saudaba was afraid of what he might say to his father. She said to herself, 'It is better that I anticipate him.' So she went to Kai Kavus and said, 'Siyavush assaulted me and clung to me, and I escaped from him.' Kai Kavus was vexed with Siyavush and there was much fierce and angry talk, until at last it was suggested to Siyavush that he should undergo ordeal by fire. Siyavush said, 'It is for the king to command; whatever he says, I am ready.' So they collected enough firewood to cover half a farsang square, and set fire to it.

When the fire had gained strength and reached the height of a mountain, they said to Siyavush, 'Now! Go in!' Siyavush was riding Shabrang. He uttered the name of God, made his horse leap into the flames, and disappeared. After some time he emerged from the far side of the fire in safety with not a hair singed either on himself or on his horse, by God's command. All the people were amazed. The priests took some of that fire and carried it to the fire-temple; and it is still alive - the fire which gave judgment correctly.

After this judgment Kai Kavus appointed Siyavush to be amir of Balkh and sent him there. But Siyavush had been offended by his father on account of Saudaba, and he lived unhappily there. He was minded not to stay in the land of Iran. He thought of going to Hindustan, or else to China and Machin [Indo-China]. Piran Wisa, who was Afrasiyab's army-commander, came to know Siyavush's secret intent. He presented himself to Siyavush and paid him compliments on behalf of Afrasiyab. Siyavush welcomed him and entered into a covenant with him. Piran Wisa said that their house was one, and their two families were one; Afrasiyab would hold him dearer than all his own sons; and if he ever wished to be reconciled with his father and return to Iran, Afrasiyab would intercede for him, and make a firm treaty with Kai Kavus, and then send him to his father with all honour and respect. So Siyavush went from Balkh to Turkistan. Afrasiyab gave him his daughter in marriage and treated him kindly. However, Garsivaz, Afrasiyab's brother, became jealous of him, and blackened him in front of Afrasiyab. Siyavush was innocent but he was slain in Turkistan. Wailing arose in Iran and her warriors were aroused. Rustam came from Sistan to the capital. Without permission he entered the women's apartments of Kai Kavus and seized Saudaba by the hair; he dragged her outside and cut her to pieces with his sword. No man dared to tell him, 'You did well,' or 'You did ill.' Then they girded themselves for war, and went to Turkistan to take vengeance for the murder of Siyavush. The war went on for many years, and on both sides many thousand men were slaughtered. And the cause of all this was Saudaba and her domination over King Kai Kavus.

Kings and men of strong judgment have always ordered their lives in such a way, and followed such a path that they never let their wives know their secrets; so they remained free from the yoke of their desires and commands and did not succumb to them; one such was Alexander.

History relates that when Alexander came from Rum and defeated Darius son of Darius, who was King of Persia, Darius was killed in flight by one of his own servants. Now Darius had a daughter perfect in beauty and charm, and she had a sister just as fair; and in his palace there were other girls of his family - all of them beautiful. People said to Alexander, 'It befits you to pass by Darius's night-quarters and see those moon-faced ones, especially his daughter, for in beauty she has no peer.' Those who said this intended that Alexander should see Darius's daughter, and having seen her with all her comeliness, marry her. Alexander replied, 'We vanquished their men; let us not be conquered by their women.' He heeded them not, and went not into Darius's night-quarters.

Another well-known story is that of Khusrau and Shirin and Farhad. Since Khusrau so loved Shirin that he put the reins into her hands and did everything that she said, then inevitably she grew bold, and though she was queen to such a great king, she began to prefer Farhad.

Buzurjmihr was asked, 'Why was it that the empire of the house of Sasan fell to ruin while you were their counsellor, for today you have no equal in the world?' He said, 'There were two reasons: firstly that the Sasanians entrusted weighty affairs to petty and ignorant officers, and secondly that instead of seeking out men of learning and wisdom, they left matters to women and boys.

This is the very opposite of prudence and wisdom, for be assured that whenever a king leaves affairs to women and boys, the kingship will surely depart from his house.'

There is a tradition that the Prophet (upon him be peace) commanded, 'Consult women, but whatever they say, do the opposite, and that will be right.' The words of the tradition are [in Arabic], 'Consult them and oppose them.' Had women possessed complete intelligence, The Prophet (upon him be peace) would not have said this.

It is reported in another tradition that when the Prophet's illness became severe, he was so weak that when the time came for obligatory prayer, the Companions were all waiting for him to begin the service; Aisha and Hafsa (may Allah be pleased with them both) were sitting at his bedside; Aisha said to the Prophet, 'O Prophet of Allah, it is time for prayer, and you are not strong enough to go to the mosque. Whom will you command to lead the prayer?' The Prophet (upon him be peace) said, 'Tell Abu Bakr to read the prayers.' Aisha said, 'O Prophet of Allah, Abu Bakr is a man of feeble spirit, who cannot possibly stand in your place.' The Prophet said, 'Tell Abu Bakr to say the prayers.' Aisha again said, 'He is a weak man and feeble-spirited.' The Prophet repeated, 'Tell Abu Bakr to say the prayers.' Aisha then said to Hafsa, 'You speak to him, as I have said several times that Abu Bakr is soft-hearted and loves him more than all other Companions do; if he should stand up to pray and see the Prophet's place empty, he would be overcome with weeping and that would spoil his own and all the others' prayers. Umar ibn al-Khattab is strong and stout of heart; if he be told to do it, nothing will go amiss.' So Hafsa spoke in this wise to the Prophet; his face flushed with anger and he said, 'You are like Yusuf and Kirsuf in the story; I shall not do what you want; I shall do what is good for the Muslims; go and tell Abu Bakr to lead the congregation.'

These are the words of the tradition; and in spite of all the nobility, the learning, the devotion and the piety of Aisha (may Allah be pleased with her), the Prophet (upon him be peace) did the opposite of what she wanted. So imagine what the opinions of other women are worth.

The story of Yusuf and Kirsuf

They say that in the time of the Sons of Israel it was the rule that if for forty years a man had preserved himself from great sins, had fasted and prayed at the proper times and harmed no one, then God would grant him three wishes. Now there was in those days one of the Sons of Israel called Yusuf, a good and pious man, and he had a wife called Kirsuf, as devout and chaste as he. He accomplished this devotional exercise and worshipped God for forty years without default. He thought to himself, 'Now what thing shall I ask from God (be He exalted)? I wish I had a friend to advise me what to ask for - something beneficial.' However much he pondered he could not think of anyone suitable. As he entered his house he caught sight of his wife. With remorse he said, 'In all the world I hold none dearer than this my wife; she is my mate and the mother of my children. My good is her good, and she more than all people desires my good. The right thing is to consult her in this matter.'

So he said to his wife, 'Know that I have now completed forty years of devotion, and three wishes will be granted to me. No one in all the world desires my good more than you. Tell me what to ask from God.' His wife said, 'You know that I have only you in all the world; my eye rejoices in you; and you know that the wife is a man's comfort; I am your comfort; your heart is always happy at the sight of me, and your life is sweet with me as companion. Ask God to give me beauty such as he has given to no other woman, and then whenever you come in at the door and see me so fair and charming, your heart will be glad; as long as we are vouchsafed to remain in this world, we will live in joy and happiness.' The man was pleased at his wife's words. He prayed saying, 'O Lord, give this woman grace and beauty such as Thou hast given to no other woman.' God heard and answered Yusuf's prayer. Next day when his wife got up from sleep, she was not the woman who had gone to bed the night before; she had changed into a form of such comeliness as mortals had never seen.

When Yusuf saw her so beautiful he was astonished and he nearly jumped out of his skin for joy. Every day his wife's beauty and excellence grew until it reached a point where the beholder could not bear to look upon her. The report of her beauty spread throughout the world, and multitudes came to catch sight of her. Then one day she looked in the mirror and saw her beauty; her heart was filled with wonder and pride. She said, 'Who is like me in all the world today? who has such grace and beauty as I have? what have I got to do with this pauper who eats barley bread and passes a miserable existence without any of the good things of this world? I am fit for the greatest kings and Chosroes of the world, and if they find me they will adorn me with gold, jewels and brocade.' Vain desires and ambitions of this sort entered the woman's head. She began to be bad-tempered and quarrelsome with her husband, and often said to him, 'You are not fit for me; you have not even got enough bread to eat.' She had three or four children by Yusuf; she ceased to look after them and became so unmanageable that Yusuf was at his wit's end and did not know what to do. He looked up to heaven and said, 'O Lord, turn this woman into a bear.' Immediately the woman turned into a bear and became a scourge, constantly prowling about the walls and roof of his house; it never went away from the house, and all day water ran from its eyes. Yusuf was at a loss to know how to look after his children; he was unable to perform his divine worship, and he constantly missed the time for prayer. Once more he was in distress; he reached such dire straits that he looked up to heaven and said, 'O God, turn this bear back into a woman just as she was before; give her a contented mind, so that she will watch over her children and care for them; then I, Thy servant, will devote myself to worshipping Thee.' Straight away the woman resumed her original form, and proceeded to attend to her children. She never remembered what had happened, and only thought that she had been dreaming. So the forty years' devotion of Yusuf was [as the Quran 25:25 says] 'blown dust' -all because of the schemes and desires of a woman. Thereafter this story became a proverbial warning against doing what women say.

The caliph al-Ma'mun one day spoke as follows: 'May there never be a king who allows the people of the veil to speak to him about the state, the army, the treasury and the government or to interfere in such matters, or to patronize particular persons; for if they are heeded, at their behest the king may promote one and punish another, or appoint one and dismiss another; [and if this happens] inevitably people will resort to the women's court and present their needs to them since they can be more easily won over. The women, finding themselves the object of attention and seeing their doors thronged with soldiers and peasants, will give way to all sorts of vain desires and initiate all kinds of corrupt practices. Soon heretics will gain access to them. Then it will not be long before the king's majesty vanishes, and the dignity and splendour of the court and the government depart; the king will lose the respect of all, and reproaches will come in from surrounding countries; the country will lapse into confusion, the troops will become disaffected, and the vizier will be powerless to prevent it.'

The best procedure is for the king to follow the established custom which great and prudent kings have practised and which God (to Him be power and glory) himself has commanded [Quran 4:38]: 'Men are rulers over women.' (He says: We appointed men over women to keep them under control.) If women had been able to control themselves, He would not have set men over their heads. So if anyone places women over men, whatever mistakes and mischiefs occur are his fault, for permitting such a thing and changing the custom.

It was a dictum of Kai Khusrau that any king who wants his house to endure, his country not to be destroyed and his own pomp and dignity not to fall to the ground, must never permit people of the veil to have any say except in matters concerning their own underlings and servants. In this way they will preserve the ancient custom and keep themselves free from all anxieties.

Umar ibn al-Khattab (may Allah be pleased with him) said, 'The words of people of the veil are, like their persons, indecent. Just as it is wrong to display their persons in public, so also it is unseemly to repeat their words.'

May that which has been mentioned on this subject be acceptable, and let it be known that these words are full of benefit.

Concerning underlings

God (be He exalted) has created the king to be the superior of all mankind and the inhabitants of the world are his inferiors; they derive their subsistence and rank from him. He must then keep them in such a position that they always know their places and do not put off the ring of service from their ears nor loose the belt of obedience from their waists. At all times he must let them know how they stand whether in merit or demerit, so that they do not forget themselves nor do whatever they like. He should know the measure and rank of every one, and be constantly enquiring into their circumstances lest they deviate from the letter of his commands or overstep the limits which are set for them.

Notes

1. Adam is considered a prophet in Islam.

SUFI HAGIOGRAPHY : DEVOUT WOMEN

['Abd al-Rahman b. 'Ali Ibn al-Jawzi, *Sifat al-safwa* (Hyderabad, 1936-38), 4:30.]

The hagiographies of devout women and men are an offshoot of the biographical genre but they differ in a number of ways. The authors of these works are less concerned with concrete biographical details such as the person's genealogy, date of death and location of activity. Even the names of many of these men and women are often omitted and they are identified by minimal and sometimes discrepant ascription. The sources of most of the tales are men, some of whom are prominent Sufis, but there is no rigorous methodology of chains of transmission as with *hadith*. The words and deeds of early Sufis are timeless models for proper or perhaps ideal behaviour for Muslims.

The earliest extant dictionary of Sufis contained a number of women to which later writers refer, but other noted Sufi authors did not include biographies of women in their collections. Abd al-Rahman b. Ali Ibn al-Jawzi (died 597/1200) was unique in that close to one-quarter of the hagiographies in his collection, 240 in number, were of women. The larger number and proportion of women is specifically cited in the introduction as one of the reasons for the superiority of his work over that of his predecessors. Men neglect to mention the female worshippers of God with their feminine shortcomings, it says, even though the noted Sufi Sufyan al-Thawri learned from the woman Rabi'a and was guided by her words.

The depiction of the daughter of Umm Hassan is typical of the stories of devout women in the Sufi collections and raises a number of questions. What are her most outstanding characteristics? To what extent is her gender relevant to the story? How do we know about the daughter of Umm Hassan and what is implied about the relations between Sufi men and women? What is this devout woman's attitude to Sufyan al-Thawri, a renowned traditionalist, legal scholar and Sufi saint?

The most famous female Sufi saint is Rabi'a al-Adawiyya (c.100-185/718-801) who is credited with having introduced the concept of unquestioning love of God to the ascetic movement. Stories of Rabi'a were transmitted to Europe in the fourteenth century, and her legend was popularized in the East and West. She was the subject of a scholarly biography in the seminal work of Margaret Smith *Rabi'a the Mystic and Her Fellow Saints in Islam* (Cambridge, 1928). Rabi'a's image is prevalent in popular culture to this day. Her life story was produced as an Egyptian musical film widely seen throughout the Middle East and (with English subtitles) in other parts of the Muslim world. Some neo-Islamic circles, however, disapprove of the film because of its graphic portrayal of Rabi'a's worldly life (replete with profane love songs and dancing girls) prior to her conversion to asceticism.

Annemarie Schimmel has devoted a number of studies to the attitude of Islamic mysticism to women, among them: 'Eros - Heavenly and Not So Heavenly - in Sufi Literature and Life,' in *Society and the Sexes in Medieval Islam,* ed. Afaf Lutfi al-Sayyid-Marsot (Malibu, CA: Undena, 1979), 119-41; 'Women in Mystical Islam,' *Women's Studies International Forum* 5 (1982) 145-51; and the introduction to the new edition of Smith's book. The subject has also been treated in Jamal J. Elias, 'Female and Feminine in Islamic Mysticism,' *The Muslim World* 78 (1988) 209-24. *Women in the Islamic Biographical Collections* (Boulder, CO: Lynne Reinner, 1993) contains a chapter devoted to an analysis of the hagiographies of Sufi women.

A number of Sufi collections are available in English. A. J. Arberry, *Muslim Saints and Mystics* (Chicago: University of Chicago Press, 1966) is a translation from Persian of thirty-eight of the seventy-two biographies in Farid al-Din Attar (died 628/1230) *Tadhkirat al-awliya,* including the lengthy hagiography of Rabi'a al-Adawiyya. Javad Nurbakhsh's *Sufi Women* (New York: Khaniqahi Nimatullahi, 1990) is based on Ibn al-Jawzi as well as some other sources. Maulana Ashraf Ali Thanawi's *Bahishti Zewar,* a guide for women composed in Urdu in the nineteenth century, contains twenty-five stories of devout women taken from al-Sha'arani's tenth/sixteenth century *al-Tabakat al-kubra.* This work has been translated and widely disseminated in English for the Muslim public. Barbara Daly Metcalf has produced a scholarly edition of parts of the *Bahishti Zewar* with extensive analysis under the title *Perfecting Women* (Berkeley: University of California Press, 1990). Parallel stories of profane medieval women have been brilliantly analysed by Fedwa Malti-Douglas in *Woman's Body, Woman's Word: Gender and Discourse in Arabo-Islamic Writing* (Princeton: Princeton University Press, 1991).

Ibn al-Jawzi, *Sifat al-safwa*

Devout Women of Basra

The Daughter of Umm Hassan al-Asadiyya

From Sufyan al-Thawri [97-161/715-778]. He said: I went in to see the daughter of Umm Hassan al-Asadiyya and she had a mark on her forehead like a goat's knee from so much prostration in prayer. I said to her: 'O Daughter of Umm Hassan, why do you not appeal to Abdallah b. Shihab b. Abdallah. If you send him a note, he might provide you with charity to improve your living conditions.' 'O Sufyan,' she said, 'Your excellence filled my heart, but God has removed it. O Sufyan, would you bid me request worldly things from one who does not own them?' Sufyan said: When the night veiled her, she entered her prayer niche, closed herself in and cried out: 'O God, every lover has secluded himself with his beloved, and I am alone with You, Î Beloved. There is no warmth but the heat of Hell for he who defies You, and no punishment but the Fire.' Sufyan said: Three days later, I went in to see her and hunger had left its mark on her face, so I said to her: 'O Daughter of Umm Hassan, you will not be granted more than was given to Moses and Khidr, peace be upon them, when they asked the people of a village for food.'[1] She said: 'O Sufyan, Say "Thank God."' I said: 'Al-hamdulillah,' Then she said: 'Have you not acknowledged Him with your gratitude?' I said: 'Yes.' She said: 'You must be grateful for recognizing gratitude, and if you experience this double gratitude, His blessing will never cease.' Sufyan said: By God, my knowledge failed me and my tongue was tied, and I turned to leave, but was not able. Then she said: 'O Sufyan, If a person boasts of his knowledge, this suffices to prove his ignorance. If a person fears God, this is enough to prove his knowledge. Know that hearts will never be cleansed of evil until all intentions are united in one concern for God.' Sufyan said: I despaired thinking of myself.'

Notes

1.The reference is to a story in the Quran, 18 *(Al-Kahf):78,* in which Moses and a servant of God came to a town, asked its people for food and were refused hospitality. The servant of God is named al-Khadir or al-Khidr by most commentators, and Sufis regard him as a saint.

12

MEDIEVAL LEARNED WOMEN

[Muhammad b. 'Abd al-Rahman al-Sakhawi, (d. 902/1497). *Al-Daw' al-lami'*
li-ahl al-qarn al-tasi'. (Cairo, 1353 AH), 10: no. 495.]

Since Islam is a legalistic religion, knowledge of the law and by extension other related fields of learning are highly-regarded. Knowledge in Arab Islamic society was transmitted orally, as we have seen, even after written works were available, and scholars travelled far and wide to gather information from the best teachers available in their time. The reputation of teachers was based to a great extent on the scholars they had studied with, creating a chain of transmission of knowledge back to the original source. Learning, therefore, was conceived of first and foremost as an informal, personal process which could take place in a mosque, a Sufi lodge, a private home or a school-building.

Primary schools *(kuttabs, maktabs),* in which the minimal knowledge needed to be a good Muslim was taught, were established wherever Islam spread, from at least the Umayyad period. The overwhelming majority of the pupils in these primary schools were boys, but there were separate girls' schools and some girls attended *kuttabs* with boys. From the tenth century, *madrasa* colleges - buildings devoted specifically to higher education, with housing and stipends for students and teachers - were established in the Middle East. To the best of our knowledge, women were not formal students at these institutions although a few may have attended lectures. Only men were appointed to salaried teaching posts in the *madrasa* colleges.

Educational institutions were founded and maintained by private individuals of means as an act of piety, and the founders determined to a great extent their character. Many of the benefactors of educational institutions were high officials or members of ruling families whose wealth was a function of their political position. Thus, although education remained essentially a private endeavour, it would not be totally accurate to conclude that the state did not provide educational services.

Despite the growing institutionalization of education, many boys and girls, men and women continued to study in their own homes and the homes of their teachers. This personal aspect of Islamic education was reflected in the fact that biographies of learned individuals rarely indicate the *madrasa* he studied in, but always cite his or her teachers.

The fifteenth-century scholar Muhammad b. Abd al-Rahman al-Sakhawi (died 902/1497) followed the example of his teacher Ibn Hajar al-Asqalani (died 852/1449) and composed a biographical dictionary devoted to over eleven thousand prominent individuals who died during the ninth Islamic century. At the end of this work, a special section is devoted to the biographies of more than one thousand women. Thirty-eight per cent of these women studied, received licenses *(ijazas)* to transmit their learning and/or taught others. Among the most prominent of these medieval learned women was Aisha, daughter of Muhammad b. Abd al-Hadi.

Who were Aisha's teachers - men or women? Were they family members or strangers? How old was she when she received a license to transmit learning from Sitt al-Fuqaha'? How would you explain naming women Sitt al-Fuqaha' (Lady of the Legists) and Sitt al-Wuzara' (Lady of the Ministers)? Only a handful of Aisha s many students are mentioned in the biography. What makes them worthy of note? Where did Aisha study? Where did she teach? One of Aisha's students received a license 'after hearing from her'; what does this imply about the other licenses granted? Why was Aisha unique in her age? What does this tell us about Islamic learning at the time? How is Aisha similar to her predecessor Sitt al-Wuzara'? In what way is Aisha superior to her? Exactly one hundred years separate the dates of death of the two female scholars. How can this fortuitous fact be interpreted?

Jonathan Berkey's *The Transmission of Knowledge in Medieval Cairo* (Princeton: Princeton University Press, 1992) provides an excellent introduction to the subject of traditional Islamic education. A medieval Islamic treatise on education *Instruction of the Student, the Method of Learning* (New York, 1947) by al-Zarnuji has been translated by G. E. von Grunebaum and Theodora M. Abel Huda Lutfi's 'Al-Sakhawi's *Kitab al-Nisa* as a Source for the Social and Economic History of Muslim Women during the Fifteenth Century A. D.,' *The Muslim World 71* (1981) deals with various aspects of the biographies of women in this important collection. A chapter in Roded's *Women in the Islamic Biographical Collections* deals with the numbers of women of learning cited in these works from the time of the Prophet to the modern period, their male and female teachers and students, and the parameters of women's learning.

495 Aisha the daughter of Muhammad son of Abd al-Hadi b. Abd al-Hamid b. Abd al-Hadi b. Yusuf b. Muhammad b. Qudama b. Miqdam, the world-renowned transmitter of traditions (musnida al-dunya), the mother of Muhammad al-Qurashi al-Umari al-Muqaddasi al-Salihi; she was born in the month of Ramadan 723 [1323] and was brought to hear al-Hajjar[1] and Abdallah b. al-Hasan[2] and Abd al-Qadir b. al-Muluk and [other] people. Among the things she heard were: first, the *Sahih,* and second, the *Sahih* of Muslim, and third, *Sira* of Ibn Hisham; and she was granted licenses by: Ibn al-Zirad, and Isma'il b. Umar b. al-Hamawi, and Sitt al-Fuqaha' [Lady of the Legists] the daughter of al-Wasiti,[3] and Yahya b. Fadlallah, and al-Burhan al-Ja'abri, and al-Burhan b. al-Furqan, and Abu al-Hasan al-Bandaniji, and Abdallah b. Muhammad b. Yusuf,[4] and al-Sharaf b. al-Barizi, and Ibrahim b. Salih b. al-Ajami[5] and others. She lived until she was unique among most of her shaykhs in hearing and stood out among the other travellers to distant places [in search of knowledge] in her license [to transmit knowledge]. She related to a great many [people], and masters *(imams)* learned from her, particularly al-Rahhala [the great traveller] and many more. She was pleasant and gentle, people told us about her. Many relate from her with a license today but in Syria only al-Khatib b. Abu Umar al-Hanbali received a license after hearing from her; he heard part of *Dhamm al-Kalam* (Disparagement of Scholastic Theology) by al-Harawi from her. Among those who frequented her was our shaykh, who mentions her in his list of teachers, and he reported that she died in Rabi' al-Awwal 816 [1413] in the Salihiyya section of Damascus after granting a license to [the Lady] Zayn Khatun and Rabi'a and Muhammad and his children. She was the last to relate Bukhari after hearing it from an excellent source. It is a remarkable coincidence that Sitt al-Wuzara' [Lady of the Ministers] the daughter of Umar b. As'ad b. al-Manja[6] was the last woman in the world who related from Ibn al-Zubayda and she died in 716 [1316]. Aisha exceeded her because no man remained on earth of those who heard from al-Hajjar, Sitt al-Wuzara's colleague, except her, and one hundred years separate the deaths of the two. She is cited in Maqrizi's *Uqud.*[7]

Notes

1. Abu al-Abbas Ahmad b. Abu Talib al-Hajjar was a famous transmitter of traditions whose biography appears in the eighth/fourteenth century biographical dictionary of Ibn Hajar al-Asqalani (1: no. 404, pp. 152-3). Students from all countries travelled to hear him, and we are told that when he died in 730/1329, the level of scholarship declined.

2. Abdallah b. al-Hasan or al-Husayn may be the Hanbali *hadith* scholar from Jerusalem

whose biography appears in the second volume of Ibn Hajar's centenary dictionary (pp. 361-362, no. 2139). He died in 732/1331.

3. Shaykha Sitt al-Fuqaha' (whose name was Amat al-Rahman), the daughter of Taqi al-Din Ibrahim b. Ali al-Wasiti, was an outstanding traditionist *(musnida)* who died in 726/1325 at the age of ninety-two or ninety-three. Biographies of her appear in the historical, chronological work of her near contemporary Dhahabi who died in 748/1347 (2:178); the retrospective, alphabetical dictionary of Safadi who died in 764/1347 (25: no. 169, pp. 117-18); and Ibn Hajar (2: no. 1789, p. 221.)

4. Abdallah b. Muhammad b. Yusuf was born in Jerusalem in 649/1251, studied with a number of teachers including his father and Shamiya daughter of al-Bakri, and later settled in Nablus. He was the last of those who related from many shaykhs in that country. He died in 737/1336. The last person to relate what he heard from him in Cairo was Qadi (Justice) Nasir al-Din Nasrallah b. Ahmad the hanbali *qadi* (judge) of Cairo. His biography appears in the second volume of Ibn Hajar (no. 2236, pp. 410-11).

5. Ibrahim b. Salih b. al-Ajami was born some time after the year 640/1242. He was the last traditionist to relate from Yusuf b. Khalil and many people travelled to study with him. He died in 731/1330 and his biography appears in the first volume of Ibn Hajar (no. 66, pp. 28-9.) who cites al-Barzali, al-Dhahabi, Ibn Habib, and his children as those who heard from him.

6. Shaykha Sitt al-Wuzara' (also named Umm Abdallah) the daughter of Qadi Shams al-Din Umar b. As'ad b. al-Manja was born in 624/1226. She heard Bukhari's *Sahih* and Shafi'i's *Musnad* collection of traditions from her father and from Abu Abdallah b. al-Zubaydi. She travelled to Egypt to pursue learning and went on the hajj pilgrimage twice. She was married four times and had three daughters. She had many pupils and was called the foremost traditionist of her age because she was the last person to have heard these works from a superior source. Several male students are named in her biographies. She died in 716/1316 or 717/1317 at the age of ninety-two or ninety-three. Biographies of her appear in Dhahabi (2:169), Safadi (25: no. 168, p. 117), Ibn Hajar (2: no. 1800, pp. 223-4), and the historical work of the eleventh/seventeenth century compiler Ibn al-Imad (6: p. 40.)

7. Among the numerous works of the medieval Egyptian historian Taqi al-Din al-Maqrizi (766-845/1364-1442), an extensive but uncompleted biographical dictionary of prominent Egyptians titled *Durar al-'Uqud* is known.

13

WOMEN IN COURT : ECONOMIC TRANSACTIONS

[Amnon Cohen and Elisheva Simon-Piqali, eds *Jews in the Moslem Court: Society, Economy and Communal Organization in Sixteenth Century Jerusalem* (Jerusalem: Yad Izhak Ben-Zvi, 1993), nos 325, 353, 334, 202.]

Judges in the Muslim courts *(qadis)* have been recording copies of their judgements (as well as other documents) in institutionalized archives *(sijills)* since the sixteenth century. These records show that women appeared regularly in the law courts as litigants in 17 to 68 per cent of the cases, depending on time and venue. They were involved in cases dealing with marriage, divorce, and guardianship, as well as a wide variety of property issues ranging from inheritance and estates to commercial transactions. Since Islamic law was the law of the land, not only Muslims, but Christians and Jews as well came to the court to settle disputes.

Amnon Cohen and Elisheva Simon-Piqali, two scholars who have researched different subjects based on the Jerusalem Muslim court records, published a selection of 452 documents involving Jews from over two hundred thousand sixteenth-century records. This collection was not focused specifically on women, yet at least fifty-five cases involve women in one way or another. The four selections translated below deal with a variety of economic activities of women: loans, property sales, rentals and a gender-specific profession, the female broker *(dalala)* who sold goods to other women in their harems.

In reading the court cases below, the following questions should be addressed. When women had to appear in court, what measures could be taken to guard their privacy or modesty? Under what circumstances did women employ these measures? How could a woman acquire ownership of costly cloth, jewellery and other moveable items of value? How could she convert these objects into cash? Does the loan given by Bila to Sultana appear to be a personal matter or a business transaction? How could a woman acquire ownership of real estate? Why would she sell it? Why would a woman rent urban property?

Why was Hanna prohibited from working as a broker? Was it because she was a woman? Could a woman serve as a guarantor for brokers?

The scope of each of the four economic activities dealt with in these documents has been assessed in quantitative and descriptive studies based on the court records of different cities and towns in different periods. Among these are: Ronald C. Jennings, 'Women in Early Seventeenth Century Ottoman Judicial Records - The Sharia Court of Anatolian Kayseri.' *Journal of the Economic and Social History of the Orient* 18 (1975): 51-114; Haim Gerber, 'Social and Economic Position of Women in an Ottoman City, Bursa, 1600-1700.' *International journal of Middle East Studies* 12 (1980): 231-44; Abraham Marcus, 'Men, Women and Property: Dealers in Real Estate in 18th Century Aleppo.' *Journal of the Economic and Social History of the Orient* 26 (1983): 137-63; Judith E. Tucker, *Women in Nineteenth Century Egypt.* (Cambridge: Cambridge University Press, 1985); Margaret L. Meriwhether, 'Women and Economic Change in Nineteenth-Century Syria: The Case of Aleppo,'Arab *Women: Old Boundaries, New Frontiers,* ed. Judith E. Tucker. (Bloomington: Indiana University Press, 1993), pp. 65-83; Miriam Hoexter,'The Participation of Women in Economic Activities in Turkish Algiers,' (unpublished paper); Elisheva Piqali, 'The Status of Muslim Women in Mid-Sixteenth Century Jerusalem according to the Sharia Court Records' (in Hebrew). MA thesis, The Hebrew University of Jerusalem, 1990.

A description of some traditional female professions based on the historical material may be found in Ahmad Abd ar-Raziq, *La femme au temps des mamlouks en Egypte* (Cairo: Institut Français d'Archéologie Orientale, 1973). Ian C. Dengler, 'Turkish Women in the Ottoman Empire: The Classical Age.' in *Women in the Muslim World,* eds. Lois Beck and Nikki Keddie (Cambridge: Harvard University Press, 1978) provides an overview from the perspective of Istanbul on women's activities in the sixteenth century.

Jerusalem Muslim Court Archives

A Loan and Pawning

Before our lord the judge *[qadi]* of the Hanafi school of law, Hisam al-Din may his virtue increase, the following occurred: Al-Shihabi Ahmad son of the late al-Rini Ya'qub al-Dhikri also known as 'black of night' sued Bila, the Jewess, daughter of Shim'on, as legal agent [*wakil*] in this matter and in the matter below on behalf of the modest lady Sultana, daughter of the most honourable governor, the late Ahmad Bey, former governor of the district of Jerusalem, may God have mercy on his soul. His power of attorney for her was legally verified in front of the aforementioned judge by the testimony of Yahya son of the late Ghanim, and al-Shihabi Ahmad son of al-Ayni Isa al-Dhikri. In his claim, he said that she has in her possession articles which belong to the woman he represents and they are: a white, stitched, silk cloth as collateral for four gold coins, one gold bracelet overlaid with metals as collateral for one and one half cubit Hurmuzi cloth valued at eleven silver para coins.[1] He also said that she [Sultana] gave her [Bila] a plate valued at five silver *para* coins, and [a debt of] six silver *para* coins remained for the rest of the Hurmuzi cloth. He demanded that she bring the silk cloth and the bracelet and that she take the gold which *both of them owe her* [RR] totalling four gold coins and six silver para coins. Bila was asked about the matter and answered, that the silk cloth was in her possession as collateral for the amount mentioned above, and she had the bracelet as collateral for the price of the Hurmuzi cloth and seven and a half gold coins that she owes her for the debt of Madam (*khatun*) Salima wife of Ali Chalabi, brother of the aforementioned woman who authorized him to represent her, by her [Sultana's] permission to her [Salima] in this matter. The *wakil* did not acknowledge what she said about the above-mentioned pawning for what Madam Salima owed. He asked the respondent to acknowledge her claim. The respondent asked the woman he represented to swear. The scribe [who wrote this document] and witnesses [whose names are listed] went to Madam Sultana's house with the aforementioned opponents. Sultana swore a legal oath by Allah that she did not pawn the aforementioned bracelet for Madam Salima's debt; she pawned it solely for the price of the Hormuzi cloth. This was a legally binding oath. Then Bila brought the aforementioned silk cloth and gave it to the claimant. The bracelet remained in her possession for four gold *sultani* coins and six silver coins until she brings the bracelet and takes her debt. Both agreed in this matter on 11 Muharram 980 [24 May 1572]. [Jerusalem Court Archives, volume 55, pp. 64-5; Cohen and Piqali, no. 325.]

Sale of a Woman's House

Before our lord, head of the honorable judges, Ahmad b. al-Diri, the acting hanafi judge in the noble city of Jerusalem, may his virtue increase, the following occurred: our lord the hanafi judge Sun' al-Din Muhammad son of Shaykh Zayn al-Din Kwan, may Allah grant him joy in this life, the master craftsman Abd al-Rahman son of Yusuf al-Tawil the builder and Shaykh Ahmad al-Nasiri testified that they legally identify the Jewish woman Lifa whose business is curing eyes (*al-kahhala*), daughter of Ya'qub the Jew, known by the name 'daughter of al-rabisa.' Our lord the judge identified the witnesses and accepted their evidence, after examining their reliablility by law and swearing them in as is customary. They also testified that on 14 Jumada al-Ula 956 [10 June 1549] she sold to Ibrahim son of Yusuf the Jewish Israelite judge the house that belongs to her, is owned by her, is used exclusively by her, is legally in her possession, that was legally bequeathed to her by her father and mother and that she has possessed until this sale. Ibrahim purchased with his money solely for himself the entire ruined house located in the noble city of Jerusalem in the Jewish neighborhood near the old gate of the city, whose borders are: on the southern side - a ruined house; and also to the east; on the north - a house owned by Abdallah the Jew; and to the west - the public road, which is where the door is located. The house was sold with all rights, paths, ruins, all that is known as part of it and attributed to it, and any additional legal right for the price of 8-1/2 gold *sultani* coins paid immediately, which she received in her hand. The matter was legally verified when a legal suit was filed in the presence of the buyer and Ubayd son of Muhammad, who brought the matter to the court and who serves here as the seller's legal agent after his power of attorney was verified by testimony ...

The matter was registered on 21 Rabi' al-Awwal 958 [29 March 1551].

[Jerusalem Court Archives, volume 24, p. 384; Cohen and Piqali, no. 353.]

House Rental

Shaykh Ahmad al-Masmudi, shaykh of the North Africans in the noble city of Jerusalem, in accordance with a noble imperial letter of appointment, legally rented to the woman Sara, daughter of Maymun, the North African Jewess, the property which beongs to the North African Endowment in the noble city of Jerusalem. She rented from him the entire house which exists and is standing in its place in the noble city of Jerusalem in the Jewish neighborhood, which was her dwelling place, with all its rights and with any legal right attached to it, for three years from the date of this document. The location of the house is well-known and there is no need to describe it and delimit it. The rent for the house is 524 *uthmani* silver coins at the rate of 168 *uthmani* silver coins for each year from the beginning of the rental period. Shaykh Ahmad legally permitted her to spend the rent money, in accordance with the conditions set down by the endowment's founder, for necessary rennovations in the house, according to legal evidence. The lease is valid and legal, and the lessee holds the house according to a previous agreement. They both legally confirmed the details of the matter to each other. The matter was registered on 10 rabi' al-awwa l955 [19 April 1548].

[Jerusalem Court Archives, volume 20, p. 319; Cohen and Piqali, no. 334.]

The Broker *(Dallala)*

Our lord the aforementioned judge[2] warned the woman Hanna the Jewess daughter of Shu'a that from this day forth she may not engage in the broker's trade *(dilala)* in the noble city of Jerusalem and she may not take goods from anyone, and if she sells without a guarantor, she will be punished. Registered 14 Safar 1004.[19 October 1595][3]
[Jerusalem Court Archives, volume 77, p. 162; Cohen and Piqali, no. 202.]

Notes

1. In mid-sixteenth century Jerusalem, gold coins, sometimes termed *sultani,* were divided into 40 silver *paras* (also known as *uthmani).* One *para* purchased about 3 kilograms of flour or one kilogram of mutton. Inflation and currency devaluation were rampant, one of the many reasons people preferred to invest their savings in precious cloths and jewelry. Data on monetary values and commodity prices at this time may be found in Amnon Cohen's *Economic Life in Ottoman Jerusalem* (Cambridge: Cambridge University Press, 1989).

2. In other words, mentioned in the previous document in the volume.

3. The court records contain a guarantee of a Jewish male cobbler to Clara daughter of Ibrahim the North African Jew to engage in the broker's trade; and a guarantee of a Jewish woman to Simha daughter of Yusuf who engaged in the broker's trade, and these two women were guarantors for another Jewish broker.

14

PROPERTY OWNERSHIP, PHILANTHROPY AND

MANAGEMENT: ENDOWMENT DOCUMENTS

['An Endowment Deed of Khasseki Sultan, Dated the 24th May 1552,' trans. St. H. Stephan. *The Quarterly of the Department of Antiquities in Palestine* 10 (1944): 175-94. Kamil al-Ghazzi, *Nahr al-dhahab fi tarikh halab* (Aleppo: al-Matba'a al-Maruniyya, 1342-1345 AH), 2: 596, 192.)]

The Islamic endowment or *waqf is* a unique institution which provides for the alienation of property and the direction of its income to charitable purposes, including the livelihood of the founder's family in succeeding generations. In the course of time, vast urban and rural properties were endowed as *waqf (pl. awqaf)*. Aside from the family aspect, *waqf* endowments provided funds for the maintenance of religious institutions as well as a variety of what we would term social services - soup kitchens, hospitals, water supply, the poor, etc. In other words, the *waqf* institution entailed vast amounts of property, generating considerable income, and the management of numerous major and minor institutions ranging from huge complexes to neighbourhood water fountains or cisterns.

Any Muslim - the ruler or members of his family, a high official, a wealthy merchant or the owner of a small apartment or part thereof – ould establish an endowment. In order to do so, he or she must first demonstrate legal ownership of the property or properties to be endowed. The details of the *waqf* would then be written down in an endowment deed *(waqfiyya)* which would generally be validated and registered in court. In the deed, the endowed property would be described in detail, and the individuals and institutions that will benefit from the revenue or use of the endowed properties would be specified. In addition, the founder must indicate how the income will be distributed in the event of the death or extinction of primary beneficiaries. Since a *waqf is* endowed in perpetuity, where benefits have been allocated to the founders' descendants, provisions are made in case of the extinction of the family - the benefits are allocated to an institution. Similarly, if the charitable institution no longer exists, the income will be transmitted to another institution. The final beneficiary is a general charitable purpose or institution which is presumed to be eternal such as the holy cities of Mecca and Medina or the poor.

Although the endowed properties are no longer privately owned, the founder designated an administrator, by name or *ex officio,* to manage the trust - frequently, the founder himself or herself in their lifetime. Like the beneficiaries, the administration must also be designated in perpetuity, so the management often passes from one individual to another. The ultimate administrator would usually be the holder of a public office or an upstanding Muslim nominated by the court. Founders of endowments frequently stipulated various conditions in their endowment deeds. These could be of a standardized nature, such as the stipulation that the *waqf* properties must be properly maintained and repaired before benefits may be distributed to beneficiaries. Other terms found in endowment documents include almost every provision the human mind can devise ranging from dormitory regulations in *madrasa* colleges to library rules for precious manuscripts; from recipes for meals distributed on Fridays and holidays to the curriculum of educational institutions; from the limitation of female kin's right to live in the family home until they marry to the exclusion of daughters and their offspring from any material benefits.

One by-product of this process is that thousands if not hundreds of thousands of waqf endowment deeds were registered in Muslim courts throughout the Middle East. In addition to newly-founded *waqfs,* court records also contain many cases relating to existing endowments such as appointment of managers, authorization of expenses and transactions, and adjudication of disputes. Sometimes, in the course of these cases, the original endowment deed or deeds would be copied into the record to substantiate a claim. Separate registers of waqf endowments or waqf cases were sometimes compiled by court personnel to facilitate their access to past records.

Although fundamentally a private enterprise, the ramifications of endowments on the public domain are clear. For this reason, the management and records of numerous endowments of various sizes would often be concentrated in the hands of a single religious functionary or government official. Also, Middle Eastern governments conducted periodic surveys of existing endowments and their terms. One of these, a register of all the endowments existing within the walls of the city of Istanbul in the year 953/1546 (with the exception of the sultans' waqfs), was published in 1970 by O. L. Barkan and E. H. Ayverdi. Similarly, data on some 1500 endowments in the northern Syrian city of Aleppo was summarized in the local bureau of *awqaf* as well as the

Muslim court at the end of the nineteenth century and published in the 1920s in a history of the city.

The fact that Muslim women are legally allowed to establish endowments and actually did so has long been evident in the names of buildings - such as the Khasseki Sultan in Jerusalem; and other geographic sites - such as the Zubayda Road for pilgrims from southern Iraq to Mecca and Medina. In the past two decades, however, quantitative studies of large bodies of *waqf* endowment records have produced some provocative findings on the ownership and management of property by women.

Studies of large numbers of endowment deeds and other documents from various regions and periods have shown that the proportion of women among founders of endowments ranges between 17 per cent and 50 per cent with a tentative mean of about 35 per cent. While this is still less than the proportion of women in the population, it indicates that large numbers of women actually owned property and apparently disposed of it according to their own wishes. This raises the question of the source of women's property. Is the common wisdom that women were precluded from the share of inheritances granted to them by the Quran totally accurate? Was the bridal dower, legally the wife's property, universally absconded by her father or other male relatives? How else could a woman amass the private property necessary to establish an endowment?

Quantitative analysis has also shown that there is little or no significant difference between the endowments of men and those of women as to size, type of property endowed and object of philanthropy. It has been suggested that women had a special interest in establishing *waqfs* to maintain control of their property in their lifetime at least, so they would not be economically dependent. It may be argued that women were more prone to endow their property than men precisely because they did not require it for their livelihood, since their fathers and husbands were required to support them financially. Extreme caution must be exercised in trying to reconstruct the motivation of founders in establishing endowments, but the fundamental similarity of endowments by men and women suggests that women founded *waqfs* for essentially the same reasons as men - a combination of philanthropic good deeds, practical economics and social status.

A separate but not unrelated issue is women's share as beneficiaries of endowments. Establishment of family *waqfs* has been regarded as one of the major vehicles for disenfranchising women from their legal Quranic share in inheritances. Some studies support this contention; others have found explicit discriminatory clauses to be rare but the outcome of the distribution of benefits favoured men in the long run; and still others have found clear attempts to make provisions for daughters in endowments. As for charitable benefits, it is clear that women were not stipended teachers or students in the madrasa colleges or religious functionaries in the mosques. There is some scanty information about charitable institutions devoted specifically to women, and clearly women benefitted from charitable endowments in ways that cannot be quantified be they religious institutions, water supply or provisions for the poor.

One of the crucial questions regarding endowments in general and those of women in particular is who controlled the *waqfs*. Gabriel Baer demonstrated that although women founded endowments in fairly large numbers in sixteenth-century Istanbul, they were less prominent among managers of *waqfs*. As time passed, control of all endowments passed into the hands of men. Moreover, in the Istanbul survey, the larger the assets the smaller the percentage of female managers. Even female founders designated men as managers in 75 per cent of the cases. At least two other studies (for Egypt and Palestine) verify Baer's findings that only a minority of endowments were managed by women. The *waqf* institution then ultimately served as a conduit for property owned by women to pass to the control of men. Large numbers of women may have been property-owners but far fewer were property managers.

Khasseki Sultan, the title of the favourite concubine of the Ottoman sultan, refers here to Khasseki Khurrem (died 1558), wife of Sulayman the Lawmaker (known in the West as the Magnificent) and mother of his heir Selim II. As a concubine, she bore the sultan four of his ten sons and Mihrima his favourite daughter. Khurrem was emancipated and was married by him. Ottoman chroniclers of the time and Western observers cite her great influence on the sultan. She is also noted for her good works which include two grand mosques in Istanbul and Edirne; two *madrasa* colleges, a hospital, two public baths, and a public kitchen in Istanbul; and soup kitchens in Mecca and Jerusalem. The latter is a complex of several buildings known as the Khasseki Sultan which was the largest and most important endowment founded by the Ottomans in all Palestine.

The first document below is a Turkish draft of an endowment deed dated 1552 (which was later rendered in Arabic and finalized) for the Khasseki Sultan complex in Jerusalem. It was found in the Khalidiyya Library, a private collection of books and manuscripts established by members of the Khalidi family, one of the oldest Muslim families in Jerusalem. The translator of the document surmises that it was drawn up in Turkish to enable Khasseki Sultan herself to read it and make the necessary corrections and additions.

The document is written in the grand imperial style of the Ottoman court at a time when the sultans ruled an empire stretching from North Africa to Persia and from the Arabian peninsula to the walls of Vienna. In addition to

Persia and from the Arabian peninsula to the walls of Vienna. In addition to the imperial hyperbole, the text abounds with religious allusions to phrases in the Quran and to Sufi mystic concepts. Large parts of the document are in rhymed prose. The deed is embellished with gilt border-lines, rosettes dividing the phrases and a richly decorated invocation of God's blessing and sultanic cypher - a rather lavish 'rough draft'. It was legally validated by 'the poor servant of Allah, to the victorious army in the flourishing province of Asia Minor,' one of the two highest-ranking judges in the Ottoman Empire (the other being for the European provinces). It would be executed after 'the poor Abu al'Su'ud' verified that its provisions were consistent with Islamic law. This Abu al-Su'ud was an eminent Ottoman legist who served as premier jurisconsult of the Empire.

The final endowment deed in Arabic (dated 1557) contains a much longer list of endowed properties (enumerated in a long addition by the translator), and contains a number of personnel changes. Salaries of the personnel are rendered in traditional Arab *dirham* rather than Ottoman Turkish *akçe*. An imperial edict dated 1560 attached to the final endowment deed lists some additions to Khasseki Sultan's Jerusalem *waqf* granted by Sultan Suleiman after her death. In that document, Khurrem is referred to as 'the Zubayda of her time and age,' referring to the wife of Harun al-Rashid who was known for her monumental good works, and 'a second Rabi'a,' alluding to the famous mystic.

Despite the convoluted style and the massive proportions of the property involved, the endowment deed of Khasseki Sultan contains all of the basic elements of a *waqf*. The deed opens with lengthy praise to God and his Prophet followed by the names of the legal authorities who have validated the *waqf*. Preceding the act of endowment are several paragraphs referring to the transitory nature of this life, the need to praise God for His bounty and perform good deeds in preparation for the Day of Judgement. This introductory material has been eliminated below although their spirit pervades the entire document. The core of the endowment deed contains: the name of the founder, the charitable foundation she has established, the endowed property whose income will finance the foundation, various conditions stipulated by the founder, and the administrator or superintendant of the *waqf*. Among the fascinating aspects of this particular endowment deed are the details concerning the food purchased, cooked and distributed in the complex. This information provides us with an indication of the diet of the residents of Jerusalem in the sixteenth century. The recipes for the rice and burghul dishes may be tried today (although it would be advisable to use smaller quantities).

The deed also enables us to address several questions about women and the *waqf*. How is Khasseki Khurrem described in the endowment deed? What types of property did she endow? How did she obtain it? What did the complex she built in Jerusalem constitute? How many people did it employ? Were they men or women? How many did it serve? Were they men or women? What conditions were included in Khasseki Khurrem's endowment? To what extent do you think she was personally involved in the foundation and management of the *waqf*? Whom did she designate to supervise the *waqf* after her death?

The second document is a single entry from chronological court records of Aleppo summarized and published by Kamil al-Ghazzi. Although far more modest than the endowment of Khasseki Sultan, it raises some of the same questions. The Qudsi widow's *waqf* also illustrates how charity and family prominence were linked.

A basic introduction to the *waqf* institution may be found in the article on the subject in the *Encyclopedia of Islam;* and the collection of articles on *Social and Economic Aspects of the Muslim Waqf* edited by Gabriel Baer and Gad Gilbar (forthcoming). Quantitative data on women's endowments may be found in the articles by Ruth Roded, 'The Waqf in Ottoman Aleppo: A Quantitative Analysis,' and Abraham Marcus, 'Piety and Profit: The Waqf in the Society and Economy of Eighteenth Century Aleppo, in Baer and Gilbar; the introduction to Barkan and Ayverdi's transcription of the sixteenth century Istanbul survey; Daniel Crecelius, 'Incidences of *Waqf* Cases in Three Cairo Courts: 1640-1802,' *Journal of the Economic and Social History of the Orient,* XXIX, 176-89; Gabriel Baer, 'Women and Waqf: An Analysis of the Istanbul Tahrir of 1546,' *Studies in Islamic Society: Contributions in Memory of Gabriel Baer* eds., Gabriel R. Warburg and Gad G. Gilbar (Haifa, Israel: Haifa University Press, 1984), 9-27; Roded, 'Quantitative Analysis of Waqf Endowment Deeds,' *Osmanli Arastirmalari,* IX (August, 1989); Judith E. Tucker, *Women in Nineteenth-Century Egypt* (Cambridge: Cambridge University Press, 1985); Margaret L. Meriwhether, 'Women and Economic Change in Nineteenth-Century Syria: The Case of Aleppo,' *Arab Women: Old Boundaries, New Frontiers, ed.* Judith E. Tucker. Bloomington: Indiana University Press, 1993, pp. 65-83; Yitzhak Reiter, *Islamic Endowments in Jerusalem Under the British Mandate* (London: Frank Cass, 1996); Reiter, *Islam in Jerusalem* (Kluwer Law, 1997).

An Endowment Deed of Khasseki Sultan

In the Name of Allah, the Merciful, the Compassionate

... It is for these clear facts and necessary premises that the pearl in the wreath of grandeur and majesty, the lucky forelock of happiness and felicity, the queen of queens, she who is of angelic dispositions, the sublime felicitous one, the beautiful person of ideal qualities, the highest of moral reputation among Muslim men and women, the quintessence of highly respected and the chief of the venerated females, the Aisha of her times, the source of a flourishing sultanate, the shell of the pearls of the glorious caliphate[1] - she who is especially adapted by the many kindnesses of the Eternal King, the mother-sultan *[Valide Sultan]* of Emir Mehmed,[2] son of the most felicitous and grand sultan and the most glorious and illustrious emperor, the holder of the great office of imam,[3] the accomplished sultan, who inherited the grand caliphate from father to son; the upholder of the shining religion, the expounder of the wonders of the pure *shari'a,* the subduer of pharaohs and giants, who causes the faces of kings and sovereigns to grow pale; the lion of the battle-fields, the conqueror of the regions of sea and land, both east and west; he, who arranges well and solidly the carpet of peace and war; the trenchant and sharp sabre, the hero, the great and generous prince, the lord of the kingdoms of the earth; the deep shade of Allah on all nations; the humiliator of emperors, the all-subduing hero and eminent prince, the sultan of all mankind, the sultan of the eastern and western parts of the world, the emperor of the four cardinal points, the sultan, son of the sultan, the sultan Suleiman Khan, may Allah - exalted be He - perpetuate the days of his flourishing caliphate and the years of his victorious reign, as long as days and years succeed each other; and may He spread his just rule over the four quarters of the inhabited world, and guard him with an unsleeping eye wherever he stays and stands, support him with His holy angels of victory wherever he goes and travels, and keep his progeny - guarded against calamities and afflictions - until the day of resurrection. May He double true happiness for him and rightly guide him to consider the actions of his glorious conduct with an appropriate mind and a sound judgement.

The Creator of the Universe - exalted be His great favours and honoured be His most comely Names - has from the very beginning distinguished her Majesty for sublime favours, and created and formed her for admirable deeds, implanted in her a high moral disposition and endowed her with excellent qualities, thus enabling her to bring forth later on the hidden virtues from behind a veiled canopy, in order that they may be publicly known, to acquire laudable moral qualities, and to perfect them with a sound knowledge which accomplishes her illustrious attributes. Yea, Allah ordained that she should be brought up in the shadow of the magnificent sultanate and in the harem of the resplendent caliphate, thus bestowing upon her all kinds of graces, both apparent and hidden, as well as bounteous blessings and gifts, so much so that the pavilion of her grandeur and felicity reaches with her crowned head to the stars, and her glorious majesty touches the highest sky.

Her Majesty having seen and beheld these endless graces and boundless favours bestowed upon her, and out of gratefulness therefor and in compliance with the noble content of the holy verse: 'Do good, as Allah has done good unto you' [Quran 28:77], unlocked the cupboards of favours and gifts and opened the doors of unlimited kindness to mankind at large, pouring out bounteous gifts and favours in abundance; thus both people of distinction and mankind at large were nurtured by her favours. Her aim thereby was that people should benefit by her kindnesses, which - in order to procure her eternal bliss - were granted freely and were intended to be perpetual as days wear into months and years into ages, and that no disorder should befall them, so that her prosperity and luck should continue unchanged to the end of time.

Her Majesty, having abandoned the desires of this world and abhorred its vanities, has had her most illustrious endeavours directed towards the most elevated stations and goal of the most sublime intentions, wishing to attain hereafter the highest heavens as reward ... while the vestiges of her devoutness should not be discontinued, nor her graceful behests abandoned, but that her legacies of kindnesses should continue to be firmly established and the traces of her gifts remain to the poor for constant use. She therefore emullates the exalted precedent set as a fine custom by Abraham, the Friend of Allah, the praiseworthy prophet[4] - may Allah, the Glorious, be graciously disposed towards him - whose carpet of prosperity was spread for comers and goers ...

Now, in order that her illustrious property may be eternal, and founded on the pillars of pious deeds and built by good actions, she ... set down in conformity with legal restrictions and stipulations, in order to withstand the vicissitudes of time and the changes of the course of ages, so that it should not be subject to the disorder of transient events ... while wishing to enregister the details of *awqaf* minutely, to comply strictly with its stipulations and requirements, and to fulfil them, has appointed as general representative of her noble self His Excellency,... who is admitted to the very exalted imperial presence, the notable of the sublime imperial realm, who is especially adapted by the grace of the Noble King, Ja'far, son of Abd al-Rahim - may Allah exalted be He, perpetuate his glory and prosperity, and may He associate his aspirations and desires with success. She has given him an unrestricted, unconditional general power of attorney and a certain, complete legal substitution, the validity of which was formally established on the witness of the two very illustrious and eminent personages, and who are especially adapted by the grace of the King of Succour, Chief Storekeeper of the Imperial Palace Yacqub Agha ibn Abd al-Rahman, and Head Butler Ya'qub Agha ibn Abd al-Hannan - may Allah, exalted be He, perpetuate their prosperity and cause their lives to end by good deeds. Both of them gave a legally valid declaration and a clear acceptable admission.

The afore-mentioned illustrious mandator - may she rejoice in this world and in that one to come - wishing to be counted amongst those believers of laudable actions and to enter their order - and on the injunction of the Grand Quran and the Noble Book: Only he repaireth the mosques of Allah, who believeth in Allah and in the Last Day' [9:18], as well as in consideration of the noble Tradition: 'Whosoever builds a mosque for Allah, shall have a house built unto him by Allah in Paradise', which contains a noble and cherished promise, has built in the protected and holy Jerusalem - may it be encompassed by the grace of Allah, exalted and blessed be He - a well-founded edifice with strongly built pillars, a lofty vaulted mosque, and a high praying-place with firm domes and has endowed it to those Muslims who would observe the prescribed prayers and continue the desirable devotion.

Seeking the pleasure of Allah, she has gratuitously built and embellished (near the Haram al-Sharif area) a building with fifty-five doors opening to high-domed rooms and pleasant dwelling-places of firm structure and strong construction. She has set them aside for those devotees who dwell [for some time] in the neighborhood [of the sanctuary] and for those pious faithful, who follow the orthodox practice of the traditional law and continue to lead a life of obedience to it, who cling to the rope of sacred law, those god-fearing monotheistic people *(muwahhidin)* who assiduously attend the devotional prayers. She has endowed them with it in order that they, dwelling there, may both in the early morning and the late afternoon busy themselves with offering prayers for the spiritual benefit of the eminent endowing lady.

Near this noble mosque, connected with the said rooms, she caused a public building of good structure to be erected, consisting of an enclosure and several roofed buildings, of high construction with a spacious courtyard - a source of abundant favours - and beside it an exquisite model of a kitchen, a bakery, a cellar, a woodshed, privies, a room for provisions, and a store room - containing many gifts.

She has set them aside for the use of the poor and needy [Sufis], the weak and the distressed. In the vicinity she has also caused a clean and fine caravanserai [inn] to be built, as well as a spacious and tidy stable for the use of travellers and those who alight and arrive from a journey, for the wayfarers, and in general for all those who travel and journey.

The illustrious bequeathing lady of sublime position, wishing the said beautiful pious foundations and exceedingly benevolent institutions to remain and endure and be of permanent and continual existence together with the objects and requisites, equipments and appurtenances, has set aside for their maintenance the revenues from:

(a)   the village of Amyun, [adding the farm Qaiqabe near by, from the Arabic *waqfiyya*] situated in the sub-district of Kura, within the district of the protected town of Tripoli,[5] which she owns as a landed estate in freehold by a royal patent, as valid property received as an imperial gift with explicit evident right, the imperial deed of possession, containing boundaries and marks set out therein in a lucid and auspicious manner and written in details in the royal letter of patent, which boundaries and marks are well known to people of esteem and famous (so that they need no further definition);

[Here the Arabic waqfiyya inserts the following additional villages, places and farms, buildings and shares set aside by Khasseki Sultan for the same purpose] :

i.   The whole village of Lydda, near Ramleh.
ii.   One share out of ten in the village of el-Jib, i.e. two thousand and five hundred *dirhem*.
iii.   The whole of two baths on a lane, leading to the Bab al-Ghawanima, the north-western gate of the Haram enclosure.
iv.   The whole of the village of Beit Iksa together with the farm of al-Kharruba.
v.   Eighteen out of twenty-four shares in the village of Kafr Jinnis.
vi.   The whole village of Kafr Ana and the farm of Kafr Tab [east of al-Kanisa (xi) mentioned below].
vii.   The whole village of Buqai' al-Din and the Buqai' al-Arnin lands.
viii. The whole village of Beit Liqya with the farms Beit Nushif and Rukubis
ix.   All the imperial share owned in Bethlehem, i.e. eighteen out of twenty-four,
x..   All the imperial share owned in Beit Jala, i.e. 18/24ths, together with the lands known as Khallat ai-Joz and Ras al-Haniyya within the boundaries of Beit Jala.
xi.   The whole village of al-Kanisa in the Ramleh sub-district.
xii.   The whole village of Birim Ma'in.
xiii. All the imperial share in the village of Subtara in the coastal plain., i.e. 12/24ths.

xiv.   The whole village of Annabeh.

xv.   All the imperial share in the village of Safiriyya, i.e. 20/24ths.

xvi.   The whole village of Kharabta [i.e. little ruin] .... Bounded on the north by lands of Deir Ammar ...

xvii.   All the imperial shares in Jindas, i.e. seven out of twenty-four.

xviii.   The whole village of Yazur.

xix.   The whole village of al-Yahudiyya.

xx.   All the share in the village of Beit Dajan, i.e. eighteen full shares out of twenty-four and a third of a share.

xxi.   The whole village of Beit Shenna.

xxii.   The whole village of Rantiyya.

xxiii.   All the imperial share in the village of Na'lin, i.e. 18/24ths.

xxiv.   The whole village of Qaqun with the farm Deir Saliam and one-fourth of the farm Heithanat ai-Jammasin in the region of Bani Sa'b (Tulkarm sub-district).

Additional endowments made by Suleiman I on 29 Shawwal 967 [23 July 1567] include:

(a)   all the imperial share in the tithes of Har village, i.e. 3830 *dirhem* ; (b) all the imperial share in the farm of al-Kanisa, i.e. 19/24ths; (c) and (d) the whole of the two farms Sufiyya and Jalbune [or Jalyube], all situated in the sub-district of Sidon.]

(b)   the caravanserai situated in the quarter of Sheikh Tutmaj (one of the quarters of the said protected town), the boundaries of which are: a public road to the south, a public road and the bank of the river Qalita [present-day Abu Ali] to the east; a public road and the sea gate to the north, and a public road to the west, at the end of which it is situated;

(c)   and the shops contiguous with it;

(d)   and a plot of land (not planted with trees);

(e)   and a vaulted market [*qisariyya*] in the selfsame protected city, situated in the quarter of Khan al-Adami, with the public road to the south, and the said Khan al-Adami to the east, and an orange grove to the north, whilst it ends in the west at the public road and the bank of the river Qalita;

(f)   and the soap factory known under the name of Sa'diyya, situated in the Zuhur quarter of the selfsame protected town, the boundaries of which are the mosque of the Samaritans in the south, and the ditch of the Sultan's Mill in the east together with the garden of Ibn Qubayya; to the north the houses of Ajim Baba Kemal and to the west the houses of the former Commandant of the citadel, Haider Agha;

(g)   and the soap factory known as *Awamid* [columns] situated in the Sabi road of the selfsame protected town; the boundaries of which are the houses of the butcher Gabrish Oghlu and of Devletbay to the south, and to the east the houses of the aforementioned Devletbay, and the public road from the north, and from the west the Sab'iyya road;

(h)   and in the village of Rash-hin in the sub-district of Zawiya attached to the district of the selfsame protected town, all the four mills known as Taitariyya and situated on the river of Rash-hin, bounded on the south by the said river Rash-hin and from the east and north by the roads leading to the orchards, and to the west the orchards;

(i)   and the four mills situated in the village of Bistanin in the said sub-district, bounded on the south and west by the river Abu Ali, and by the mill ditch on the east, and the public road on the north; which mills are known as Ra'iyye [Trabiyya in the Arabic deed] and are driven by the said river Abu Ali;

(j)   and outside the outskirts of the aforementioned protected town the three windmills known as Sahyun, which need no further description nor definition, and of which one is known as the main mill;

The whole of these *awqaf* mentioned above together with their boundaries, rights, appurtenances, and annexations in general as well as their appendants have been bequeathed by her Majesty, who has stipulated that, during her lifetime, she herself would administer and manage all the affairs of the above-mentioned endowments according to her own wish; that revenues accruing there from should be spent in the manner she chooses to direct; that their administration should lie in her hands undisputably, so that she may change the conditions of the bequest, its rules and regulations and alter them, reduce or increase them, and that her decisions in this connexion be neither objected to nor hindered, nor be the subject of strife or question by anyone soever; and that, after the ray of light and gift of grace of her soul soars from this bodily world to the spiritual one of paradise, and ascends to the gardens of eternal bliss, all the affairs of the *awqaf* should be administered by the sultan of East and West, subject to his enlightened behest. His Majesty would then order the different posts and offices to be given in charge to those trust-worthy Muslims and reliable faithful people, who are most fit for them;

Further her Majesty has ordered that the trustee be a person renowned for his deep attachment to religion and known for his appearance of integrity and honesty. He should be a pious, religious, acceptable, and religiously minded person who would not deviate from the straight path, and whose hands are clean from committing sins, a man of serious endeavours in carrying out his duties, who would welcome guests and not turn them away. He should strive and show his aptitude and should guard himself as much as possible from negligence and carelessness. He should observe with integrity the laws of collecting the revenues and should endeavour to make the awqaf prosper through all kinds of laudable efforts, following the prescriptions of efficiency, increasing and repairing it from time to time and making it a habit to disburse sufficiently for that purpose; and to pay the greatest attention to it, so that all vestiges of her illustrious personage should thus grow and increase day by day.

An upright and honest clerk should be employed to put down in writing all the business transactions of the said *awqaf* and to note them down without delay nor postponement. He should be well versed in accountancy, proficient in writing, and of a sound judgement.

Also a tax-collector, possessed of the said laudable qualities and noble character, able to carry out his duty, and upright, pious, and religiously minded, free from vice and devoted to his duty, should be employed. Whatever he collects and obtains he should hand over and deliver to the trustee without delay.

Enlisting the help and assistance of the said clerk and tax-collector, the trustee should put all the said *awqaf* to profitable use according to the usual practice, the ordinary method, and the lawful ways as well as the well-known manner.

After having duly observed and followed the above-mentioned stipulations laid down, and the restrictions and conditions imposed, the daily fixed wages payable to the trustee should be twenty *akçe;*[6] his clerk should be paid six *akçe* a day, and the tax-collector five *akçe* per day.

What remains hereafter from the revenues should be spent, whenever necessity calls for it and in sufficient amounts, on the real estates mentioned above, for the repairs and reconditioning of the said buildings the afore-mentioned noble mosque, the noble rooms the beautiful caravanserais and the high and lofty building, in general on the main endowments and benevolent institutions.

The illustrious bequeathing lady - may Allah, exalted be He, perpetuate her protecting qualities, and make her exalted rank and eminence endure forever - has thus ordered, that a virtuous *imam* should be appointed for the aforementioned noble mosque. He should be one of the Muslim jurisprudents and a God-fearing believer, known for his religious knowledge, asceticism, and piety, endued with forbearance, orthodox belief, and spiritual prosperity; mastering the knowledge concerning the pillars of prayer, the religious duties, the rules of action conforming with the Prophet's precepts, the works deemed to be canonically laudable, the principles and elements of knowledge in religious matters, good behaviour, and beneficent acts. He should be a Sunnite, following the school of Abu Hanifa. He should lead the Muslim congregation in prayers as prescribed, and also serve as *mu'ezzin,* calling for prayers. He should be paid three *akçe* per day.

She has also stipulated that a sheikh should be in charge of the said imperial building. He should be of pure character traits, God-fearing, conforming to the canonical law, content, trusting in Allah, piously scrupulous, and not greedy; of kind words and agreeable speech, forbearing, free from vices, of good demeanour, refraining from hurting one's feeling, pious and of mild and forbearing disposition. He should receive as wages five *akçe* per day.

Also an under-steward should be employed. He should be known for his honesty and religiosity. He should buy (under the directions of the trustee and the sheikh) the requisite foods for the public kitchen, and hand these to the stores and the larder. He should receive four *akçe* per day as wages.

Also a trustworthy and upright keeper for the store room and another for the pantry should be employed. They both should be virtuous and honest people, and should be put in charge of the store room and the pantry, respectively, which they should keep and guard with honesty and integrity. Each of them should receive four *akçe* per day.

A trustworthy and upright clerk should especially be employed for these duties. He should be free from moral faults, not deviating from the right path, and of a morally sound character. He should keep account of receipts and expenditure, both large and small down to the veriest trifle, without changing or altering the facts, neither neglecting his duty nor failing to enter these details in an account book. He should receive four *akçe,* too, per day.

Two serious, active master cooks and master bakers, respectively, should also be employed. They should cook the foods in the manner followed by all the imperial public kitchens, and bake the *fodula* [brown] bread accordingly. Of the cooks one should be the head, and should receive six *akçe* per day, while the other should receive four *akçe* daily. Both of them should have an apprentice under them, who should be always in their service. He should be paid two *akçe* per day.

Of the bakers, too, one should be the head and receive five *akçe* per day, while the other should get four *akçe* a day. Three apprentices should work under them, each receiving two *akçe* a day.

Two inspectors of food and bread should also be employed, who should pursue their duties with honesty, in the usual manner. Each of them should receive four *akçe* daily.

Two persons should be employed to wash dishes and plates, and whose wages should be two *akçe* per day for each.

Further, two persons should be placed in charge of the earthenware dishes; they should be held responsible for cups, bowls, and basins of the whole public kitchen building, each receiving as daily wages two *akçe*.

Three additional persons should be employed, one for cooking the food. He is to receive two *akçe* per diem. The two others should wash and cleanse the wheat and rice to be cooked as food. Each of them should receive fifteen *akçe* per month as wages.

Two other persons should be employed, one for carrying the wheat destined for bread from the store to the mill, and transporting the flour from the mill to the store. He should receive daily three *akçe*. The other person should fetch water for the kitchen in sufficient quantity, also sprinkle water in front of the aforementioned benevolent institution. His wage should be two *akçe* a day.

Two honest, religiously minded persons, pious and able to carry out their duty, should further be employed: the one as guardian of the noble mosque and the living rooms (also to be in charge of pots and pans), and to light and extinguish the lamps in due time, to open the doors in the morning, and to close them in the evening, and sweep and clean the mosque and rooms whenever cleaning is needed. He should receive four *akçe* per day. The other one should carry out the duties of innkeeper of the said caravanserai, as well as doorkeeper and general servant; and guard the khan and keep it in good order and be responsible for carrying out all the necessary relevant services. He should receive daily two *akçe*.

Furthermore, two persons should be employed: one as doorkeeper of the public kitchen and the refectory, receiving two *akçe* a day, and the other as general servant for the public kitchen, the refectory, and the building of the sanctuary, cleaning any refuse or rubbish. He should receive as wages two *akçe* daily.

Another three persons, well versed in miller's works, should be appointed, in order to work at the above-mentioned three windmills in the usual manner, performing there whole-time duty, and carrying out the necessary repairs if and when required. The miller in charge of the main mill should receive daily six *akçe*, while the others would get three *akçe* each a day.

A master repairer should be employed to carry out all important repairs connected with the works. He would be required to repair all apparent defects in whatever *waqf*, be they small or large, without delay, and restore them. He should receive four *akçe* per day.

For lights and lamps two *akçe* should be spent per day.

She has therefore apportioned and estimated the following rations for the imperial public kitchen, where food should be cooked twice daily, in the evening and in the morning. On the nights preceding Fridays a *zerdé* rice dish should be cooked; and on all other nights a rice soup for the following morning should be cooked with clarified butter and for the evening meals a burghul soup. Rice for the said dish should be measured out in the Istanbul kilé [roughly an English bushel or 36 liters], and five kilé [180 liters] each time accordingly, sixty *uqiyya*[7] [17 kilograms] mutton, sixteen *uqiyya* [5 kilograms] clarified butter, two *uqiyya* [600 grams] chick peas, four *uqiyya* [1.2 kilograms] onions, five *uqiyya* [1.4 kilograms] salt, one hundred and twenty *uqiyya* [34.6 kilograms] fuel wood, and thirty *dirhem* [96 grams] pepper.

As for the *zerdé* dish two kile and four *uqiyya* [75 kilogram] rice, six *uqiyya* [1.7 kilograms] clarified cooking butter, twenty *uqiyya* [5.8 kilograms] honey, and saffron for ten *akçe* worth have been apportioned by her.

With regard to the said rice soup one kilé and four *uqiyya* [38 kilograms] rice, four *uqiyya* [1.2 kilogram] clarified cooking butter, and two *uqiyya* [600 grams] chick peas together with four *uqiyya* [1.2 kilograms] onions and five *uqiyya* [1.4 kilograms] salt as well as one hundred and twenty *uqiyya* [34.6 kilograms] fuel wood; and during the seasons squash, and dried, cooked fruits and yoghurt and vinegar and lemon juice and pepper should be bought for the value of twelve *akçe*, as estimated by her;

As to the burghul (cracked wheat) soup two kilé and one-eighth [77 kilograms] - according to the Istanbul measure - burghul, together with four *uqiyya* [1.2 kilograms] clarified cooking butter, two *uqiyya* [600 grams] chick peas, four *uqiyya* [1.2 kilograms] onions, one hundred and twenty *uqiyya* [34.6 kilograms] fuel wood, five *uqiyya* [1.4 kilograms] salt, and half an *uqiyya* [150 grams] coriander have been estimated by her;

She has also stipulated that Fodula bread should be baked daily in the bakery mentioned above, the net weight of a baked Fodula being ninety *dirhem* [300 grams]; and that for the daily baking of these Fodula breads ten kilé [360 kilograms] flour, five *uqiyya* [1.4 kilograms] salt, and eighty *uqiyya* [23 kilograms] fuel wood have been set aside by her.

She has further stipulated that a ration from the above-named dishes should be issued to each devotee and pious person living in the holy precincts: a basting-ladle full of cooked food and a Fodula bread per head, to which a lump of cooked meat should be added on Friday eve.

Cooked rations should also be issued in the same manner to the preacher of the noble mosque, the clerk of the *awqaf,* the sheikh of the building, the under-steward and his clerk, the keepers of the store room and the pantry, to each of the two cooks and their apprentice, the two bakers separately, as well as to their three apprentices, to each of the two wardens, to each of the washers of plates and pans, and those in charge of the dishes, and of cleaning rice and wheat, and to him who carries the wheat to the mill and retransports the flour thence, and to the person carrying water to the kitchen section, and to the guardian of the mosque, the innkeeper, the doorkeeper at the kitchen and the refectory, the general servant, the three millers separately, and to the repair-master: each time a basting-ladle full of food and two Fodula breads, and on Friday eve a lump of cooked meat should be issued in addition thereto.

She has further stipulated that food should be distributed in the said refectory to the poor and needy, the weak and destitute, to four hundred persons at a time, each of them receiving one Fodula bread and each two of them a bowl of food, a basting-ladle full, and in addition to that a lump of cooked meat on Friday eve.

She has also stipulated that except for the above-mentioned servants and other employees no food may be set aside to any one person on the request and intervention of anyone, nor may it be taken outside in a copper bucket. Thus food set aside for such a purpose and taken out would be considered by her to have been stolen, and the person doing so as having committed a crime and a sin against Allah, the eternal King.

Furthermore she has also stipulated that whosoever be *ex officio qapu aghasi* at the Gate of Felicity [chief white eunuch in charge of the imperial palace in Istanbul] should be superintendent of the said *awqaf*.

At the end of each year he should take the accounts of the said *waqfs* from the administrator, who, submitting them, should after due deduction of the estimated expenses and the fixed personal emoluments, pay the rest of the revenues to the superintendent. This one, in his turn, would accept, receive, and keep them, so that they may be ready to be spent on the freehold property, in accordance with the principles followed, if and when vicissitudes and misfortunes happen as months wear into years, ages pass by, and times and hours change.

This arrangement of stipulations and setting of regulations having been settled, the model of noble and eminent persons, and the chief of the general and illustrious people, who is especially adapted by the grace of the All-Bounteous King, Haider Kiahya b. Abd al-Rahman was appointed by Her Noble Self to be the joint administrator. She handed over to him all the revenues of the said *waqfs*, to administer them in accordance with the endowment deed until the registration of them has been completed.

The said Haider Kiahya has wholly and completely acknowledged and confirmed the said words and written stipulations and all regulations, completed and fulfilled them and duly observed and kept them. He signed the details of the said *awqaf* with regard to their legal validity and usefulness, the regulations fixed and the necessity of the written stipulations and their purpose; having been legally decreed, pronounced and confirmed and signed by him.

These sentences have been arranged, set up, and written down on the thirtieth day of Jumada the First, nine hundred and fifty nine [24 May 1552].

Kamil al-Ghazzi's, History of Aleppo Volume II

Dhu al-Qada 1274 Shawwal 1275
... 1275 [1858 AD] : Banba daughter of Abdallah wife of Ahmad Efendi al-Qudsi endowed buildings of the smallest size to the Madrassa al-Salahiyya college, then to the poor of the Haramayn [holy cities of Mecca and Medina,], [p. 596.]

Suwayqa Ali Quarter

... [The Salahiyya Madrasa] known in our times as the Baha'iyya, west of the Khayr Bey Khan, is named for Amir Salah al-Din Yusuf b. al-As'ad al-Dawatdar. He endowed it in the year 737 [1336], and it was his house, known previously as the Ibn al-Adim house. The said Salah endowed it as a *madrasa* college to the four schools of Islamic law and stipulated that the Shafi'i and the Hanafi *qadi* judges of Aleppo would be instructors in it. The *madrasa* receives an allotment of about 5000 *qurush* per year from the Aleppo Bureau of Waqfs. In the days of the Ottoman Empire, it was used as a court for the shafi'is for a long time. Then it was left, and it was on the verge of ruin, and its *waqfs* were neglected until its administrator the late Baha al-Din Efendi ibn Taqi Efendi al-Qudsi restored it in the year 1260 [1844]. He reinstated it as a *madrasa* as it had been before but the yield of its *waqf* was still very little so that the rent did not support its functionaries - students, prayer-leader, instructor and other providers of liturgical services. In the year 1275 [1858], *Hajja* [the pilgrim] Banba daughter of Abdallah b. Abd al-Manan, wife of the late Baha al-Din mentioned above, endowed a house in the Firafara quarter [home of the Qudsi family] near the Zaynabiyya grand mosque to the *madrasa*. The *madrasa* stands high now ... and the prayers are held in it. [p. 192]

Notes

1. Khurrem is so termed because she was the mother of the heir-presumptive.
2. He was the first-born of Khasseki Sultan but had three elder half-brothers. He was

born on 29 January 1523; died 6 November 1543.

3. The sultan is referred to as *imam* in the sense of ruler. The Ottomans sultans assumed the title of caliph after the conquest of Egypt where the last (titular) Abbasid caliph resided.

4. Abraham is considered a prophet by the Muslims.

5. The Ottomans applied this term to nearly all large towns.

6. At this time, the Ottoman *akçe* was valued at one-half a silver *para*. An *akçe* was worth about 1-1/2 kilograms flour, 1/2 kilogram mutton, and 1/4 kilogram olive oil or soap in mid-sixteenth century Jerusalem. These values were calculated based on data in Amnon Cohen's *Economic Life in Ottoman Jerusalem*. Since the Ottoman Empire was plagued by inflation, within a relatively short time, the real value of the salaries would be meaningless.

7. The Jerusalem *uqiyya* equalled 90 *dirhams* weight; each *dirham* weighed 3.2 grams. The weights and measures in the following recipes have been calculated based on these values as well as estimations of the weight of a liter of cereal. The proof of the values is in the eating.

8. The endowment became binding and was registered in the middle of the month of Sha'ban 964 [14 June 1557]. The deed was witnessed by several notables of the Ottoman Empire, including the trustee and Rustem Pasha, son-in-law of Khasseki Khurrem.

15

ISLAMIC VIEWS ON SEXUALITY

[Madelain Farah, *Marriage and Sexuality in Islam: A Translation of al–Ghazali's Book on the Etiquette of Marriage from the Ihya'*. (Salt Lake City: The University of Utah, 1984), pp. 106-13.]

Islam regards sexuality as a natural part of human relations which must be regulated within the spiritual, ethical and social framework of the religion. Like the prophets of the Bible, Muhammad had a regular sex life with his wives and concubines, and his superior sexual prowess is regarded as one of the signs of his excellence among men. Similarly, early biographies of the Prophet's wives relate to female sexuality quite frankly. The sex act does, however, bring the man and the woman to a state of ritual impurity from which they must cleanse themselves. This attitude probably derives from the ancient concept that any bodily discharge renders the individual 'unclean'. The prohibition of full sexual intercourse with a menstruating woman is apparently also related to a primordial taboo. As we have seen, in Islam, a variety of sexual acts, short of full penetration, are permitted with a menstruating woman. These regulations reflect attitudes towards menstruation and towards sex.

In the Quran, sex is limited to legally sanctioned relations between a man and a woman, that is, in marriage or concubinage. Fornication *(zina')* is explicitly forbidden, but two separate verses relate to this offense differently. In one verse (4 *(al-Nisa'):15)*, only women are mentioned as fornicators and their punishment is incarceration in their home for a period of time which may be until their death. Another verse (24 *(al-Nur):2)* refers to fornicating men and women both of whom are to be punished by 100 lashes. A famous passage of the Quran on slander requires that an accusation of fornication be proven by four witnesses and prescribes a harsh penalty for false accusations. The implication of this injunction is that it is difficult if not impossible to legally prove adultery short of a confession by the guilty party.

Homosexuality *(al-lawata)* and sodomy *(lut)* are discussed in the Quran in the many references to Lot and his family, the only ones of their people who repented their lewd acts and were spared by Allah. Those who did not change their ways are severely condemned, and both parties to a homosexual relationship are to be strictly punished [7 (al-A'raf):81; 4 *(al-Nisa'):16*]. A saying of the Prophet specifies the death sentence for both parties to an act of sodomy. Other *hadiths* forbid homosexuality, including lesbianism, and transvestitism.

The precedent of the Prophet's life as well as an explicit saying attributed to him precludes the institution of celibacy in Islam. Nevertheless, mystic writers continued to deal with the tension between marriage and sexuality on the one hand and the quest for gnosis and unity with Allah on the other. Human sexuality was also dealt with in the vast Islamic medical literature in the context of prevention and treatment of disorders. In some of these works, the permissibility of birth control is discussed and various methods are enumerated. Of course, human sexuality, including relations considered illicit by Islamic ethics and law, is a prominent theme in the profane literatures of Islamic societies. It is from these works that Europeans drew their fantasies that all Muslims lived lives of 'one thousand and one nights'.

Abu Hamid al-Ghazali (1058-1111) was a brilliant Persian jurist who was sent by Nizam al-Mulk to teach at his *madrasa* college in Baghdad where he lectured to an audience of hundreds of thousands. After four years of this prominent scholarly career, Ghazali experienced some sort of crisis which led him to leave Baghdad to live as a poor Sufi travelling to various holy places in the Islamic world. At this time, he wrote the *Ihya' ulum al-din,* 'The Revival of the Religious Sciences', designed to suggest a golden mean between the extreme passion and excessive practices verging on heresy of the mystic movement and the sterile scholasticism and hypocrisy to which orthodox scholars had deteriorated. Although Ghazali wrote many other works, returned to academic life for a time, and established a mystic centre in his hometown, it is the depth, breadth and originality of the *Ihya'* which established his reputation as one of the most influential reformers in Islamic history.

The *Ihya'* is a guide for the devout Muslim to every aspect of life. It is divided into four 'quarters' or volumes: ritual practices *(ibadat),* social customs *(adat),* vices *(muhlikat)* and virtues *(munjiyat).* Each of these comprises ten 'books' or chapters. The second book of volume two deals with customs of marriage including sexual relations. The bulk of this chapter recapitulates the arguments of mystics for and against marriage and reconciles the clear directives of the Quran and words and deeds of the Prophet advocated by orthodoxy with the aspirations of the ascetics. The ascetic is not complete, Ghazali concludes, unless he marries and overpowers desire. A Sufi should marry a devout woman who will assist him in his spiritual endeavors.

In the following selection from Madelain Farah's translation of the Book of Marriage, sexual relations and coitus interruptus are discussed. Why does Ghazali recommend reciting prayers before and during sexual intercourse? What is the implication of this practice? Why should the couple try to be as quiet as possible? What attitude to nudity is reflected in this passage? How does Ghazali relate to women's sexual needs? What view of menstruation is reflected in this passage? How does Ghazali interpret the Quranic verse (2:223) 'go to your tilth as ye will'? What is the attitude toward sodomy or anal sex? What is the attitude toward masturbation? What factors does Ghazali take into consideration in discussing whether coitus interruptus as a form of birth control is permitted? Note that the translator has indicated the eulogy formulae that Muslims append to every mention of the name of the Prophet or his Companions by an asterisk.

The noted Moroccan sociologist and feminist Fatima Mernissi compares Ghazali's attitude to sex to that of Freud in her influential book *Beyond the Veil* (Cambridge, Mass.: Schenkman, 1975).

Further information on the Islamic legal and medical treatment of coitus interruptus and other forms of birth control may be found in B. F. Musallam's *Sex and Society in Islam: Birth Control Before the Nineteenth Century* (Cambridge: Cambridge University Press, 1983).

al-Ghazal's, 'The Revival of the Religious Sciences'

Book on Etiquette of Marriage

[Etiquette of Intimate Relations]
The tenth: on the etiquette of intimate relations. It is desirable that it should commence in the name of God and with the [following] recitation: Say, 'He is God, the One and Only' [Quran 112:1]; then he should glorify and exalt His name saying, 'In the name of God, Most High, Most Great; O God, cause it to be a good progeny if you cause it to issue forth from my loins.' The Prophet* said, 'If one of you say when he comes upon his wife, "O God, avert the devil from me and avert the devil from what You have granted us." Then should a child result, the devil shall not hurt him.'

When you near ejaculation, say to yourself without moving your lips: "Praise be to God Who has created humans out of fluid, and made thereof relatives and in-laws, for thy Lord is omnipotent." One of the men of *hadith* used to raise his voice in praise to the extent that the members of the household could hear his voice. Then he would turn away from the *qibla* [direction of prayer], and would not face the *qibla* during coitus out of deference for the qibla. He should also cover himself and his wife with a garment. The Messenger* of God used to cover his head and lower his voice, saying to the woman, "Remain quiet." A [transmitter] says, "If one of you should have intimate relations with his wife, you should not denude yourselves completely like two onagers," that is, two donkeys.

Let him proceed with gentle words and kisses. The Prophet* said, "Let none of you come upon his wife like an animal, and let there be an emissary between them." He was asked, "What is this emissary, O Messenger of God?" He said, "The kiss and [sweet] words." He* also said, "There are three qualities which are considered deficiencies in a man: one, that he should meet someone whose acquaintance he wishes to make but parts from him before learning his name and lineage; second, that he should be treated kindly and reject the kindnesses done unto him; and third, that he should approach his concubine or wife and have sexual contact with her before exchanging tender words and caresses, consequently, he sleeps with her and fulfills his needs before she fulfills hers."

Intimate relations are undesirable during three nights of the month: the first, the last, and the middle. It is said that the devil is present during copulation on these nights, and it is also said that the devils copulate during these nights. It was related that Ali, Mu'awiya, and Abu Hurayra also frowned upon it [during those nights]. Certain *ulama* [scholars] recommended intimate relations on Friday and the night before it [Thursday] in fulfillment of one of the two interpretations of the Prophet's* words, "May God bless the one who purifies and performs the ablution, etc."

Once the husband has attained his fulfillment, let him tarry until his wife also attains hers. Her orgasm *(inzal)¹* may be delayed, thus exciting her desire; to withdraw quickly is harmful to the woman. Difference in the nature of [their] reaching a climax causes discord whenever the husband ejaculates first. Congruence in attaining a climax is more gratifying to her because the man is not preoccupied with his own pleasure, but rather with hers; for it is likely that the woman might be shy.

It is desirable that he should have intimate relations with her once every four nights; that is more just, for the [maximum] number of wives is four which justifies this span. It is true that intimate relations should be more or less frequent in accordance to her need to remain chaste, for to satisfy her is his duty. If seeking intimate relations [by the woman] is not established, it causes the same difficulty in the same demand and the fulfillment thereof.

He should not approach her during menstruation, immediately after it, or before major ablution *(ghusl),* for that is forbidden according to the decree of the Book [Quran 2:222]. It has been said that it would engender leprosy in the offspring. The husband is entitled to enjoy all parts of her body during menstruation but not to have sodomy; intercourse during menstruation is forbidden *(haram)* because it is harmful, and sodomy will cause permanent harm; for that reason it [sodomy] is more strongly prohibited than intimate relations during menstruation. The words of the Almighty state, 'so go to your tilth as ye will' [Quran 2:223]; that is, 'any time you please.' He may achieve emission by her hand and can enjoy what is concealed by the loincloth *(izar)* short of coitus. The woman should cover herself with a loincloth from her groin to [a point just] above the knee during the state of menstruation. This is one of the rules of etiquette. He may partake of meals with the woman during her period of menstruation; he may also sleep beside her, etc. He should not avoid her.

If the husband wishes to have intimate relations with one after having had coitus with another, then he should wash his genitals first. If he has nocturnal emission, then he should not have intercourse before washing his genitals or urinating. Sexual intercourse is frowned upon at the beginning of the night for he should not sleep in an impure state. Should he seek sleep or food, then let him perform first the limited ablution *(wudu'),* for that is a recommended practice of the sunna. The son of Umar related,'I said to the Prophet,* "Should any of us sleep in a state of major ritual impurity *(junub)?"* And he replied, "Yes, if he has performed the limited ablution *(wudu').* " 'However, a dispensation was given in this regard: Aisha* said, 'The Prophet* used to sleep in a state of major ritual impurity having not touched water.'

Whenever he returns to his bed, he should wipe the covers or shake them, for he does not know what might have taken place thereon during his absence. He should not shave, trim his fingernails, sharpen the blade [with which he shaves], cause blood to flow, or reveal any part of him while in a state of major ritual impurity; for all parts of his body would be restored to him in the hereafter, and he would thus return to a state of major ritual impurity. It is said that every hair will demand an account for the infraction it committed.

[Coitus Interruptus]

Other etiquettes include refraining from coitus *(azl)* and not ejaculating except in the place of tilling, which is the womb, for there is not a soul whose existence God has decreed but that will exist. To that effect were the words of the Messenger* of God. As pertains to coitus interruptus, the *ulama* have split into four groups over whether it is permissible or reprehensible: (a) There are those who consider it unconditionally permissible under all circumstances; (b) there are those who forbid it in all circumstances; (c) there are those who say it is permissible with her consent; evidently those proponents consider the harm [caused to the woman], which is forbidden rather than coitus interruptus it self; (d) there are those who say it is permissible with the bondmaid but not with the free woman.

As far as we are concerned, it is permissible. As to a reprehensible act, it applies to cases where unlawfulness is disregarded, where uprightness is ignored or where virtue is abandoned. It [coitus interruptus] is reprehensible according to the third stipulation; in other words, it involves abandonment of a virtue, as it is said: It is reprehensible for someone in the mosque to sit without being preoccupied with *dhikr* [remembrance of God] or prayer; and it is reprehensible for someone residing in Mecca not to perform the pilgrimage every year; this reprehensibility applies to the abandonment of what should take precedence and is more convenient, nothing more. This is firmly established in what we have explained concerning the virtue of [having] offspring, and in what has been related concerning the Prophet': 'A man has intimate relations with his wife, and is thus decreed for him the reward of a male offspring who fights for the cause of God and is killed [martyred].' He said so because if such a son is born to him, he would receive the reward of being the cause for his [son's] existence, even though Almighty God is his creator, his sustainer, and the one who strengthens him for jihad. His part in causing [the child] to exist is the act of coitus at the time of ejaculating in the uterus. We have stated that there is no reprehensibility in terms of prohibition and purification, for upholding prohibition is possible only by text or by analogy with a text; there is no text without a basis for analogy. Rather, we have here a basis for analogy - namely, abstaining from marriage altogether, abstaining from intimate relations after marriage, or avoiding emission after penetration; all such abstentions are more preferable, but they do not constitute acts of unlawfulness or disagreement. For the progeny is formed by the sperm being deposited in the uterus, which comes from four causes: marriage, then copulation, then patience until emission takes place after intercourse, then waiting until the sperm is implanted in the uterus. Some of these causes are more closely related than others. [Thus] abstaining from the fourth is like abstaining from the third; likewise, the third is similar to the second, and the second is like the first. All that is not the same as abortion or the burying of girls alive *(wa'd)*.[2]

These two things, in effect, constitute a crime against an already existing person; and that also has stages: The first stage of existence is that the sperm should lodge in the uterus, merge with the fluid of the woman, and become thus receptive to life; to interfere with this process constitutes a crime. If it develops into an embryo and becomes attached [a fetus], then the crime becomes more serious. If the spirit is breathed into it and the created being takes form, then the crime [of abortion] becomes more serious still. The crime is most serious after the fetus is born alive [then buried if it is a girl]. We have said that the initial stage of existence is the planting of the sperm in the uterus, not emission from the urethra; for the offspring is not produced by the sperm of the male alone but from the agglutination of the mates, either from both his and her fluid or from his fluid and the blood of menses, and that the blood plays, in relation to it, the same role as milk to its coagulator; the sperm from the man is necessary in coagulating the blood of the menses as the thickening agent *(rawbah)* is for milk since through it the coagulator gels. However that might be, a woman's fluid is a fundamental element in coagulation.

The two fluids are likened unto an offer and related acceptance which result in the consummation of a contract. Whoever makes an offer and goes back on it before it is accepted has breached the contract by rendering it null and void. Whenever an offer and related acceptance take place, rescission becomes a nullification, an annulment, and a severance. As no child can issue forth from a sperm in the vertebra, likewise [a child would not be created] after the expulsion [of the sperm] from the urethra unless it mixes with the fluid or the blood of the woman. This is, therefore, a clear analogy.

Should you say: 'But coitus interruptus is not reprehensible on account of opposing the existence of a child, it is likely to be reprehensible on account of the motive behind it; for it cannot be motivated except by a corrupt intention which is blemished by concealed polytheism.' I would answer that the motivations for coitus interruptus are five:

The first pertains to concubines who serve to preserve property from the destruction entailed by the right to manumission; the purpose of maintaining property by avoiding manumission and heading off its causes is not prohibited.

The second, preserving the beauty of the woman and her portliness in order to maintain enjoyment, and protect her life against the danger of childbirth; and this, too, is not prohibited.

The third, fear of excessive hardship on account of numerous offspring, and guarding against the excessive pursuit of gain and against the need for resorting to evil means. This, too, is not prohibited, because encountering fewer hardships is an aid to religion [faith]. Without doubt, perfection and virtue ensue from dependence on and faith in God's guaranty which is expressed in His words, 'No creature is there crawling on the earth, but its provision rests on God' [Quran 2:6³]. Falling short of the apex of perfection, and abandoning what is preferable is not a criminal act. However, we cannot say that taking consequences into account as well as preserving possessions and hoarding them are prohibited, even though they are contrary to dependence [on God].

The fourth, fear of having female children because of the stigma involved in getting them married, as was the custom of the Arabs in burying their female progeny *(fi qatlihim al-inath)* .This would be an evil intention if marriage or coitus are to be abandoned on its account; a person would be guilty of the intention but not of abstinence from marriage and coitus; so likewise in coitus interruptus. Corruption engendered by belief in disgrace is stronger in the sunna of the Prophet*. Such would be comparable to the circumstance of a woman who avoids marriage out of disdain for having to lie under a man and thus attempts to emulate them. Undesirability [in this case] is not due to abstinence from marriage per se.

The fifth, that the woman might abstain from having children on account of arrogance, excessive cleanliness, fear of labor pains, childbirth, and nursing. Such was the custom of the Kharijite [Seceder] women in their excessive use of water to the point that they used to perform the prayers during the days of menses and would not enter the bathroom except naked [because] of their excessive cleanliness. This too is an innovation which contradicts the sunna and manifests a corrupt intent. One among them sought permission to see Aisha* when she came to Basra, but she [Aisha] did not grant it. Thus it is the intent and not the prevention of having children which is corrupt.

If you should say that the Prophet* said, 'Whoever abandons marriage for fear of having dependents is not one of us in the least,' I would say that coitus interruptus is like abstinence from marriage. By 'he is not one of us' is meant that he does not concur with our sunna and our path: Our sunna is the pursuit of the more preferable deed. Should you point out the fact that the Prophet* said regarding coitus interruptus, 'That constitutes a secret form of burying children alive' and [also] recited, 'and when the girl-child that was buried alive is asked,' which is reported in the *Sahih* [of Muslim], we would reply [that] in the *Sahih* are also authentic reports concerning the lawfulness [of coitus interruptus]. His expression 'secret form of burying children alive' is like unto his words 'secret polytheism,' and that is an act which constitutes undesirability but not unlawfulness.

If you should point out the fact that Ibn Abbas said, 'Coitus interruptus constitutes the lesser degree of burying children alive, as conception is prevented by coitus interruptus,' then we would reply, 'He is equating the prevention of existence to cutting it off, and that is a weak form of analogy.' For that reason Ali* denounced this act upon hearing this saying, 'A child is not buried alive until after the seventh, or seven phases have been completed,' and he recited the Quranic verse pertaining to the stages of creation [23:12-14]: 'Verily We created man from a product of wet earth; then placed him as a drop (of seed) in a safe lodging,' up to 'and then produced it as another creation'; that is to say, we breathed a spirit into him. Then he recited the Almighty's words in [another] verse [81:8]: 'And when the girl-child that was buried alive is asked.' If you examine what we have already stated concerning analogy and point of view, you will perceive the difference between the method of AH* and that of Ibn Abbas* in seeking hidden meanings and pursuing knowledge.

It appears that the two *Sahihs* [of Bukhari and Muslim] concur in relating what Ibn Jabir had said, 'We used to have coitus interruptus in the days of the Prophet* while the Quran was being revealed.' In another transmittal: 'We used to have coitus interruptus; the Prophet* heard about it, but he did not enjoin us against it.' There is also a report that Jabir had said: 'A man came to the Prophet* and said, "I have a bondmaid who is our servant and who brings us water [to drink] during the date-picking season. I do have intimate relations with her, but I am undesirous that she should conceive."' He* replied, 'Have coitus interruptus if you wish; for she shall receive what has been destined for her.' The man was absent for some time, then he came back to him [the Prophet] and said, 'The bondwoman is pregnant.' He replied, 'I told you that she will receive what has been destined for her.' All this can be found in the two *Sahihs* [of Bukhari and Muslim].

Notes

1.   Arabic has one term, *inzal,* which is here translated as 'orgasm', 'climax', 'ejaculation', or 'emission'.

2.   A pre-Islamic, pagan custom, forbidden in the Quran.

3.   Arberry translation.

16

FOLK TALES : JUHA AND HIS WIFE; AISHA AND

HER HUSBAND

[*Juha,* ed. Rahamin Rejwan (Tel Aviv: Zmora, Bitan, 1984), 123, 129, 130-1, 136. (translated from Hebrew); 'Who's Cleverer: Man or Woman?' trans. Fatima Mernissi in Margot Badran and Miriam Cooke, eds. *Opening the Gates: A Century of Arab Feminist Writing* (Bloomington: Indiana University Press, 1990), pp. 318-27.]

Information about women among the popular classes may be cautiously gleaned from folk tales and the popular view of women may be deciphered. Although clearly folk tales are meant to portray the fantastic, they must be anchored in reality for them to be credible.

Juha is said to be a real historic figure who lived in the city of Kufa, Iraq in the fourteenth century. Some of the stories connected to Juha take place in Turkestan and their hero is Khawaja Nasraddin who lived at the time of the Mongol conqueror Timurleng. Alternately, Nasreddin Hoca is said to originate from Aksehir in Turkey, and an annual festival devoted to him is still celebrated there. Stories of Juha and Nasreddin merged into the most popular figure in Middle Eastern folklore.

Juha represents the poor people who have to live by their wits and contend with everyday problems and figures of authority. He is witty and foolish, the actor and the victim. Under the humour and irony of these stories, realities of social life and popular attitudes may be discerned. Juha's wives (as well as his donkey) often appear in these stories.

The first story should be read in light of the verse of the Quran (4:34, see above) which explicitly permits a man to beat his wife (and H. H. Jessup's evidence and attitude on this subject). Is it reasonable to assume that women beat their husbands? What facts do we learn about the behaviour of women of the popular classes from incidental information in the other stories? What images of women and their relationships with men are projected in them?

The tale of Aisha the Carpenter's Daughter has been circulating in Morocco for a long, long time *(min zaman)*. The sociologist and feminist Fatima Mernissi transcribed it and published it in Arabic and in French. Israeli Jews of Moroccan origin know the story in slightly different versions, and add that the tale is much more effective when related orally by a master storyteller. Margot Badran and Miriam Cooke (with translation assistance from Elise Goldwasser) included the story in their anthology *Opening the Gates: A Century of Arab Feminist Writing* in the section titled 'Activism.'

How is Aisha depicted in this Moroccan folk tale? Why did Fatima Mernissi decide to publicize this particular story? Why did Badran and Cooke include it in their anthology? What morals may be learned by Moroccans from this story?

To further explore the fascinating subject of women in folk tales, the following collections may be analysed: Hasan M. El-Shamy, ed. *Folktales of Egypt* (Chicago: The University of Chicago Press, 1980); Inea Bushnaq, ed. *Arab Folk-Tales* (New York: Pantheon Books, 1986); Ibrahim Muhawi and Sharif Kanaana, *Speak Bird, Speak Again: Palestinian Arab Folktales* (Berkeley: University of California Press, 1989); Barbara K. Walker, trans. *The Art of the Turkish Tale*, 2 vols. (Lubbock: Texas Tech University Press, 1990,1993).

Juha

Lengthening

While in the marketplace, Juha heard the crier announce that a sword was for sale for thirty dinars. Juha examined the sword and saw that it was not worth the price. But when he inquired, he was told that the sword lengthens by five cubits when one strikes with it.

The next day, he took long tongs and offered them in the marketplace for thirty dinars. The people laughed at him and said that the tongs were not worth a farthing.

'You err,' Juha told them. 'You said that the sword lengthens by five cubits when one strikes with it, and asked thirty dinars for it. These tongs lengthen by more than ten cubits when my wife beats me with them.'

The Cause

The preacher was telling the people how God created the world in six days. Juha's wife, hearing that God created woman on the last day, was offended and asked the preacher:

'Tell me, sir, why did God create woman at the end of the week - she is the most beautiful of all creatures?'

Juha immediately interrupted and answered her:

'My wife! If God had created you on the first day, you would have prevented Him from creating the rest of the creatures with all your chattering.'

No Equality

Juha's wife used to go out every evening to visit with women neighbours and leave him at home to watch the house. The wife kept coming home very late until it angered Juha and he decided to teach her a lesson.

One night when she returned, she knocked on the door again and again, but Juha would not open it for her. She began to complain and promise him that she wouldn't stay out late at nights any more. But Juha persisted and didn't open the door. In desperation, she said that if he did not open the door for her, she would throw herself in the well near the house. As she said, she threw a large stone into the well and hid nearby.

When Juha heard the sound of the stone hitting the water, he was sure that his wife had thrown herself into the well. He opened the door and went out to the well, but he saw no sign of her.

His wife saw him searching, entered the house and closed the door after herself.

When Juha realized what had happened, he demanded that she let him in the house. But she stood by the window and began to yell at him, curse him, and accuse him of spending his nights with a wanton woman, neglecting her and returning home very late. She was not satisfied with making these accusations, but even threatened to sue him in court in order to reveal his true face to all in public.

Hearing her terrible shouting, the neighbors gathered round and began to reprove Juha for his immoral behavior. But he turned them away, saying it was a personal matter. When he finally entered the house, he asked his wife what was the meaning of the shameful thing she had done to him, and she answered:

'I had to teach you a lesson. Now we are equals.'

'That is true, woman,' Juha answered her. 'But there is no equality between a man and his wife in Islam.'

Each Person's Role

Passersby noticed smoke and flames bursting out of Juha's house. They immediately ran to him and told him what was happening. But Juha didn't budge.

'Run already ... ! What are you waiting for? Your house is about to burn down,' they pleaded with him. But Juha answered them:

'Gentlemen! I do not wish to quarrel with my wife. We divided the chores between us. I am responsible for matters outside the house and she is responsible for household affairs. Do you want me to mix in her realm?'

Who's Cleverer: Man or Woman?

> There was and there was
> There was basil and there were lilies
> which grew everywhere.

Once upon a time there was a carpenter who had a daughter named Aisha. She gave great care to the basil she was growing on her terrace and she watered it incessantly. The son of the king noticed the young woman and got into the habit of spying on her. He wanted to know her name and found out she was called Aisha. He, therefore, decided to speak to her.

He said to her:

> Lalla Aisha, daughter of the carpenter,
> you who tend and water the basil,
> Do you know how many leaves does the stem hold?

She said to him:

> Sidi Muhammad, son of the king
> you who have studied the book of God
> tell me how many stars are in the sky
> how many fish in the water
> And dots in the Quran!

The prince was surprised and upset by her rejoinder. 'She's mocking me,' he said to himself. He shut the window from which he watched the terrace and he went away. She did the same. The next day she watered the basil again. The prince watched as he had before. On this day Aisha's household was preparing *anhamca*. Someone called her but she wanted to eat the soup on the terrace. It was brought to her in a bowl. She was eating it when a dumpling fell on her breast. She caught it and ate it. The prince was elated. 'I will remind her of this incident.' The next day as she was going up to water the basil, he said:

> Lalla Aisha, daughter of the carpenter
> you who tend and water the basil
> do you know how many leaves does the stem hold?

She replied :

> Sidi Muhammad, son of the king
> you who have studied the book of God
> tell me how many stars are in the sky
> how many fish in the ocean
> and dots in the Quran!

He said to her:

> Remember, you ill-bred glutton
> you didn't hesitate to gobble up a poor lost dumpling
> that fell on your breast
> and you ate it up.

'This young man is always watching me,' she thought. And so for two days she stayed out of sight. She passed much of her time spying on the prince. Finally, she surprised him at a merchant's where he was eating pomegranates. She watched him carefully. He ate happily. Suddenly a seed fell and rolled on the ground to the door of the store. He stooped, retrieved the seed and ate it. Lalla Aisha hurried home. The next morning she rushed up to the terrace to water her basil. The prince was there and said:

> Lalla Aisha, daughter of the carpenter
> you who tend and water the basil
> do you know how many leaves does the stem hold?

She replied:

> Sidi Muhammad, son of the king
> you who have studied the book of God
> tell me how many stars are in the sky
> how many fish in the ocean
> and dots in the Quran!

He said to her:

> Remember, you ill-bred glutton
> You didn't hesitate to gobble up a poor lost dumpling
> that fell on your breast
> and you ate it up!

She responded to him:

> Remember, you ill-bred glutton!
> You didn't hesitate to gobble up a poor pomegranate seed
> that had rolled to the store door
> And you devoured it!

My God! This young woman is spying on me ...' He spied on her more discreetly. One day when he was in front of his home, a Jew showed up with a donkey loaded with fish to sell. The prince offered to buy everything - the donkey, the fish and even his clothes. The merchant gladly accepted the deal. The prince, disguised as a Jewish merchant, went to sell his fish in front of Lalla Aisha's home. 'Fish! Fish! Who wants to buy fish!' He praised his goods loudly until Aisha appeared on the doorstep:

> Hey, Jew! Are you selling fish!
> Yes, Lalla! That's what I'm selling.
> How much?
> A kiss on the cheek will be enough.

She was tempted: 'No one's looking. Why not?' She offered her cheek and in return he offered her the donkey and all of the fish. Then he left. She returned to her home with the fish, distributed it to everyone, and let the donkey go free in the street. After this adventure, she didn't do anything for two days. The third day she went up to the terrace and the prince said to her:

> Lalla Aisha, daughter of the carpenter
> you who tend and water the basil
> do you know how many leaves does the stem hold?

She replied:

> Sidi Muhammad, son of the king
> you who have studied the book of God
> tell me how many stars are in the sky

how many fish in the ocean
and dots in the Quran!

He said to her:

Remember, you ill-bred glutton
You didn't hesitate to gobble up a poor lost dumpling
that fell on your breast
and you ate it up.

She responded to him:

Remember, you ill-bred glutton!
You did not hesitate to gobble up a poor pomegranate seed
That had rolled to the store door.
And you devoured it!

He said to her:

There was a fish-vendor
and he kissed the cheek of the carpenter's daughter.

'Lord have mercy!' She cried in amazement. The next day she asked her father to
buy her black dye. For seven days she applied it and her skin became black like
that of an African woman, a real African slave. She asked her father to take her to
the market to sell her. Her father was afraid and absolutely refused. But she
insisted, 'Please take me to the market and sell me. Don't worry about me.' So the
next day he took her to market and sold her. And guess who bought her? The
prince! He took her home, gave her to one of his slaves to be washed and prepared
and be brought up to his rooms. But Lalla Aisha refused to be washed. She
assured everyone that she was perfectly clean. She prepared herself for the prince
and in the evening she was taken up to his rooms. She spent pleasant moments
with him. They played and amused each other very much. The prince never
suspected that she had brought with her a razor, a mirror, rouge, a long radish and
a sleep inducing herb called *sikran*. When she prepared his tea she put several
drops *oisikran* in the brew. As soon as he tasted it he fell fast asleep. She took
out her razor and removed the prince's fine beard. She then put rouge on his
cheeks, put kohl in his eyes and put the radish in his bottom. Finally she put the
mirror in front of his face and left quickly.

It was a long time before the prince opened his eyes. He had been asleep for
three long days. When he finally awoke, he looked in horror at his image in the
mirror: his shaven beard, his painted eyes and cheeks. He also felt the harsh

presence of the radish. He searched for the woman who had been his companion. Nowhere was she to be found! 'God knows who could have pulled this on me!' And the prince locked himself in for seven days, while he waited for his beard to grow back. He carefully got rid of every trace of the make-up and paid special attention to his attire.

During this time Aisha had returned to her home. Each day, she went up to the terrace to inspect her neighbour's windows. When would they open again? Finally, sure enough! He showed up. He said to her:

> Lalla Aisha, daughter of the carpenter
> you who tend and water the basil
> Do you know how many leaves does the stem hold?

She replied:

> Sidi Muhammad, son of the king
> you who have studied the book of God
> tell me how many stars are in the sky
> how many fish in the ocean
> and dots in the Quran!

He said to her:

> Remember, you ill-bred glutton
> You didn't hesitate to gobble up a poor lost dumpling
> that fell on your breast
> and you ate it up.

She responded to him:

> Remember, you ill-bred glutton!
> You didn't hesitate to gobble up a poor pomegranate seed
> That had rolled to the store door.
> And you devoured it!

He said to her:

> There was a fish-vendor
> and he kissed the cheek of the carpenter's daughter.

She replies:

> There was a slave

sold in the market
who messed with the prince's face and bottom ...

The prince was stupefied. 'So she's the one who mocked me like this.' On the next day, he went to ask his father, the sultan, to ask for the hand of the carpenter's daughter. The sultan was surprised:

'You ignore the daughters of viziers, you neglect your own cousins and you choose the daughter of a carpenter!'

'I will marry no one but her,' his son replied firmly. 'I want her, no matter the price. No matter what the conditions!'

Therefore, the king asked for the hand of the carpenter's daughter for his son. The carpenter told his daughter the news immediately. 'Father, give him my hand,' she told him. He tried to dissuade her. She insisted, 'Give him my hand.' He agreed but demanded a fairly high dowry. The king gave it to him immediately. When the marriage was confirmed, Aisha gave her father instructions:

'You know the king's palace. Well, you must dig a tunnel between our house and the palace.'

And so it was done. The carpenter hired some masons who dug a tunnel that connected the two homes. A little while afterwards the prince set the wedding date. He brought his fiancée and moved her into the palace.

When they were alone he said to her: 'You have mocked and ridiculed me!'

'Yes! I'm the one who did it.'

'And now tell me,' he said to her, 'Who is cleverer, man or woman?'

'Woman, my Lord,' she replied.

He was angry and decided to lock her up in the grain room underground. Each day he went to see her in her prison. He brought her a loaf of barley bread, some olives, a jar of water and asked her: 'Aisha, the Defeated, living in the grain room, who is cleverer man or woman?'

'Woman, my Lord.'

As soon as he heard this, he left her. Days and days passed this way. The carpenter, alarmed at his daughter's silence, searched for some news. He found that the prince had locked up Lalla Aisha in a cellar. He met with the masons and told them to unblock the entrance to the tunnel that connected the house to the palace. He demanded that they dig it to the cellar where his daughter was imprisoned. So it was. Lalla Aisha could now come home to sleep comfortably in her father's home. She re-entered the cellar at dawn and the prince never knew. He continued to visit her regularly and each time asked the ritual question.

'Who is cleverer, man or woman?'

'Woman, my Lord.'

One day he came to see her and told her that he was going on a *nzaha* in Sour. She wished him good luck and asked when he was leaving. He told her Friday after next. She went by way of the tunnel to her father and said, 'You must find me a woman to henna my hands for a wedding. I also want a very pretty tent and people to guard it.'

Her father granted her wishes. That Thursday evening, when the prince told his wife he was leaving, she solicitously wished him good luck again and never let on about her plan. When he left, she returned to her father's home.

'My tent must be up in Sour before the prince's is.'

So it was. When the prince arrived at Sour, he saw a beautiful tent set in the middle of the fields and guarded by slaves. 'But who beat me to it here?' he asked, very intrigued. His tent was pitched nearby. The prince called one of his slaves and sent him to find out who was the owner of this mysterious tent. The slave was stopped by Lalla Aisha's guards. He asked them who was there. 'Our mistress,' they replied. The messenger told the prince that the tent owner was a woman. The prince summoned Lalla Aisha. She told the messenger that the prince should know a woman never goes to a man. It is the man who must always go to the woman.

So the prince prepared himself and went to join her in her tent. They talked for a long time, they drank ... They denied themselves nothing. They stayed together for three days ... or perhaps seven. When the prince finally decided to leave, he offered one of his rings to Lalla Aisha. When he left, the young woman ordered camp to be struck before the prince had time to leave the area. Before leaving, he glanced over and the famous tent had simply disappeared into thin air. 'Where's this woman now?' he asked his servants. 'She has disappeared,' was all they could answer.

As soon as he had returned to the palace, he visited Lalla Aisha in her cellar and said: 'Aisha the defeated, living in the grain room, you missed a beautiful *nzaha!*

'I'm glad, my Lord, you had a good time', she replied.

'You should have seen the marvel I met. What a woman!'

'I am thrilled that my Lord had such a charming *nzaha!*

He left. As for her, she realised she was pregnant and some months later she gave birth to a son, whom she named Sour. At night she kept herself busy with the baby, during the day she left it in her father's home and stayed in her cellar. The prince visited regularly. He never forgot to bring barley bread, olives and water and he always asked the ritual question,'Who is cleverer, man or woman?'

Invariably she answered 'Woman, my Lord'.

One morning he came to announce that he was leaving right away for a *nzaha* in Dour. Aisha again asked her father for the services of a woman to dye her hands with henna, a tent and some people. The tent was to be different from the first one. She decorated her hands, and put on her most beautiful garments. She ordered the tent to be set up before the prince's arrival and settled in. The prince was as surprised as he had been at Sour that someone had preceded him. He sent a messenger to find out who was in the tent. He was told it was a woman. The prince invited her to join him. But she sent a message to him: 'I do not go to another's home. Whoever wants to see me must come to me.' So he went and stayed with her for seven days. On the day he left he gave her his dagger.

No sooner had he left than Lalla Aisha ordered everything to be taken down, and she left before the prince. When the prince's slaves awoke, they could find no trace of the mysterious woman. 'A woman who acts like that must be, without a doubt, a jinn! She can't be human!' they said.

The prince left Dour and returned to his palace where he visited Lalla Aisha in her cellar. He brought her the usual black bread, olives and water and asked her the eternal question: 'Aisha, the Defeated, living in a grain room, who is cleverer, man or woman?'

'Woman, my Lord.'

He said to her: 'The *nzaha* was terrific. Even better than last time. I met a wonderful woman. I've never seen such beauty.'

'My Lord is worthy of it.'

He left her, quite pleased with himself. A few days later she knew she was pregnant again. When she was reaching the end of her term, she went to her father's home and she gave birth to a second boy whom she named Dour. A little later, the prince came to see her and as always asked the same question. 'Aisha, the Defeated, living in a grain room, who is cleverer, man or woman?'

'Woman, my Lord,' she answered.

'I am going on a *nzaha* to Lalla Hammamat Laqur,' he told her.

'Have fun,' she said.

She asked when he was leaving. He told her the next week. So Lalla Aisha prepared and set up a tent as before. His response was the same. As before, the prince sent a messenger to her. He returned to his master and announced that it was the same woman. The prince told his messenger to have her come to him this time. Lalla Aisha said, 'I will go to no one. If the prince wants to see me, he will come here.'

They spent a very pleasant week together. When he announced his plans to leave, Lalla Aisha wished him a good trip. He gave her his *dalil* before leaving.

Lalla Aisha returned home. She was pregnant a third time. She gave birth to a little girl and named her Lalla Hammamat Laqur.

Months passed. One day, the sultan decided his son should marry. The prince protested, 'I don't really feel like getting married, father.' But the sultan insisted. 'It's absolutely necessary that you marry. I've asked for your cousin's hand.' When the marriage date was set, the prince went to visit his wife.

'Aisha, the Defeated, who lives in a grain room, do you know that my father is marrying me off?'

'To whom?' she asked.

'My cousin!'

'Good luck, my Lord,' she answered.

She inquired about the date of the marriage and found out it was to be the very next day. She gathered her children and carefully fixed their hair and dressed them in their nicest clothes. She gave the ring to the first child, the dagger to the second and the *dalil* to the third. She ordered them to go to the palace where preparations for the wedding were going on, and to turn things upside down, to take the covers off the cushions and to do as much damage as possible. And if anyone tried to stop them they were to repeat the following words:

'This is our father's home and some sons of bitches are driving us out of it.'

And if someone demand that they leave? Lalla Aisha taught them a phrase by which they were to address each other:

'Come, Sour, come, Dour, come, Lalla Hammamat Laqur. Let's go to our mother, Aisha the Defeated, who lives in a grain room.'

When all was ready, Lalla Aisha asked her father to take her children to the palace and leave them at the front entrance. And so it was. When the three children entered the palace, people remarked on their elegance and finery. 'Are they children of viziers? Children of a friend of the king?' The children set about their task according to their mother's instructions. They attacked and tore up the cushions in the salon prepared for the prince's fiancée. The palace servants tried to stop the children, but in vain. They didn't dare slap the children but tried to persuade them to stop. All they would say to those who tried to reason with them was:

'This is our father's home, and some sons of bitches are driving us out of it.'

Tired of the battle, the palace servants called the prince. He heard the children say to each other:

'Come, Sour, come, Dour, come, Lalla Hammamat Laqur. Let's go to our mother, Aisha the Defeated, who lives in the grain room.'

Intrigued, he asked who they were and they said:

'We are the children of Aisha the Defeated who lives in the grain room.'

More and more intrigued, he asked their names:

'Sour,' responded the first.

'Dour,' said the second, 'and this is my sister Lalla Hammamat Laqur.'

The prince was dumbfounded. He recognised his ring on the first, his dagger on the second, and his *dalil* on the little girl. Then he understood and ran to the grain room. He leant toward Lalla Aisha:

'Aisha the Defeated, who lives in a grain room, who is cleverer, man or woman?'

'Woman, my Lord,' she replied.

'Then give me your hand and come with me.'

She gave her hand to the prince. He freed her from her prison. Lalla Aisha took a long bath, scrubbed herself and put on her finest clothes. It was only minutes before the prince's cousin was to take the place prepared for her! It was then that Lalla Aisha appeared. The prince pushed his cousin aside to make room for Lalla Aisha. And on that day there was an extraordinary feast that woke the dead and they said: 'Get up to celebrate the feast of Lalla Aisha the Defeated, daughter of the carpenter, who had been held prisoner in the cellar.'

Khalinahum kaiaklu ihdid
w-hna jina naklu trid.
They were left there to eat iron
And we came here to eat pancakes.

PART FIVE

TWENTIETH-CENTURY VICISSITUDES

The twentieth century brought major changes to the Middle East which impinged on women no less than men. One of these was the increasing contact of Middle Easterners with the West, a cultural interchange (often overshadowed by political and economic power relations) in which the status of women has been a central issue. From the onset, Middle Easterners have been less than enthusiatic about women's role in western society, and Europeans have brought their own gender biases to the Middle East.

Another change has been the expanding roles of government and greater involvement in the public sphere and in individual's private lives. Areas such as education, which had been regarded to a great extent as a private endeavor, increasingly became the responsibility of the state. In the last two decades, there has been a growth of public, non-governmental activity. Both neo-Islamic movements and feminist organizations have entered this space.

Innovations in transportation and communications produced quantitative changes with qualitative implications. Gender differences in social mobilization have opened new vistas for women but have not always improved their situation.

Middle Eastern Muslim women's voices have been heard for the first time without the mediation of male compilers as in the past. Women have expressed themselves in public lectures, autobiographies, political platforms, essays and poetry, to name but a few.

17

HISTORICAL STATISTICS ON EDUCATION

[Justin McCarthy, *The Arab World, Turkey and the Balkans (1878-1914): A Handbook of Historical Statistics*. (Boston: G. K. Hall, 1982.), pp. 116-7,123-5, 134.]

There is a tendency to assume that the gathering of statistical information is a phenomenon of modern society. In fact, the Ottoman Empire (which ruled most of the Middle East and parts of Europe from the sixteenth century to World War I) was a vast bureaucratic state. In their heyday, the Ottomans undertook regular, reliable surveys of population, lands, endowments and other resources deemed important for the management of their empire. Loss of control by the Ottoman centre over the periphery during the seventeenth and eighteenth centuries was reflected in a decrease in the frequency and devaluation in the quality of these surveys. One aspect of the Ottomans' nineteenth-century attempts to strengthen the empire and regain control over the provinces was the production of a wide variety of government statistical yearbooks. Why were some of these reports styled *Istatistik* in Ottoman Turkish (see: source, Table V.l) rather than a traditional, indigenous title?

Justin McCarthy, the author of a number of important demographic studies of various regions of the Middle East in the late nineteenth and early twentieth centuries, based on Ottoman figures, has transcribed statistics on a number of subjects for the benefit of those who do not know Ottoman Turkish and do not have access to Ottoman government yearbooks. This important resource book includes data on: climate; population; medical, educational and judicial institutions; state budgets; manufacturing; transportation; foreign trade; minerals; agricultural and animal husbandry.

The tables below, taken from the chapter on education, provide valuable indicators of the scope of women's education in the Ottoman provinces of the Fertile Crescent and Turkey at the turn of the century and up to the First World War.

In order to evaluate the participation of women in the Ottoman educational system in the waning years of the empire, it is necessary to briefly explicate the contribution of the Ottomans to the development of traditional education and the changes they introduced in the nineteenth century. Like Muslim rulers before them, the Ottomans patronized traditional religious higher education by endowing and maintaining *madrasa* colleges to do good works, to immortalize their names, and no less important, to provide properly-educated manpower for the civil service. For this purpose, they brought Islamic higher education to a greater degree of bureaucratization and hierarchization than any other traditional Islamic state. Just as women did not serve as state-appointed jurisconsults, judges, college professors or mosque functionaries, they did not attend Ottoman state-regulated *madrasa* colleges. Moreover, learned women are noticeably absent from the biographical dictionaries of the Ottoman period. The Ottomans also developed the training of the military-bureaucratic elite into a hierarchical system of state education. The acme of this system was the palace school which provided its students with an excellent professional education as well as the religious knowledge and cultural polish deemed necessary for an Ottoman gentleman. Since women were neither soldiers nor ministers, they were not recruited to or trained in this system. There is some indication, however, that women who served as functionaries in the sultans' harems may have been trained in a manner somewhat similar to that of their male counterparts in the palaces.

By the nineteenth century, the classical Ottoman educational system no longer fulfilled its original functions properly not to mention the challenges posed by the growing cultural, political and military impingement of the European powers. The first attempts to rectify this situation was the establishment of a series of higher professional training schools such as a military academy, a civil service school, a law school, etc. In order to prepare students for these new state colleges, a system of public secondary, preparatory and elementary schools was gradually built up under the auspices of a newly-founded Ministry of Education. The establishment of teachers training schools was a natural outcome of these developments. Finally, in the Galatasaray palace - the site of one of the sixteenth century palace schools - a European-style, lycée college where French was taught, was established. At the same time, schools of the indigenous non-Muslim population as well as foreign missionary schools of every denomination and order increased in number and attracted some Muslim students as well. The broad outlines of these educational developments were paralleled in Egypt and Iran at roughly the same time.

From the biographies of women who grew up at this time, we know that women (particularly of the upper classes) continued to be educated in their homes by private teachers. Towards the end of the nineteenth century, it became fashionable to employ European nannies to teach the girls French, English or German in addition to their classical Islamic education. Of course, no statistics are available on the scope of this and other forms of informal education of women, and the level and breadth of education of girls must have differed widely from family to family.

Statistical tables embody as much information as a discerning eye can reveal. The following questions relating to the five tables below will guide the reader to a few of the many fields of inquiry that the figures address.

Table V.1

1. What kind of higher Ottoman professional schools did women attend in 1895/96? How can this be explained?
2. What proportion of the pupils in state high schools, secondary schools and elementary schools were girls? How can these figures be explained?
3. How many non-Muslim women and non-Muslim men attended state schools? How many Muslim women and Muslim men attended non-Muslim schools? How do you interpret these figures?
4. What proportion of the students in foreign schools were women? What proportion of the women in these schools were Muslim and non-Muslim?

Table V.2

In what geographical region are the greatest number of elementary schools located? What modern states are located in that region? What proportion of elementary school pupils were girls in Siirye province? Beirut province? Kuds-i Şerif (Jerusalem)? Bagdad? Basra?

Table V.8

1. What proportion of the Ottoman state schools were 'mixed,' rather than male or female? To what extent did boys and girls or men and women actually intermingle in these schools? What type of state schools were 'mixed'?
2. Were more non-Muslim or foreign schools 'mixed' than Ottoman schools? How can these findings be explained?
3. What was the proportion of female educational personnel in the Ottoman Empire in 1905-6? Was the proportion of female personnel greater in non-Muslim or foreign schools? What is the implication of these findings?

Table V.9

1. What was the proportion of private schools in Sürye province? Beyrut? Kuds (Jerusalem)? Bagdad? Basra? Medina? Hicaz (Hejaz)?
2. To what extent is the number of female teachers in a province a good indicator of the number of female pupils in that province? Compare the proportion of female teachers in the following provinces: Surye, Beyrut, Kuds, Bagdad, Basra, Medina, Hicaz.
3. Compare the proportion of female teachers in state and private schools.

Table V. 15

1. According to Ottoman official statistics, how many women were studying abroad in 1913-14? What proportion were they of all registered students abroad? Do you think these figures represent all Ottoman subjects studying abroad?
2. What subjects did the women study? Were they similar or different from those that the men studied?
3. In what countries did the women study? Was there a gender difference in the country of study? Why do you think women chose to study in these particular countries? How did study abroad influence these women?

Further information on education in the Ottoman Empire, nineteenth-century Egypt and Iran, and the twentieth-century successor states may be found in J. S. Szyliowicz *Education and Modernization in the Middle East* (Ithaca: Cornell University Press, 1973).

Table VI Students in the Ottoman Schools, 1313 (1895-96)

Type of Schools	Number of Schools	Total Students	Students			
			Muslim		Non-Muslim	
			Male	Female	Male	Female
Civil Service School	1	446	415	-	31	-
Law School	1	372	334	-	38	-
Medical School	1	453	127	-	326	-
Teacher Training (Male)	1	125	125	-	-	-
Fine Arts School	1	143	57	-	86	-
Commerce School	1	118	114	-	4	-
Galatasaray & similar lycées	1	699	382	-	317	-
Teacher Training (Female)	1	350	-	350	-	-
Orphans' School	1	421	421	-	9	-
Veterinary School	1	60	51	-	14	-
Agricultural School	1	73	59	-	32	-
Industrial School	1	252	220	-	527	-
Preparatory (High) School	55	5,419	4,892	-		-
Secondary School	412	31,469	27,207	4,262	-	-
Elementary Teachers Training	14	277	277	-	-	-
School for Dumb and Blind	1	16	16	-	-	-
Elementary Schools	28,594	848,943	600,206	248,737	-	-
Istanbul Private Schools	20	5,898	5,818	-	80	-
Non-Muslim Schools	6,739	404,168	-	-	299,817	104,351
Foreign Schools	383	31,541	-	-	17,002	14,539
Total	**36,230**	**1,331,243**	**640,721**	**253,349**	**318,283**	**118,890**

(Source: 1313 *Istatistik*, p. 54)

Table V.2 Number of Elementary Schools and Elementary School Pupils in Provinces of the Ottoman Empire, 1313 (1895-96)

	No. of Schools	Number of Students		
		Total	Muslim Males	Muslim Females
Istanbul & Surroundings	263	19,792[a]	13,806	5,906
Edirne	1,925	64,205	40,652	23,653
Salonik	1,058	36,111	23,034	13,077
Yanya	127	6,399	5,792	607
Aydin	2,571	90,618	64,749	25,869
Hüdavendigar	3,417	112,235	72,441	39,794
Kastamonu	3,374	89,542	57,690	31,852
Trabzon	2,619	80,272	57,117	23,155
Ankara	2,092	17,725	10,410	7,315
Sürye	291	8,164	6,637	1,527
Beyrut	386	15,891	13,291	2,600
Adana	597	12,911	10,661	2,250
Konya	1,996	89,314	59,146	30,168
Sivas	1,637	49,955	35,437	14,518
Diyarbakir	196	3,966	3,966	–
Haleb	633	12,981	11,192	1,789
Cezair	70	3,278	2,059	1,219
Manastir	451	19,809	13,960	5,849
Erzurum	850	16,320	16,320	–
Çatalca	49	1,984	1,133	851
Kosova	445	15,687	14,023	1,664
Izmir	670	15,704	9,529	6,175
Biga	444	13,697	8,417	5,280
Mamuretülaziz	401	12,632	12,632	–
Kuds-i Şerif	248	11,586	10,828	758
Bagdad	49	1,822	1,726	96
Mosul	392	3,130	2,737	393
Işkodra	101	3,319	2,419	900
Van	125	1,954	1,803	151
Basra	116	2,124	2,124	–
Zor	4	290	234	56
Bitlis	263	5,838	4,573	1,265
Trablusgarb	401	10,229	10,229	–
Yemen	279	3,784	3,784	–
Bengazi	74	1,553	1,553	–
Total	**28,614**	**854,921**	**606,104**	248,737

(Source: *1313 istatistik,* p. 63)

[a]Includes 80 male non-Muslims in Istanbul (elementary) schools.

Table V. 8 Schools, Students and Educational Personnel in the Ottoman Empire in the 1323-24 School Year (1905-6) Provinces Outside of Istanbul, Istanbul, and Totals

	Schools				Students			Personnel		
	m.	f.	mixed	total	m.	f.	total	m.	f.	total
Official										
Preparatory Schools	70	-	-	70	9,553	-	9,553	970	-	970
Secondary Schools (M)	129	-	-	129	5,399	-	5,399	350	-	350
Secondary Schools (F)	-	31	-	31	-	2,140	2,140	-	86	86
Elementary Schools	2,554	203	2,388	5,145	162,859	43,661	206,520	6,104	342	6,446
Elem. Teacher Training	23	-	-	23	541	-	541	60	-	60
Special Muslim Schools	725	86	1,305	2,106	59,276	28,102	87,378	3,111	124	3,235
Total	**3,501**	**310**	**3,693**	**7,504**	**237,628**	**73,903**	**311,531**	**10,595**	**552**	**11,147**
Non-Muslim										
Preparatory Schools	45	12	8	65	8,778	3,206	11,984	609	63	672
Secondary Schools	233	68	90	391	33,463	15,296	48,759	1,183	433	1,616
Elementary Schools	1,105	269	1,125	2,499	71,912	30,386	102,298	3,383	1,027	4,400
Teacher Training Schools	2	-	-	2	158	-	158	20	3	23
Seminaries	1	-	-	1	40	-	40	-	-	-
Total	**1,386**	**349**	**1,223**	**2,958**	**114,351**	**48,888**	**163,239**	**5,185**	**1,526**	**6,711**

Table V. 8 continued

	Schools				Students			Personnel		
	m.	f.	mixed	total	m.	f.	total	m.	f.	total
Foreign										
Colleges	1	-	-	1	11	-	11	4	-	4
Preparatory Schools	35	22	4	61	6,550	5,705	12,255	488	270	758
Secondary Schools	28	19	12	59	2,955	3,060	6,015	210	111	321
Elementary Schools	61	44	66	171	7,538	8,296	15,834	325	218	543
Teacher Training	3	2	-	5	139	144	283	32	8	40
Total	127	87	82	297	17,193	17,205	34,398	1,059	607	1,666
Total in Provinces	5,015	746	4,998	10,759	369,172	139,996	509,168	16,839	2,685	19,524
Total in Istanbul	94	56	344	494	40,782	23,470	64,252	3,036	663	3,699
Empire Total	5,109	802	5,342	11,253	409,904	163,466	573,420	19,875	3,348	23,223

Table V.9 Elementary Schools: Number of State and Private Schools by Province, 1329-30 (1913-14) and Number of Teachers in State and Private Schools, by Province*

| | Number of Schools | | | Number of Teachers | | | | | | |
| | State | Private | Total | State | | Private | | Total | | |
				M	F	M	F	M	F	
Istanbul	116	158	274	411	198	569	349	980	547	
Edirne	204	329	533	286	56	377	117	663	173	
Adana	159	50	209	247	53	144	60	391	113	
Ankara	291	50	341	366	43	77	53	443	96	
Aydin	439	241	680	773	204	447	327	1,220	531	
Bagdad	63	10	73	137	19	98	28	235	46	
Beyrut	136	421	557	253	58	421	288	674	346	
Haleb	213	147	360	358	69	249	212	607	281	
Hüvendigar	212	1,098	1,310	334	56	1,058	124	1,392	180	
Diyarbakir	60	10	60	75	11	10	-	85	11	
Sürye	129	32	129	206	45	84	-	290	45	
Sivas	167	278	425	269	50	255	43	529	93	
Trabzon	229	85	314	284	26	102	4	386	30	
Kastamonmu	261	1,114	261	364	33	-	-	364	33	
Konya	317	148	465	436	37	163	78	599	115	
Mamuretülaziz	185	191	376	264	27	257	126	521	153	
Mosul	56	84	140	91	8	122	21	213	29	
Urfa	23	32	55	41	6	35	25	76	31	
Izmid	45	6	51	57	15	8	3	65	18	
Bolu	117	9	126	153	22	4	5	157	27	
Teke	89	31	120	111	5	33	8	144	13	

Table V.9 Continued

	Number of Schools			Number of Teachers						
	State	Private	Total	State		Private		Total	
				M	F	M	F	M	F
Canik	71	147	218	122	27	172	23	294	50
Çatalca	46	35	81	51	9	35	22	86	31
Zor	39	-	39	49	2	-	-	49	2
Kuds	30	290	320	75	18	398	70	473	88
Karahisar-i Sahib	43	6	49	74	10	13	1	87	11
Karasi	125	86	211	242	29	116	35	358	64
Kale-i Sultaniye	40	132	172	62	17	138	13	200	30
Kayseri	46	40	86	72	4	80	29	152	33
Medina	11	-	11	21	3	-	-	21	3
Menteşe	42	8	50	64	19	16	6	80	25
Erzurum	198	-	198	268	29	-	-	268	29
Bitlis	83	80	163	117	14	73	16	190	30
Basra	28	-	28	38	4	-	-	38	4
Hicaz	61	-	61	79	1	-	-	79	1
Van	51	47	98	63	4	93	28	156	32
Yemen	96	-	96	124	1	-	-	124	1
Asir	1	-	1	1	-	-	-	1	-
Total	**4,522**	**5,395**	**9,917**	**7,038**	**1,232**	**5,647**	**2,114**	**12,685**	**3,346**

*Some forms of these statistics may differ from those given here. They are taken from a hand-corrected copy of the *1329-30 Maarif* which contains a number of corrections in the 'Private School' categories. The original, for example, listed 994 private schools in Kayseri, rather than the 40 given here. (Source: *1329-30 Maarif*, Table 7)

Table V.15 Ottoman Students in Europe, by Fields of Study, and Sex, 1329-30 (1913-14)

	France		Germany		Switz.		Austria		Belgium		England		America		Italy		Russia		Total	
	m.	f.	m.	f.	m.	f.	m.	f.	m.	f.	m.	f.	m.	f.	m.	f.	m.	f.	m.	f.
Natural Sciences*	15	–	5	–	4	–	–	–	–	–	–	–	–	–	–	–	–	–	24	–
Jurisprudence	12	–	–	–	3	–	–	–	–	–	1	–	–	–	–	–	–	–	16	–
Fine Arts	11	–	2	–	–	1	4	–	–	–	–	–	–	–	3	–	–	–	20	1
Mathemathics	10	1	11	–	6	–	–	–	1	–	1	–	–	–	–	–	–	–	29	1
Medicine	8	1	9	–	7	–	–	–	3	–	–	–	1	–	–	–	–	–	28	1
Agriculture	5	–	1	–	–	–	1	–	–	–	–	–	–	–	–	–	–	–	7	–
Electric	5	–	–	–	2	–	10	–	2	–	2	–	–	–	–	–	–	–	21	–
Literature	4	–	–	–	–	–	–	–	–	–	–	–	–	–	–	–	–	–	4	–
Printing	2	–	–	–	–	–	–	–	–	–	–	–	–	–	–	–	–	–	2	–
Mineralogy	2	–	–	–	–	–	–	–	–	–	–	–	–	–	–	–	–	–	2	–
Commerce	2	–	–	–	2	–	–	–	4	–	–	–	–	–	–	–	1	–	9	–
Dentistry	1	1	–	–	1	–	–	–	–	–	–	–	–	–	–	–	–	–	2	1
Deaf Education	1	–	–	–	–	–	–	–	–	–	–	–	–	–	–	–	–	–	1	–
Home Economics	1	3	–	–	1	2	–	–	–	–	–	1	–	–	–	–	–	–	2	5
Music	1	2	1	–	–	1	3	–	–	–	–	2	–	–	–	–	–	–	5	5
Engineering	–	–	2	–	1	–	–	–	5	–	–	–	2	–	–	–	–	–	10	–
Economics	–	–	1	–	–	–	–	–	–	–	–	–	2	–	–	–	–	–	3	–
Industrial Arts	–	–	–	–	–	–	–	–	–	–	1	–	–	–	–	–	–	–	1	–
Total	**81**	**8**	**32**	**–**	**27**	**4**	**18**	**–**	**15**	**–**	**5**	**2**	**5**	**–**	**3**	**–**	**1**	**–**	**187**	**14**

(Source: *1329-30 Maarif*, Table 77). *McCarthy provides no explanation for the double entries here and below.

194

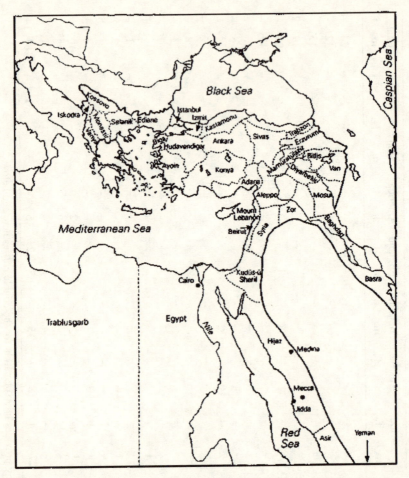

The Provinces of the Ottoman Empire in the late Nineteenth Century

Source: Selim Deringil, *The Well-Protected Domains: Ideology and the Legitimation of Power in the Ottoman Empire, 1876-1909* (London: I.B.Tauris, 1998).

The transliteration of Ottoman place names on this map sometimes differs from that used in McCarthy's tables. Readers who wish to compare the statistics in tables V.2 and V.9 should note that the Ottoman Empire lost its provinces in the Balkans (Iskadora, Kosova, Salonik, Manastir and Yanya) following the Balkan Wars of 1912-13. In addition, by 1913-14, when the statistics shown in Table V.9 were gathered, the Ottoman government had created new administrative divisions in Anatolia. Those relevant to a reading of Table V.9 are as follows: Bolu (formerly part of Kastamonu), Canik (formerly part of Trabzon), Karasý (formerly part of Hüvendigar) Kayseri (formerly part of Ankara), Menteþe (formerly part of Aydin), Urfa (formerly part of Haleb/Aleppo).

OUT OF THE HAREM: WOMEN'S

AUTOBIOGRAPHIES

[H. Edib, *The Memoirs of Halidé Edib* (London: John Murray, 1926), pp. 11-14, 85-8, 142-8. Halidé Edib, *The Turkish Ordeal: Further Memoirs* (London: John Murray, 1928), pp. 25-34.]

Halidé Edib was representative of a whole generation of women whose lives spanned the old world of palaces harems and slaves and the new world of journalism, public speaking and nationalist politics. She was a unique woman because she came from a privileged background and achieved a position of national leadership. Halidé was born in 1884 in Istanbul to a highly-placed Ottoman family. Her father Edib Bey was secretary to Sultan Abdul Hamid II, the last of the autocratic Ottoman sovereigns. She hardly saw her sickly mother who died when she was very young; the mother is referred to in the memoirs as 'the pale woman,' with long, coiled plaits of hair, 'dressed in white.' It is against this background that the first excerpt below should be read. It reveals a great deal about Halidé's childhood experiences and personality.

Halidé's grandfather, although illiterate and from a rural Anatolian family, held a high position in the retinue of one of the royal princes. Her grandmother was from an old, wealthy Istanbul family who were keepers of one of the main religious shrines in the city. In the second selection below, the beginning of Halidé's education is described. Fikriyar is a slave-girl of the household, and Mahmoure is Halidé's older sister. What do we learn about the education of women in Istanbul of the nineteenth century from these passages? Can this description shed light on the biography of the learned Aisha daughter of Muhammad b. Abd al-Hadi (selection 12 above)? How does it relate to the Ottoman educational statistics of this period (selection 12)?

Halidé's father had remarried after her mother's death; a relatively short time later, he took a second wife. Halidé's description of the event (in the third selection below) seems fairly typical of the circumstances and implications of polygamy for all members of the extended family. Halidé's mildly critical, even apologetic attitude to polygamy (which is expressed even more directly in other parts of the book) is surprising because, at the time of these events, a number of male and female Turkish authors had already opened the debate on the status of women in the Ottoman family. Moreover, about the time these memoirs were published, the critics of polygamy had gained enough ground so that the practice was prohibited in Turkey. Halidé's personal and public life, however, is full of such seeming conflicts and ambiguities.

Shortly after these events, Halidé attended the American College for Girls in Istanbul, although she was underage. A year later, she was graduated from the school and married a noted scientist of her father's age who had been her tutor. Halidé's description of her married life is pretty grim, and in fact, after about one year, she suffered a nervous breakdown. The birth of two sons and other family matters are interspersed in her memoirs with her literary interests and the growing impingement on her life of political affairs.

The Young Turk revolution of 1908 opened an era of lively, public debate on political and social issues, and of organization of national, cultural and social clubs. Halidé, who knew most of the prominent politicians and intellectuals, began her literary career writing for the newspaper *Tanine,* one of the most outstanding of the many journals established at this time. She relates that a Turkish literary and cultural club gave her the title 'Mother of the Turk' at this time, preceding Mustafa Kemal's taking of the surname Ataturk or father of the Turks. Halidé was also elected the only woman on the general congress of the Turk Ojak, or Turkish Hearth organization. This cultural, national club began to establish a network of centres throughout the country where mixed audiences met for the first time and women appeared as speakers. At about the same time, Halidé also founded the Society for the Elevation of Women a primarily cultural and philanthropic association. One of about a dozen women's associations founded after the 1908 revolution, her group comprised a limited number and class of women. It had some feminist tendencies and links to the British suffragette movement.

Halidé Edib's first volume of memoirs describes events up to the middle of the first world war. Although the first part relates to her personal life, from about 1908 on, she focuses on the turbulent political and ideological developments in the last years of the Ottoman Empire to which she was a witness. A section on her husband's taking a second wife (which she condones) is sandwiched between more momentous public events.

Her second volume of memoirs, titled *The Turkish Ordeal,* is devoted to the Turkish struggle for independence from the end of World War I in 1918 to the establishment of the Turkish republic in 1922. It is even less of a personal diary than the first volume, and does not even mention the termination of her first marriage and second marriage to Dr. Adnan Adivar, a prominent nationalist. Halidé Edib Adivar was part of the inner circle which led the national struggle with Mustafa Kemal Ataturk, but she was critical of Ataturk on a number of issues. Ataturk was a strong leader who breached little opposition, and as his government became more dictatorial, she found it prudent to move to England. Her description of the war of independence, published in English in 1928, did not appear in Turkey until the 1960s because it differed from the official version.

As befits a novelist and playwright, Halidé Edib opens her description of the Turkish struggle with a number of dramatic incidents illustrating the Allies control of Istanbul at the end of the first world war and humiliation of the Turks. The nationalist movement had already started in eastern Anatolia, and Mustafa Kemal embarked on his famous journey to marshal these forces. On May 15,1919, news came that the Greeks had occupied Smyrna (Izmir) under the umbrella of Allied military power. Halidé Edib began her career as a nationalist leader with the public speech related so dramatically below. How does Halidé Edib describe her entry into politics? What gave her the confidence to deliver her speech? What is her attitude toward the sultan and the palace (compared to the earlier story from her childhood)? What is her attitude toward Islam (in light of her educational background)?

Halidé Edib's memoirs may be compared to the diary of her Egyptian contemporary Huda Shaarawi (who is dealt with in the introduction to chapter 19). This work has been unearthed and translated with an excellent introduction about Shaarawi's life work by Margot Badran under the title *Harem Years: The Memoirs of an Egyptian Feminist* (1987). The memoirs of a Persian princess, Taj al-Saltana (1884-1914) appeared in English translation in 1993. Autobiographies of some other Middle Eastern Muslim women such as Selma Ekrem, Fadwa Tuqan, Fatima Mernissi, Nawal El Saadawi, Jihan Sadat and Ashraf Pahlavi have also been published in English.

In the Ottoman, Turkish context, Halidé Edib may be compared to Khurrem Sultan, the influential wife of Suleiman I who established the endowment documented in chapter 14. She may also be compared to her male contemporary Mustafa Kemal Ataturk whose lengthy speech, the delivered in 1924 has been published in English. It is interesting to place the two leaders, their oratory styles and their view of the events they took part in apposition. The Turkish living memory of their struggle for independence features Halidé Edib's famous speech rendered in popular genres such as cartoon pamphlets and a television docudrama *Kurtulus*.

Some additional information may be found in 'The Novelist Halidé Edib Adivar and Turkish Feminism' by Emel Sonmez in *Die Welt des Islams* 14 (19XX). One of her novel's was translated into English with the title *The Daughter of Smyrna* and another - *The Clown and His Daughter* - originally appeared in England in 1935 (and was later published in Turkish).

'The Memoirs of Halidé Edib'

This is the Story of a Little Girl

It was now that the event which is somewhat like a symbol of her lifelong temperament occurred. On the long divan, covered with white cloth, sat the old lady housekeeper, a kind and hard-working creature, leaning over her darning continually; the young Circassian sat at the table, lost in his books, for he was getting ready for a school education. (Her father had a mania for taking poor young men under his protection and sending them to school.) She, the little girl, was left to herself. There was no one scolding her or filling her mouth with black pepper for telling about things she did not know. There was complete silence. The father was no longer shedding tears by the flicker of a single candle. Her loneliness seemed suddenly to have taken the form of a tangible hardness in her throat. The woman with the long coiling plaits and wonderful eyes was no more. What was this silence about? Why had she no one to cuddle close to and go to sleep with? There was no answer to her unspoken questioning. Still only that dead silence. The next moment she stood in the middle of the room and spoke her mind out:

'I want my father!'

'He is at the palace.'

'I want my father!'

'He will come back tomorrow.'

'I want my father!'

'He cannot come, dear. The gates of the palace are closed at night, and the whole place is kept by guards.'

'I want my father!'

Gradually the little voice rose and rose in hoarse and piercing howls of pain which she herself internally noted as strange. On and on it went, rising and howling till the Greek neighbours came in one by one to help the old lady housekeeper to calm and soothe her, their voices making a still greater noise than the little girl. The place was a Christian quarter - Armenians and Greeks were the only neighbours - and the Greeks of Constantinople talk louder than anybody else, especially if they are women. But there were twenty wild beasts ranging in the little girl's breast, making her howl and howl with pain till she caught sight of a pail of cold water brought by a Greek woman to stop her crying.

'She may catch cold.'

'But she will burst if she goes on like that.'

'O Panagia' (Holy Mother), 'pour it on her head.'

And pour it they did, which gave the old housekeeper the extra trouble of changing her clothes, but for the rest caused a sudden catch in her breath which stopped her for an instant only to begin louder and louder, wilder and wilder, the next moment.... It was the symbol of the force of her desires in later years, the same uncontrollable passion for things, which she rarely wanted, but which, once desired, must be obtained at all costs; the same passionate longing although no longer expressed by sobbing or howling.

Finally the old lady housekeeper and the Greek women beg the young Circassian to take the child to the palace.

It was almost midnight as the young man carried her in his arms through the guarded streets of Yildiz. He stopped at each tall soldier whose bayonet flashed under the street oil-lamps.

'Who goes there?'

And the young Circassian placed the little girl in the lamplight and showed her swollen face:

'It is Edib Bey's daughter. She would have died with crying if I hadn't promised to bring her to her father. Her mother died....'

And the soldier, who probably had seen the mother's coffin pass not long ago, let them go on.

The little girl began to watch calmly and with pleasure the dimly lighted white road, the long shadows of the guards, while she heard the distant bark of the street dogs. She was not going to be knocked down by loneliness and dead silence any longer.

Before the gigantic portals which led immediately to the quarters where her father worked she and the Circassian youth were stopped once more. No one was allowed to pass the palace gates after midnight... But sometimes a little girl and her heart's desire are stronger than the iron rules of a great despot. The guards are human and probably have little daughters of their own in their villages. There is a long wait. A man in black dress comes to the door. He looks at the little girl by the lamplight and lets her pass on. At last they reach the father's apartment. He looks at her with astonishment and perhaps with pain. He has just jumped out of bed because there is a rumour of some little girl at the palace door crying for her father ... On a bed opposite the father's lies a fat man with an enormous head who is blinking at the scene. (He is Hakki Bey, later on the famous grand vizier.) Every one no doubt expects her to jump into her father's arms, but her attention is caught by the quilt on her father's bed. It is bright yellow ... and the night is closed in her memory with that bright patch of the hated colour.

When the Story Becomes Mine

One night about this time I begged granny to allow me to learn to read. 'Thy father does not want thee to learn before thou art seven,' she said. 'It is stupid of him. *I* started at three, and in my days children of seven knew the Quran by heart.' In spite of this I kept bothering her and even speaking to father about it, so that he at last consented, although I was not fully six yet. Thereupon the house began to get ready to celebrate my *bashlanmak,* my entrance into learning.

Little children in Turkey started to school in those days with a pretty ceremony. A little girl was dressed in silk covered with jewels, and a gold-embroidered bag, with an alphabet inside, was hung round her neck with a gold-tasselled cord. She sat in an open carriage, with a damask silk cushion at her feet. All the little pupils of the school walked in procession after the, carriage, forming two long tails on either side. The older ones were the hymn-singers, usually singing the very popular hymn, 'The rivers of paradise, as they flow, murmur, 'Allah, Allah.' The angels in paradise, as they walk, sing, 'Allah, Allah.' ' At the end of each stanza hundreds of little throats shouted, *'Amin, amin!'*

They went through several streets in this way, drawing into the procession the children and waifs from the quarters they passed through until they reached the school. In the school the new pupil knelt on her damask cushion before a square table, facing the teacher. Kissing the hand of the instructor, she repeated the alphabet after her. Some sweet dish would then be served to the children, and each child received a bright new coin given by the parents of the pupil to be. After this sort of consecration, the little one went every day to school, fetched by the *kalfa,* an attendant who went from one house to another collecting the children from the different houses.

The ceremony was as important as a wedding, and fond parents spent large sums in the effort to have a grander ceremony than their neighbours. Each family who could afford a costly *bashlanmak* would arrange for a few poor children of the quarter to share the ceremony and would thenceforward pay their schooling, as well as that of their own child. The old systematic philanthropy of the Ottomans, although fast disappearing, was not entirely dead yet.

The sight of a children's procession with the grand carriage had always caused me certain excitement, mixed, however, with a longing to be the little girl in the carriage and a fear of being the centre of attraction in public.

Father had arranged that I was not to begin by going to school, but a hodja was to come and give me lessons at home. The *bashlanmak* too in my case was not to be the usual one. There was to be a big dinner at home for the men, and the ceremony was to take place at home after the night prayers.

Granny had her own way about my dress for once. She could not bear to have me begin my reading of the holy Quran in a blue serge dress. I remember well the champagne-coloured silk frock with lovely patterns on it, and the soft silk veil of the same colour, that she got for me instead.

A large number of guests arrived, both from our own neighbourhood and also from the palace.

Some one held a mirror in front of me after I was dressed, and I looked strange with the veil over my hair and bedecked with the really beautiful jewels of the palace lady. Fikriyar was moved to tears. 'Thou shalt wear a bride's dress and I will hold thy train one day,' she said. She was wishing me the one possible felicity for a Turkish woman.

Then hand in hand with Mahmouré Abla, who was unusually subdued, I walked to the large hall where every one had assembled for the ceremony. A young boy chanted the Quran while our hodja sat by the low table swaying himself to its rhythm. Mahmouré Abla had already been to school, and so she only knelt, while I had at the same time to kneel and to repeat the first letters of the alphabet, frightened to death at the sound of my own voice. As I rose I forgot to kiss the hand of the hodja, but some tender voice whispered behind me, 'Kiss the hodja's hand.' All ceremonies in Turkey, even marriages and Bairams, tend to take on a sad and solemn tone; always the women with wet eyes and the men in softened silent mood. What makes other people rejoice makes the Turk sad.

My lessons took place in the same room in the selamlik, before the same table and in the same kneeling attitude as at the *bashlanmak*. My teacher, who was a regular schoolmaster and busy with his own school in the daytime, could only come to our house in the evenings. Two candles therefore were placed on the table and burned under green shades, while I struggled with the Arabic writing of the holy book. Of course it was difficult to go on without understanding the meaning of the words one read, but the musical sound of it all was some compensation.

Our hodja and his wife were recent immigrants from Macedonia and had built a tiny house behind our own. She taught little girls at home, while his school was in one of the poor quarters of Beshiktash.

Our Various Homes in Scutari

One day soon after, Abla went to spend a week with some old lady friends in Beshiktash, and in her absence father married Teizé. I cannot say that the event either pleased or comforted me, although there was no longer the danger of her leaving me.

The event was received coldly by the household, and with the marriage ceremony there settled upon the hitherto serene atmosphere of the house an oppressive feeling, a feeling of uneasiness and wonder at the possibility of unpleasant consequences, which never left it again. Sympathy and pity, as well as conjectures as to how Abla would receive the news, filled all our minds, and I fancy a rather violent scene was expected.

If there is an ecstasy and excitement in times of success, there is a deeper feeling of being singled out for importance when a great and recognized misfortune overtakes one. When a woman suffers because of her husband's secret love-affairs, the pain may be keen, but its quality is different. When a second wife enters her home and usurps half her power, she is a public martyr and feels herself an object of curiosity and pity. However humiliating this may be, the position gives a woman in this case an unquestioned prominence and isolation. So must Abla have felt now. The entire household was excited at her return. As she walked upstairs and entered the sitting-room, she found only Teizé standing in the middle of it. But the rest must have been somewhere in the corridors, for every one witnessed the simple scene of their encounter. Teizé was the more miserable of the two. She was crying. Abla, who had somehow learned what awaited her homecoming while she was still away, walked up to her and kissed her, saying, 'Never mind; it was Kismet.' Then she walked away to her own room while her servant Jemilé wept aloud in the hall. Hava Hanum, whose heart was with Abla, probably because of her own past experience, scolded Jemilé: 'Is it thy husband or thy lady's who was married? What is it to thee?'

Although this dramatic introduction to polygamy may seem to promise the sugared life of harems pictured in the 'Haremlik'[1] of Mrs. Kenneth Brown, it was not so in the least. I have heard polygamy discussed as a future possibility in Europe in recent years by sincere and intellectual people of both sexes, 'As there is informal polygamy and man is polygamous by nature, why not have the sanction of the law?' they say.

Whatever theories people may hold as to what should or should not be the ideal tendencies as regards the family constitution, there remains one irrefutable fact about the human heart, to whichever sex it may belong. It is almost organic in us to suffer when we have to share the object of our love, whether that love be sexual or otherwise. I believe indeed that there are as many degrees and forms of jealousy as there are degrees and forms of human affection. But even supposing that time and education are able to tone down this very elemental feeling, the family problem will still not be solved; for the family is the primary unit of human society, and it is the integrity of this smallest division which is, as a matter of fact, in question. The nature and consequences of the suffering of a wife, who in the same house shares a husband lawfully with a second and equal partner, differs both in kind and in degree from that of the woman who shares him with a temporary mistress. In the former case, it must also be borne in mind, the suffering extends to two very often considerable groups of people - children, servants, and relations - two whole groups whose interests are from the very nature of the case more or less antagonistic, and who are living in a destructive atmosphere of mutual distrust and a struggle for supremacy.

On my own childhood, polygamy and its results produced a very ugly and distressing impression. The constant tension in our home made every simple family ceremony seem like a physical pain, and the consciousness of it hardly ever left me.

The rooms of the wives were opposite each other, and my father visited them by turns. When it was Teizé's turn every one in the house showed a tender sympathy to Abla, while when it was her turn no one heeded the obvious grief of Teizé. It was she indeed who could conceal her suffering least. She would leave the table with eyes full of tears, and one could be sure of finding her in her room either crying or fainting. Very soon I noticed that father left her alone with her grief.

And father too was suffering in more than one way. As a man of liberal and modern ideas, his marriage was very unfavourably regarded by his friends, especially by Hakky Bey, to whose opinion he attached the greatest importance.

He suffered again from the consciousness of having deceived Abla. He had married her when she was a mere girl, and it now looked as if he had taken advantage of her youth and inexperience. One saw as time went on how patiently and penitently he was trying to make up to her for what he had done.

Among the household too he felt that he had fallen in general esteem, and he cast about for some justification of his conduct which would reinstate him. 'It was for Halidé that I married her,' he used to say. 'If Teizé had married another man Halidé would have died.' And, 'It is for the child's sake I have married her father,' Teizé used to say. 'She would have died if I had married any one else.' Granny took the sensible view. 'They wanted to marry each other. What has a little girl to do with their marriage?'

The unhappiness even manifested itself in the relation between granny and

Hava Hanum. The latter criticized granny severely for not having put a stop to it before things had gone too far, and granny felt indignant to have the blame thrown upon her by a dependent for an affair she so intensely disliked.

Teizé, with her superior show of learning and her intellectual character, must have dominated father at first, but with closer contact, the pedantic turn of her mind, which gave her talk a constant didactic tone, must have wearied him. For in the intimate companionship of everyday life nothing bores one more than a pretentious style of talk involving constant intellectual effort. Poor Teizé's erudition and intelligence were her outstanding qualities, and she used and abused them to a maddening degree. When, after her dull and lonely life, she gave herself, heart and soul, to a man, the disillusionment of finding herself once more uncared for rendered her very bitter; and she either talked continually of her personal pain or else of some high topic, too difficult to be understood by the person she was talking to. Somehow her efforts to dethrone her rival from the heart of her husband lacked the instinctive capacity of the younger woman's, and it was only granny and poor me that sympathized and suffered with her in a grief which did not interest any one else.

The wives never quarrelled, and they were always externally polite, but one felt a deep and mutual hatred accumulating in their hearts, to which they gave vent only when each was alone with father. He wore the look of a man who was getting more than his just punishment now. Finally he took to having a separate room, where he usually sat alone. But he could not escape the gathering storm in his new life. Hava Hanum not inaptly likened his marriage to that of Nassireddin Hodja. She told it to us as if she was glad to see father unhappy. The hodja also wanted to taste the blessed state of polygamy, and took to himself a young second wife. Before many months were out his friends found the hodja completely bald, and asked him the reason. 'My old wife pulls out all my black hairs so that I may look as old as she; my young wife pulls out my white hair's so that I may look as young as she. Between them I am bald.'

The final storm, kept in check for some time by the good-mannered self-control of the ladies, broke out in the servants' quarter. Fikriyar and Jemilé were always running down each other's mistresses. Fikriyar called Abla common and ignorant, and Jemilé called Teizé old and ugly. 'Besides, she is a thief of other women's husbands,' she added. One day the quarrel grew so distracting that the ladies had to interfere, and for the first time they exchanged bitter words. That evening father went up to Abla's room first, and he did not come down to dinner. The next morning it was announced that father was going with Abla and her little girls to Beshiktash to the wisteria-covered house, and we, the rest of the composite family, were to take a house near the college,[2] and my education was to begin seriously.

Halidé Edib, The Turkish Ordeal

The Occupation of Smyrna

I had another telephone call the next morning. It was from the Ojak.

'Come at once,' said the voice. 'We are going to have a meeting to protest against the massacres in Smyrna; all the student associations have joined.'

I started for the Ojak immediately. The president of the Ojak was Ferid Bey. He had been exiled by the Union and Progress in the remote past, and that fact (which he naturally made the most of) was in his favour in the eyes of the present government. He pretended to be - perhaps he actually was - one of the extreme absolutists, and he insisted that Turkey should go back to absolutism. All this gave him a chance to get a place in the new cabinet. But the misfortune of Ferid Bey was that no one would take him very seriously, and every one considered his political opinions to be so many methods of obtaining a position.

Besides Ferid Bey there were some old members of the Ojak present, and they looked extremely despondent. I remember one of these saying that if he had thirty pounds in his pocket he would pass on to the Smyrna mountains. 'Going to the mountain' is a Turkish term which means the raising of the standards of revolt. I had a profound sympathy with any 'going to the mountain' feeling at the moment. I was feeling most bitter not only against the Allies, who had inaugurated their policy of spoliation in Turkey with such ugly bloodshed, but also against all the Turkish leaders, past and present, who had driven the poor Turks into the adventure of the great war, or who were now at each other's throats from more or less personal motives, complicating and endangering the people's chances of ever standing on their feet. Somehow neither the presence of the Allied armies nor the sorry state of Turkish politics prevented a great number of Turkish youths from going to the Smyrna mountains before many months had passed after the events I am recording.

The idea of the meeting was at first simply the making of some sort of protest against the Smyrna massacres; but from the way Ferid Bey was speaking, I gathered that there was also a desire to send a delegation to the sultan demanding a cabinet composed of more independent and Nationalist elements. The political part did not interest me, although the protest seemed entirely natural and necessary. I remember a young member of the Ojak humorously whispering, 'Is not Ferid Bey the ideal independent and Nationalist member for the coming cabinet?' All I could see after a great deal of speaking was that Ojak had chosen no speaker, and no one seemed to be willing to speak. Ferid Bey, who as the president ought to have spoken, said with a significant air that he had been called away by Ali Kemal Bey (who was the minister of interior as well as of public instruction - from whom Ferid Bey had strong hopes of office), and that he would come back before the end of the meeting and speak and propose the national cabinet business. Every one there somehow felt that he was taking this meeting, which was conceived by the student unions, as a move in his own personal political game and that he was trying to force Ali Kemal Bey's hand to give him a seat in the cabinet - failing which he would address the crowd and try to bring about the change of cabinet by popular pressure. All this seemed to me futile and only superficial. I was concerned with the pain and the disaster, which could no longer be ignored.

When the talk came round to the choosing of a speaker for Ojak, each one looked at the other nervously and seemed to be hesitating.

'I will speak,' I said at last, which pleased every one. Fatih, where the speaking was going to take place, was already crowded, and it was a serious and hazardous undertaking to address an excited monster meeting, with the Allies and the government looking on suspiciously and policing it with aeroplanes. Although I had been a public speaker since 1908, I had never addressed an outdoor meeting, having always considered such meetings undignified in the extreme, after witnessing the speakers in the streets shouting to the mob in 1908. But for the moment I was too much worked up to bother about ridicule, so we decided to start at half-past one for Fatih.

The people had gathered in big groups before the square in front of the municipality building. They were to be addressed from the balcony. As I looked up and realized how far my voice would have to carry, over a mass of people estimated at fifty thousand, I quailed; but at that instant, by a dramatic coincidence, something happened which engulfed me in a great storm of sorrow, to the exclusion of every other feeling. There, over the red flags and their white crescents, which were hanging down and waving in the gentle breeze, an enormous black drapery was being lowered. This sight, so sudden and so dramatic, roused such emotion - coming as it did on top of my small material fear for my voice - that I immediately had the poignant feeling of a woman who sees her most beloved covered with a shroud. As the soft black draperies swayed, patches or bits of brilliant red slits appeared and disappeared like streaks of flowing blood. Some one evidently with an unconscious feeling for the psychology of the masses had conceived the idea. But I was caught by its symbolic tragedy as much as any simple man in the street; the palpitation and its pain were so strong that I had actually to lean against the railings of the garden and wait before I could proceed. Then we walked up to the large halls of the building. I was to speak first and I had not prepared a word.

Leaning over the black draperies on the railings of the balcony I fell under the spell of a sea of faces.

The centre of the mass was formed by a compact group of soldiers and officers. In the front and around the soldiers was a thick circular human wall composed of women dressed in black, mostly young, and their faces, the drapery of their black veils shading them from the shimmering sun, were strangely quivering with emotion and ecstasy. The rest seemed all white turbans, red fezzes, and a few hats. But one had a very dim impression of the coloured tops - the necks seemed to be screwed backward, all the faces seemed to be screwed upward and kept in that position with absolute immobility. And there were eyes, thousands of them, glistening, shooting their message and their desire. This feeling of what they wanted me to say was so clear that I had the sense of repeating what they were thinking. I realized that their supreme demand was identical with mine. We all longed for hope, for absolute belief in our rights and in our own strength, and I gave them what they wanted: 'Brothers, sisters, countrymen, Moslems: When the night is darkest and seems eternal, the light of dawn is nearest.' I began thus, and my voice as I spoke struck against the broken column opposite, a memorial for the airmen killed in the war, and came back to me in a distant echo. It was a strange coincidence that this column should be the agent which kept my voice in the square and made it audible to each one in the crowd. Somehow, between my voice and the faces screwed round on the necks below, there was a wonderfully intimate communication. I hardly thought it was my voice speaking. I listened to what it said as a creature aloof, believing in and feeling comforted by its message as much as any one of the crowd down below. The voice was telling them to trust in their own rights and to lean on their own strength, the strength which is not of machines but of brave hearts and unconquerable ideals. We were hardly conscious of two aeroplanes which policed the crowd and flew so low sometimes that in ordinary circumstances we would have been terrified. As I finished the speech a tattered old man with a white beard began to tear his clothes and cry in very loud and distressed tones, 'Allah, Allah, help us!' It was then that one of the aeroplanes almost descended on the right end of the mass, which swayed and opened, and I remember for the time seeing bits of pavements on the right. But in the centre the women seemed to be nailed to the ground.

A military voice shouted up, half entreatingly and half in command:

'Speak again!'

I went on. I do not know what I said, but it was like holding the hand of a frightened child in the middle of a dreadful storm and telling it stories to keep its mind off the possible danger and disaster. In a moment the crowd was thickening.

It was Selaheddine Bey, the much beloved professor of international law in the university, who summed up the resolution of the meeting. The people unanimously demanded representatives who would go to his Majesty the sultan and ask him to take the side of the people.

Ferid Bey came back about this time. The Ministry of Public Works had been proposed to him by Ali Kemal Bey. Ferid Bey's attitude had been distinctly modified in consequence. He was no longer anxious to ask the sultan for a new cabinet.

The organizers went to the university at Bayazid to draft the resolution and to choose the representatives to be sent to the sultan.

Accompanied by two students, I was to go to the palace and present the prayer of the people to his Majesty.

It was quite dark when our carriage climbed the hill of Yildiz leading to the royal palace, and the lamps were already lighted: the hill of Yildiz, where I had so often wandered as a child. A man in black - one of the secretaries, I believe - led us to the great reception hall. He looked furtively and hesitatingly at my companions and myself. I found myself wondering if we were repugnant to them in the same way that the French crowd were to Louis XVI. The rumours of the meeting had preceded us, and naturally nothing is so likely to upset a royal palace, with strong ideas about hereditary and divine rights, as the assertion of the people's will in some outward demonstration.

Two aides-de-camp, one naval and the other a major in the army, received us very cordially; one could feel at once the suppressed sympathy and hope aroused in their hearts by the meeting, although they said no words to express it.

Yaver Pasha, the first chamberlain of his Majesty, came hurriedly forward, rubbing his hands apologetically. He seemed most uneasy, especially in front of the young students who seemed to enjoy their position as the people's envoys immensely. Yaver Pasha went to his Majesty's apartment several times: he was ill, and to his great regret he could not receive us, but he let us know that 'He would consider the pleasure of his children' and do whatever he could. Yaver Pasha added some very kind words himself and seemed to be happy addressing himself to my more moderate manner, for the students repeated several times, 'We are the envoys of the people and want to be admitted,' the mere idea of which evidently made poor Yaver Pasha shudder inwardly. He must have pondered on the changing times, when a young man would try to dictate to the All-Powerful, at prayer time in the evening. I gave a message from his Majesty's children to Yaver Pasha, and felt extremely glad when I left the palace. Outside I felt a sudden sadness: the hill of Yildiz seemed completely deserted, the lights gleamed on the royal road, so dusty and so different from the time of Abdul Hamid. In some curious way I had the feeling that the house of Osman had fallen.

On the following Friday the medical students in Haidar Pasha, together with the residents of Kadi-Keuy, organized another protest meeting at which they wanted me to speak. It was a stormy and rainy day, but that did not prevent a large crowd gathering on the quay of Haidar Pasha. I addressed them from the balcony of the big town hall. There was a sea of umbrellas in slow and perpetual movement under a drear, watery atmosphere. The faces looking up through the gray and drifting mist seemed sometimes very near and sometimes distant and blurred. A wild wind swayed the human sea, and the Marmora looked far away, strange, its brilliant blue toned to a dull and colourless expanse and its white foam undulating in large and rhythmic motion. The populace stood in the rain nearly three hours.

It was more or less Fatih over again. These months were months of almost continuous public speaking for me. But the meeting of the revolution was to be in Sultan Ahmed, the Friday after. And whenever people speak in Turkey about the meeting they mean the one at Sultan Ahmed on June 6,1919.

I entered the Hippodrome through the narrow street called 'Fuad Pasha Turbessy.' I cannot tell how many people accompanied me. I could hardly stand on my feet, so fast and loud was my heart thumping: it was only when I entered the huge square that this violent thumping was stopped by the mere surprise of the spectacle. The minarets of Sultan Ahmed mosque rose into the brilliant white flutes of magic design. From their tiny balconies high in the air the black draperies waved softly, flying like long, black detached ribbons in the sky. Down below, just in front of the mosque railings, rose the tribune, covered with an enormous black flag on which was inscribed in huge white letters, 'Wilson's Twelfth Point.'[3] Not only the square but the thoroughfares down to St. Sofia and Divan Yolou were blocked with a human mass such as Istanbul had never seen and will probably never see again. 'Two hundred thousand,' said the staff officers.

Besides this mass of humanity, hardly able to move, railings, domes, roofs, and the grand old elms in the yard of the mosque were filled with human bunches. How I reached the tribune I have no idea. Two soldiers with bayonets walked at my side, and four more marched in front, opening the way in as friendly a manner as they could -I have an unforgettable impression of their kindness and brotherly feeling on that day. I do not know whether these soldiers were asked to escort me or whether they had sprung from nowhere and wanted to help me in their own way.

As I set foot on the tribune I knew that one of the rare, one of the very rare, moments of my life had come to me. I was galvanized in every atom of my being by a force which at any other time would have killed me, but which at that crisis gave me the power to experience - to know - the quintessence of the suffering and desire of those two hundred thousand souls.

I believe that the Halidé of Sultan Ahmed is not the ordinary, everyday Halidé. The humblest sometimes can be the incarnation of some great ideal and of some great nation. That particular Halidé was very much alive, palpitating with the message of Turkish hearts, a message which prophesied the great tragedy of the coming years.

Flutelike voices from the minarets chanted, and hundreds of low bass voices, the voices of a myriad of ulemas and religious orders, took up the refrain from below – that refrain which is the hallelujah of the Moslem Turks: 'Allah Ekber, Allah Ekber, La Ilaheh Illa Allah, Vallahu Ekber, Allah Ekber, Ve Lillahil Harnd.' As Halidé was listening to this exquisite chant, she was repeating to herself something like this:

Islam, which means peace and the brotherhood of men, is eternal. Not the Islam entangled by superstition and narrowness, but the Islam which came as a great spiritual message. I must hold up its supreme meaning today. Turkey, my wronged and martyred nation, is also lasting: she does not only share the sins and the faults and virtues of other peoples, she also has her own spiritual and moral force which no material agency can destroy. I must also interpret what is best and most vital in her, that which will connect her with what is best in the universal brotherhood of men.

Halidé's voice could not have been heard beyond a certain area, I am sure. She must have seemed a mere speck to those human bunches above and to the human sea below. But there was a profound and almost an uncanny silence as she began to speak. Each one seemed to listen to his own internal voice. And Halidé was perhaps nothing more than a sensitive medium which was articulating the wordless message of the Day.

She began by pointing out that years of glory and beauty looked down from the minarets, and when she said this she was appealing to their sense of continuity in history. When she repeated the sentence - which became afterward something like a national slogan - 'The peoples are our friends, the governments our enemies,' she was expressing the proper sentiment of a Moslem nation, highly conscious of its democratic principles. When she was asking them to take the sacred oath, which they were to swear three times, that they would be true to the principles of justice and humanity, and that they would not bow down to brute force on any condition, she was formulating that moral characteristic without which no people can survive in the human family of the new world which is to come.

'We swear,' answered thousands of voices. And there was a mighty swaying and a continual human thunder which made the frail boards of the tribune sway under her feet. In the meantime, the Allied aeroplanes flew in and out of the minarets, policing the crowd. They buzzed like mighty bees and came down as low as they could in order, I believe, to intimidate the crowds. But no one was conscious of brute force: there was that in the heart of the crowd which comes to a people at moments, a thing which is far above machines and death; and had the aeroplanes fired, I still believe the crowd would have stood in absolute stillness, in absolute communion with the spirit of the new revolution which was coming to life. The last time she stood and gazed in front of her, she saw that there were a mighty crowd of mutilated soldiers forming the head of the mass. All of them were dressed with religious care. A younger group holding each other's hands formed a semi-circle around the throne to prevent the crowd surging forward. In this semicircle, nearest to the tribune, there was a slender man with a beautiful and refined face, dressed in a French uniform. It was General Foulon a Frenchman by birth but a Turk at heart, who was standing there with the rest of the Turkish youth, tears rolling down his cheeks.

The tension was broken at last by a young student of the university, who started to cry out in a hysterical voice, and who all of a sudden fell and fainted. 'My nation, my poor nation,' he sobbed. That woke Halidé from her trance, and becoming her ordinary self she hurried down from the tribune to help the sufferer.

And my story comes back to the first person again, for that unnatural detachment which had created a dual personality was no more. At the foot of the steps an apparition in green robes and a turban took hold of me. It was a simple Anatolian hodja, with a round beard and black eyes streaming with tears.

'Halidé Hanum, Halidé Hanum, my daughter?' he cried quietly, holding my hands. I made him sit on the steps of the tribune, and he leaned his old face on my hand and went on crying. As some one else was speaking at the time, I sat down also and patted his hand. I think I was also crying. Then I pushed him up the platform, very gently. 'Go and pray,' I said. And he did go up and pray, in Turkish, very simply and beautifully, I thought, and that ended the meeting.

Notes

1. The word haremlik does not exist in Turkish. It is an invented form, no doubt due to a mistaken idea that 'selamlik' (literally, the place for salutations or greeting, i. e., the

reception-room, and therefore, among Moslems, the men's apartments) could have a corresponding feminine form, which would be 'haremlik.' The word is, however, a verbal monstrosity. 'Harem' is an Arabic word with the original sense of a shrine, a secluded place (cf. Harem Sherif, the Holy of Holies in the Kaaba at Mecca). Hence it came to be identified with the seclusion of women, either by means of the veil or by confinement in separate apartments; and hence again it came to be used for those apartments themselves.

2. The American College for Girls as it was then called; an institution founded by American missionaries for educating girls in the Orient. It is now represented by the Constantinople College for Girls, but it is no longer connected with any missionary societies. It was at first housed in an old picturesque Armenian house in Scutari.

3. 'The Turkish portions of the present Ottoman Empire should be assured a secure sovereignty, but the other nationalities which are now under Turkish rule should be assured an undoubted security of life and an absolutely unmolested opportunity of autonomous development, and the Dardanelles should be permanently opened as a free passage to the ships and commerce of all nations under international guarantees.'

19

AN EARLY PUBLIC LECTURE ON WOMEN'S

LIBERATION

[Bahithat al-Badiya, 'A Lecture in the Club of the Umma Party, 1909,' *Opening the Gates: A Century of Arab Feminist Writing* ed. Margot Badran and Miriam Cooke. Bloomington: Indiana University Press, 1990, 228-38.]

Just as Westerners (like H. H. Jessup and Mark Twain) did not fail to cite the differing status of women in the Islamic East compared to the West, so Middle Easterners who travelled to the West or came into contact with Westerners noted this difference in their writings. Muslims who wrote about Western culture (in growing numbers from the early nineteenth century) did not necessarily regard the Western model of women's role in society as superior to their own values. Shaykh Rifa'a Rafi' al-Tahtawi (1801-73), who lived in Paris from 1826 to 1831 as religious officer for Egyptian military missions, wrote that in the West, 'men are slaves of their women'. Yet this same Shaykh Tahtawi wrote in support of girls' education in the 1870s while working in the Egyptian Ministry of Education, shortly after the first government school for girls was established in Cairo (1873). Ambivalent attitudes toward the role of women in Islamic Middle Eastern society, and toward the West - the political and cultural enemy of Islam, but also the arbiter of modernity and a model to be mimicked - continued to permeate the works of Middle Eastern intellectuals and policy-makers.

After education (and related to it), an important innovation of the nineteenth century in the Middle East which contributed to the proliferation of the discussion on woman's roles in society as well as other subjects was the establishment of newspapers and magazines. From the 1890s, womens' journals began to appear in Cairo and Istanbul, and in 1910, the first Persian magazine for women was published.

Calls for the liberation of Muslim women emerged from and were influenced by an ideological movement which Western scholars term Islamic reform but whose members defined as the *salafiyya,* those who aspire to return to the true, early, untainted Islam. The intellectual leader of this movement was the Egyptian Shaykh Muhammad Abduh (1849-1905) who tried to reinterpret the primary sources of Islam in order to address Egypt's social problems. In the area of women's rights, he is best known for his determination that the verse in the Quran (4 (The Women): 3) which appears to permit a man to marry up to four wives in fact indicates that monogamous marriages should be the norm. On the question of the hijab, however, he refused to take a stand.

There is some disagreement as to who was the first feminist in the Middle East, a woman or a man, a Turk or an Egyptian Arab. As early as the 1850s and 1860s, Young Ottoman intellectuals wrote plays and articles in Turkish criticizing the traditional family and calling for the education of women.

Aisha al-Taymuriyya, daughter of an Egyptian-Turkish upper class family, is considered the first to raise the idea of gender equality by some, but her appeal for women's education, published in 1889, is based on quite conservative premises. Fatima Aliye Hanim, daughter of a prominent Ottoman reformist legist, argued against polygamy, publishing a book on *Muslim Women (Nisvani Islam)* in 1891. The best-known Middle Eastern feminist is Qasim Amin who published two books on the subject in 1899 and 1901.

Qasim Amin was one of Shaykh Abduh's students (and a French-educated lawyer by profession) whose interest in the role of women in modern Egypt was sparked by a critique written by the French intellectual le Duc d'Harcourt. Amin's first response, published in French in 1894, was to defend the role of women in Egypt (including the custom of veiling) and to attack the free relations between the sexes prevalent in Europe. After further study of the matter, Amin came to the conclusion that some reforms were required in the status of women — in education, veiling, seclusion, relations between the sexes, marriage and divorce — within the framework of Islam in order to promote the progress of Egypt. His two later books were extremely influential and opened a fierce debate on the role of women in Muslim society which has not abated to this day.

Another innovation introduced in the Middle East in the early twentieth century was the first series of public lectures by women for women. Huda al-Sha'arawi, who would later found the first politically-oriented woman's organization in Egypt, wrote in her diary about the visit of the French feminist Marguerite Clement to Egypt. Clement told Sha'arawi about her travels and lectures, and asked if Egyptian women also gave lectures. Sha'arawi admitted that it was not customary but invited Clement to speak on the differences between Eastern and Western womens' lives. The event took place at the new

Egyptian university, on a Friday when there were no other classes, under the patronage of Her Royal Highness Ayn al-Hayyat, wife of the crown prince. After Clement's lecture series, a number of Egyptian women also gave talks, among them the poet and writer Malak Hifni Nasif (1886-1918) known as Bahithat al-Badiya.

Malak Hifni Nasif was the daughter of an Egyptian intellectual associated with Muhammad Abduh's circle who held important government posts and taught in institutions of higher education. She studied at the womens' teacher training school, and in 1900 was one of the first women to receive a government teaching license, after which she began a career teaching in government schools. She left teaching when she married the shaykh of a bedouin tribe and went to live with him in the Fayyum oasis. Upon arrival, she discovered that he already had a wife and a daughter whom he expected her to tutor. Her pseudonym, which means 'seeker in the desert' was taken from this experience. Among the subjects she wrote about in her articles are 'A View of Marriage - Woman's Complaints Against It,' 'The Use or Disuse of the Veil,' 'The Education of Girls at Home and in School,' polygamy, and marriage age.

The following lecture by Bahithat al-Badiya concludes with a platform of ten suggestions or demands which she later presented to Egyptian nationalist leaders and to the legislative assembly which functioned during the British conquest of Egypt. In the 1909 lecture (published a year later), Malak Hifni Nasif takes what would be considered a radical stand for her time on certain issues but seems fairly conservative on others. Why should women be educated? Under what circumstances may women work outside the home, and what kinds of work may they do? What arguments does Bahithat al-Badiya bring to support the notion of women's work? Who are her female role models? What changes in women's dress does Malak Hifni Nasif attest to in her time? What is her attitude to these changes? How does she justify her position? Under what circumstances may a couple meet before their marriage? What do we learn from Bahithat al-Badiya's extensive treatment of the negative consequences of marriages between Egyptian men and European women? What do we learn about the women of Istanbul at this time? How would you describe Malak Hifni Nasif's attitude towards Western culture?

For many years, Qasim Amin was depicted as the father of the woman's liberation movement in the Arab world and his opponents were regarded as relentless conservatives. Thomas Philipp has dealt with the thirty-year debate about women's liberation which took place in Egypt up to the 1919 national revolution in 'Feminism and Nationalist Politics in Egypt' (in Beck and Keddie, 1978). He emphasizes that the opposition to Amin's demands was not restricted to conservative religious circles but also characterized part of the nationalist leadership. Juan Ricardo Cole's 'Feminism, Class, and Islam in Turn of the Century Egypt,' *(International Journal of Middle East Studies,* 1981) views the issue from an interesting, new perspective. The English-reader may now read Qasim Amin's *The Liberation of Women (Tahrir al-Mar'a),* and *The New Woman (Al-Mar'a al-Jadida).*

More recent studies of the emergence and evolution of Egyptian feminism forefront women intellectuals and activists. Badran's *Feminists, Islam and Nation* (1994) deals with the feminist movement in depth from its origins to the mid-twentieth century. Baron's *The Women's Awakening in Egypt* (1994) takes the women's press as a point of departure to discuss broader issues of the period. On the Persian women's press, see: Eliz Sanasarian, *The Women's Rights Movement in Iran: Mutiny, Appeasement and Repression from 1900 to Khomeini* (New York: Praeger, 1981).

Huda Sha'arawi's fascinating diary of her early years, before she entered political life, has been unearthed and translated with an excellent introduction about Sha'arawi's life work by Margot Badran under the title *Harem Years: The Memoirs of an Egyptian Feminist* (1987). Readers may wish to compare this diary to the published memoirs of Halidé Edib Adivar.

Another article by Bahithat al-Badiya appears in *Opening the Gates: A Century of Arab Feminist* Wnrmgwhich includes a number of other works by Arab women of this period. A concise biography of Malak Hifni Nasif'Bahithat al-Badiya: Cairo Viewed From the Fayyum Oasis,' by Evelyn Aleene Early appeared in *The Journal of Near Eastern Studies* 40 (1981): 339-41.

A Woman's Lecture in the Umma Party Club (1909)

Ladies, I greet you as a sister who feels what you feel, suffers what you suffer and rejoices in what you rejoice. I applaud your kindness in accepting the invitation to this talk where I seek reform. I hope to succeed but if I fail remember I am one of you and that as human beings we both succeed and fail. Anyone who differs with me or wishes to make a comment is welcome to express her views at the end of my talk.

Our meeting today is not simply for getting acquainted or for displaying our finery but it is a serious meeting. I wish to seek agreement on an approach we can take and to examine our shortcomings in order to correct them. Complaints about both women and men are rife. Which side is right? Complaints and grumbling are not reform. I don't believe a sick person is cured by continual moaning. An Arab proverb says there is no smoke without fire. The English philosopher, Herbert Spencer, says that opinions that appear erroneous to us are not totally wrong but there must be an element of truth in them. There is some truth in our claims and in those of men. At the moment there is a semi-feud between us and men because of the low level of agreement between us. Men blame the discord on our poor upbringing and haphazard education while we claim it is due to men's arrogance and pride. This mutual blame which has deepened the antagonism between the sexes is something to be regretted and feared. God did not create man and woman to hate each other but to love each other and to live together so the world would be populated. If men live alone in one part of the world and women are isolated in another both will vanish in time.

Men say when we become educated we shall push them out of work and abandon the role for which God has created us. But, isn't it rather men who have pushed women out of work? Before, women used to spin and to weave cloth for clothes for themselves and their children, but men invented machines for spinning and weaving and put women out of work. In the past, women sewed clothes for themselves and their households but men invented the sewing machine. The iron for these machines is mined by men and the machines themselves are made by men. Then men took up the profession of tailoring and began to make clothes for our men and children. Before women winnowed the wheat and ground flour on grinding stones for the bread they used to make with their own hands, sifting flour and kneading dough. Then men established bakeries employing men. They gave us rest but at the same time pushed us out of work. We or our female servants, used to sweep our houses with straw brooms and then men invented machines to clean that could be operated by a young male servant. Poor women and servants used to fetch water for their homes or the homes of employers but men invented pipes and faucets to carry water into houses. Would reasonable women seeing water pumped into a neighbour's house be content to fetch water from the river which might be far away? Is it reasonable for any civilised woman seeing bread from the bakery, clean and soft, costing her nothing more than a little money, go and winnow wheat and knead dough? She might be weak and unable to trouble herself to prepare the wheat and dough or she might be poor and unable to hire servants or to work alone without help. I think if men were in our place they would have done what we did. No woman can do all this work now except women in the villages where civilisation has not arrived. Even those women go to a mill instead of crushing wheat on the grinding stones. Instead of collecting water from the river they have pumps in their houses.

By what I have just said, I do not mean to denigrate these useful inventions which do a lot of our work. Nor do I mean to imply that they do not satisfy our needs. But, I simply wanted to show that men are the ones who started to push us out of work and that if we were to edge them out today we would only be doing what they have already done to us.

The question of monopolising the workplace comes down to individual freedom. One man wishes to become a doctor, another a merchant. Is it right to tell a doctor he must quit his profession and become a merchant or vice versa? No. Each has the freedom to do as he wishes. Since male inventors and workers have taken away a lot of our work should we waste our time in idleness or seek other work to occupy us? Of course, we should do the latter. Work at home now does not occupy more than half the day. We must pursue an education in order to occupy the other half of the day but that is what men wish to prevent us from doing under the pretext of taking their jobs away. Obviously, I am not urging women to neglect their home and children to go out and become lawyers or judges or railway engineers. But if any of us wish to work in such professions our personal freedom should not be infringed. It might be argued that pregnancy causes women to leave work, but there are unmarried women, others who are barren or have lost their husbands or are widowed or divorced or those whose husbands need their help in supporting the family. It is not right that they should be forced into lowly jobs. These women might like to become teachers, doctors with the same academic qualifications. Is it just to prevent women from doing what they believe is good for themselves and their support? If pregnancy impedes work outside the house it also impedes work inside the house. Furthermore, how many able-bodied men have not become sick from time to time and have had to stop work?

Men say to us categorically, 'You women have been created for the house and we have been created to be breadwinners.' Is this a God-given dictate? How are we to know this since no holy book has spelled it out? Political economy calls for a division of labour but if women enter the learned professions it does not upset the system. The division of labour is merely a human creation. We still witness people like the Nubians whose men sew clothes for themselves and the household while the women work in the fields. Some women even climb palm trees to harvest the dates. Women in villages in both Upper and Lower Egypt help their men till the land and plant crops. Some women do the fertilising, haul crops, lead animals, draw water for irrigation, and other chores. You may have observed that women in the villages work as hard as the strongest men and we see that their children are strong and healthy.

Specialised work for each sex is a matter of convention. It is not mandatory. We women are now unable to do hard work because we have not been accustomed to it. If the city woman had not been prevented from doing hard work she would have been as strong as the man. Isn't the country woman like her city sister? Why then is the former in better health and stronger than the latter?

Do you have any doubt that a woman from Minufiya (a town in the Delta) would be able to beat the strongest man from al-Ghuriya (a section of Cairo) in a wrestling match? If men say to us that we have been created weak we say to them, 'No it is you who made us weak through the path you made us follow.' After long centuries of enslavement by men, our minds rusted and our bodies weakened. Is it right that they accuse us of being created weaker than them in mind and body? Women may not have to their credit great inventions but women have excelled in learning and the arts and politics. Some have exceeded men in courage and valour, such as Hawla bint al-Azwar al-Kindi who impressed Umar ibn al-Khattab with her bravery and skill in fighting when she went to Syria to free her brother held captive by the Byzantines. Joan of Arc who led the French army after its defeat by the English encouraged the French to continue fighting and valiantly waged war against those who fought her nation. I am not giving examples of women who became queens and were adept in politics such as Catherine, Queen of Russia; Isabel, Queen of Spain; Elizabeth, Queen of England; Cleopatra; Shajarat al-Durr, the mother of Turan Shah, who governed Egypt. Our opponents may say that their rule was carried out by their ministers who are men but while that might be true under constitutional rule it is not true under monarchies.

When someone says to us that's enough education it discourages us and pushes us backwards. We are still new at educating our daughters. While there is no fear now of our competing with men because we are still in the first stage of education and our oriental habits still do not allow us to pursue much study, men can rest assured in their jobs. As long as they see seats in the schools of law, engineering, medicine, and at university unoccupied by us, men can relax because what they fear is distant. If one of us shows eagerness to complete her education in one of these schools I am sure she will not be given a job. She is doing that to satisfy her desire for learning or for recognition. As long as we do not work in law or become employed by the government would our only distraction from raising children be reading a book or writing a letter? I think that is impossible. No matter how much a mother has been educated or in whatever profession she works this would not cause her to forget her children nor to lose her maternal instinct. On the contrary, the more enlightened she becomes the more aware she is of her responsibilities. Haven't you seen ignorant women and peasant women ignore their crying child for hours? Were these women also occupied in preparing legal cases or in reading and writing.

Nothing irritates me more than when men claim they do not wish us to work because they wish to spare us the burden. We do not want condescension, we want respect. They should replace the first with the second.

Men blame any shortcomings we may have on our education, but in fact our upbringing is to blame. Learning and upbringing are two separate things - only in religion are the two connected. This is demonstrated by the fact that many men and women who are well educated are lacking in morals. Some people think that good upbringing means kissing the hands of women and standing with arms properly crossed. Good upbringing means helping people respect themselves and others. Education has not spoiled the morals of our girls, but poor upbringing, which is the duty of the home not the school, has done this. We have to redouble our efforts to reform ourselves and the young. This cannot happen in a minute as some might think. It is unfair to put the blame on the schools. The problem lies with the family. We must improve this situation.

One of our shortcomings is our reluctance to take advice from each other. When someone says something, jealousy and scorn usually come into play. We also are too quick to ridicule and criticise each other over nothing, and we are vain and arrogant. Men criticise the way we dress in the street. They have a point because we have exceeded the bounds of custom and propriety. We claim we are veiling but we are neither properly covered nor unveiled. I do not advocate a return to the veils of our grandmothers because it can rightly be called being buried alive, not *hijab* not correct covering. The woman used to spend her whole life within the walls of her house not going out into the street except when she was carried to her grave. I do not, on the other hand, advocate unveiling, like Europeans, and mixing with men, because they are harmful to us.

Nowadays the lower half of our attire is a skirt that does not conform to our standards of modesty *(hijab)* while the upper half like age, the more it advances the more it is shortened. Our former garment was one piece. When the woman wrapped herself in it her figure was totally hidden. The wrap shrunk little by little but it was still wide enough to conceal the whole body. Then we artfully began to shrink the waist and lower the neck and finally two sleeves were added and the garment clung to the back and was worn only with a corset. We tied back our headgear so that more than half the head including the ears were visible and the flowers and ribbons ornamenting the hair could be seen. Finally, the face veil became more transparent than an infant's heart. The purpose of the *izar* is to cover the body as well as our dress and jewellery underneath, which God - has commanded us not to display. Does our present *izar,* which has virtually become 'a dress' showing the bosom, waist, and derriere, conform with this precept? Moreover, some women have started wearing it in colours - blue, brown and red. In my opinion we should call it a dress with a clown's cap which in fact it is. I think going out without it is more modest because at least eyes are not attracted to it.

Imams have differed on the question *of hijab.* If the get-ups of some women are meant to be a way to leave the home without the *izar* it would be all right if they unveiled their faces but covered their hair and their bodies. I believe the best practice for outdoors is to cover the head with a scarf and the body with a dress of the kind Europeans call *cache poussiè re* dust coat to cover the body right down to the heels, and with sleeves long enough to reach the wrist. This is being done now in Istanbul, as I am told, when Turkish women go out to neighbourhood shops. But who will guarantee that we will not shorten it and tighten it until we transform it into another dress? In that instance, the road to reform would narrow in front of us. If we had been raised from childhood to go unveiled and if our men were ready for it I would approve of unveiling for those who want it. But the nation is not ready for it now. Some of our prudent women do not fear to mix with men, but we have to place limits on those who are less prudent because we are quick to imitate and seldom find our authenticity in the veil. Don't you see that diamond tiaras were originally meant for queens and princesses and now they are worn by singers and dancers.

If the change that some women have made in the *izar* is in order to shed it when they go out that would be all right if these women would only uncover their faces but keep their hair and figures concealed. I think the most appropriate way to dress outside is to cover the head and wear a coat with long sleeves which touches the ground the way the European women do. I am told this is the way women in Istanbul dress when they go out shopping. But who can guarantee that we are not going to shorten it and tighten it until we transform it into something else?

The way we wear the *izar* now imitates the dress of Europeans, but we have outdone them in display *(tabarruj)*. The European woman wears the simplest dress she has when she is outside and wears whatever she wishes at home or when invited to soirées. But our women are just the opposite. In front of her husband she wears a simple tunic and when she goes out she wears her best clothes, loads herself down with jewellery and pours bottles of perfume on herself... Not only this , but she makes a wall out of her face - a wall that she paints various colours, she walks swaying like bamboo in a way that entices passers-by or at least they pretend to be enticed. I am sure that most of these showy women *(mutabarrajat)* do this without bad intentions: but how can the onlooker understand good intentions when appearances do not indicate it?

Veiling should not prevent us from breathing fresh air or going out to buy what we need if no one can buy it for us. It must not prevent us from gaining an education nor cause our health to deteriorate. When we have finished our work and feel restless and if our house does not have a spacious garden why shouldn't we go to the outskirts of the city and take the fresh air that God has created for everyone and not just put in boxes exclusively for men. But, we should be prudent and not take promenades alone and we should avoid gossip. We should not saunter moving our heads right and left. If my father or husband will not choose clothes I like and bring them to the house, why can't he take me with him to select what I need or let me buy what I want?

If I cannot find anyone but a man to teach me should I opt for ignorance or unveiling in front of that man along with my sisters who are being educated? Nothing would force me to unveil in the presence of the teacher. I can remain veiled and still benefit from the teacher. Are we better in Islam than Sayyida Nafisa and Sayyida Sakina - God's blessings be upon them - who used to gather with *ulama* and poets. If illness causes me to consult a doctor and there is no woman doctor should I abandon myself to sickness, which might be right but could become complicated, through neglect or should I seek help from a doctor who could cure me?

The imprisonment in the home of the Egyptian woman of the past is detrimental while the current freedom of the Europeans is excessive. I cannot find a better model of today's Turkish woman. She falls between the two extremes and does not violate what Islam prescribes. She is a good example of decorum and modesty.

I have heard that some of our high officials are teaching their girls European dancing and acting. I consider both despicable - a detestable crossing of boundaries and a blind imitation of Europeans. Customs should not be abandoned except when they are harmful. European customs should not be taken up by Egyptians except when they are appropriate and practical. What good is there for us in women and men holding each other's waists dancing or daughters appearing on stage before audiences acting with bare bosoms in love scenes? This is contrary to Islam and a moral threat we must fight as much as we can. We must show our disdain for the few Muslim women who do these things, who otherwise would be encouraged by our silence to contaminate others.

On the subject of customs and veiling I would like to remind you of something that causes us great unhappiness - the question of engagement and marriage. Most sensible people in Egypt believe it is necessary for fiancés to meet and speak with each other before their marriage. It is wise and the Prophet himself, peace be upon him and his followers, did not do otherwise. It is a practice in all nations, including Egypt, except among city people. Some people advocate the European practice of allowing the engaged pair to get together for a period of time so that they can come to know each other, but I am opposed to this and am convinced this is rooted in fallacy. The result of this getting together is that they would come to love each other, but when someone loves another that person does not see the faults of that person and would not be able to evaluate that person's morals. The two get married on the basis of false love and without direction and soon they start to quarrel and the harmony evaporates. In my view, the two persons should see each other and speak together after their engagement and before signing the marriage contract. The woman should be accompanied by her father, or an uncle or a brother and she should wear simple clothing. Some might protest that one or two or more meetings is not enough for the two persons to get to know each other's character, but it is enough to tell if they are attracted to each other. However, anyone with good intuition can detect a person's moral character in the eyes and in movements and repose and sense if a person is false, reckless and the like. As for a person's past and other things one should investigate by talking with acquaintances, neighbours, servants, and others. If we are afraid that immoral young men would use this opportunity to see young women without intending marriage her guardian should probe the behaviour of the man to ascertain how serious he is before allowing him to see his daughter or the young woman for whom he is responsible. What is the good of education if one cannot abandon a custom that is not rooted in religion and that is harmful. We have all seen family happiness destroyed because of this old betrothal practice.

By not allowing men to see their prospective wives following their engagement we cause Egyptian men to seek European women in marriage. They marry European servants and working class women thinking they would be happy with them rather than daughters of pashas and beys hidden away in 'a box of chance'. If we do not solve this problem we shall become subject to occupation by women of the West. We shall suffer double occupation, one by men and the other by women. The second will be worse than the first because the first occurred against our will but we shall have invited the second by our own actions. It is not improbable, as well, that these wives will bring their fathers, brothers, cousins and friends to live near them and they would close the doors of work in front of our men. Most Egyptian men who have married European women suffer from the foreign habits and extravagance of their wives. The European woman thinks she is of a superior race to the Egyptian and bosses her husband around after marriage. When the European woman marries an Egyptian she becomes a spendthrift while she would be thrifty if she were married to a Westerner.

If the man thinks the upper class Egyptian wife is deficient and lacking in what her Western sister has why doesn't the husband gently guide his wife? Husband and wife should do their utmost to please each other. When our young men go to Europe to study modern sciences it should be to the benefit, not the detriment, of Egypt. As these men get an education and profit themselves they should also bring benefit to their compatriots. They should bring to their country that which will profit it and dispense with whatever is foreign as much as possible. If a national manufacturer of silk visits the factories of Europe and admires their efficiency he should buy machinery that would do work rapidly rather than introduce the same European-made product because if he does he will endanger his own good product.

If we pursue everything Western we shall destroy our own civilisation and a nation that has lost its civilisation grows weak and vanishes. Our youth claim that they bring European women home because they find them more sophisticated than Egyptian women. By the same token, they should bring European students and workers to Egypt because they are superior to our own. The reasoning is the same. What would be the result if this happens? If an Egyptian wife travels to Europe and sees the children there with better complexions and more beautiful than children in Egypt would it be right that she would leave her children and replace them with Western children or would she do her best to make them beautiful and make them resemble as much as possible that which she admired in those other children? If the lowliest Western woman marrying an Egyptian is disowned by her family shall we be content with her when she also takes the place of one of our best women and the husband becomes an example for other young men? I am the first to admire the activities of the Western woman and her courage and I am the first to respect those among them who deserve respect, but respect for others should not make us overlook the good of the nation. Public interest is above admiration. In many of our ways we follow the views of our men. Let them show us what they want. We are ready to follow their views on condition that their views do not do injustice to us nor trespass on our rights.

Our beliefs and actions have been a great cause of the lesser respect that men accord us. How can a sensible man respect a woman who believes in magic, superstition, and the blessing of the dead and who allows women peddlers and washerwomen, or even devils, to have authority over her? Can he respect a woman who speaks only about the clothes of her neighbour and the jewellery of her friend and the furniture of a bride? This is added to the notion imprinted in a man's mind that woman is weaker and less intelligent than he is. If we fail to do something about this it means we think our condition is satisfactory. Is our condition satisfactory? If it is not, how can we better it in the eyes of men? Good upbringing and sound education would elevate us in the eyes of men. We should get a sound education, not merely acquire the trappings of a foreign language and rudiments of music. Our education should also include home management, health care, and childcare. If we eliminate immodest behaviour on the streets and prove to our husbands through good behaviour and fulfilment of duties that we are human beings with feelings, no less human that they are, and we do not allow them under any condition to hurt our feelings or fail to respect us, if we do all this, how can a just man despise us? As for the unjust man, it would have been better for us not to accept marriage to him.

We shall advance when we give up idleness. The work of most of us at home is lounging on cushions all day or going out to visit other women. How does the woman who knows how to read occupy her leisure time? Only in reading novels. Has she read books about health or books through which she can profit herself and others? Being given over to idleness or luxury has given us weak constitutions and pale complexions. We have to find work to do at home. At a first glance one can see that the working classes have better health and more energy and more intelligent children. The children of the middle and lower classes are, almost all of them, in good health and have a strong constitution, while most of the children of the elite are sick or frail and prone to illness despite the care lavished on them by their parents. On the other hand, lower class children are greatly neglected by their parents. Work causes poisons to be eliminated from the blood and strengthens the muscles and gives energy.

Now I shall turn to the path we should follow. If I had the right to legislate I would decree:

1. Teaching girls the Quran and the correct Sunna.
2. Primary and secondary school education for girls, and compulsory preparatory school education for all.
3. Instruction for girls on the theory and practice of home economics, health, first aid, and childcare.
4. Setting a quota for females in medicine and education so they can serve the women of Egypt.
5. Allowing women to study any other advanced subjects they wish without restriction.
6. Upbringing for girls from infancy stressing patience, honesty, work and other virtues.
7. Adhering to the *Sharia* concerning betrothal and marriage, and not permitting any woman and man to marry without first meeting each other in the presence of the father or male relative of the bride.
8. Adopting the veil and outdoor dress of the Turkish women of Istanbul.
9. Maintaining the best interests of the country and dispensing with foreign goods and people as much as possible.
10. Make it incumbent upon our brothers, the men of Egypt, to implement this programme.

20

THE FEMINIST MOVEMENT

[Nawal El Saadawi, 'The Arab Women's Solidarity Association,' *Women of the Arab World* ed. Nahid Toubia (London and New Jersey: Zed, 1988), pp. 1-7.]

The history of the woman's liberation movement in Egypt (as well as the woman's movement in the Arab world which emanated from it) may conveniently be divided into generations that roughly parallel larger political events. Although women's philanthropic organizations were formed in Egypt as early as 1908, it was in 1919, at the height of Egypt's national revolution against the British, that the first women's political organization was established under the aegis of the nationalist movement. Huda al-Sha'arawi (1879-1947), a woman from an upper-class family active in Egyptian politics, was selected to head the women's committee. In 1923, (shortly after the death of her husband), Sha'arawi founded the Egyptian Feminist Union and succeeded in leading a delegation of Egyptian women to a meeting of the International Union of Women in Rome. Upon her return, she dramatically removed her veil in public. In the same year, minimum marriage ages for men and women were fixed by law.

In 1924, Sha'arawi left the Wafd nationalist party and devoted herself fully to the Egyptian Feminist Union. In the next two decades, the union expanded its membership in numbers and among middle-class women, and attempted to reach out to rural and urban lower-class women. Two journals were published, one in French and one in Arabic, and a youth organization was founded. The union worked for various social and political goals but was unsuccessful in obtaining the right of suffrage for Egyptian women Š a right which was granted to women in Turkey in 1930.

The first Arab women's conference was organized in Cairo in the late 1930s as a by-product of the transformation of the Palestine question into an all-Arab issue and the rise of pan-Arabism in general. In 1944, parallel with steps toward the establishment of the League of Arab States, the Arab Feminist Union was founded. In opening the pan-Arab woman's conference, Sha'arawi cited two standards which the liberation movement raised. She said: 'The Arab woman who is equal to the man in duties and obligations will not accept, in the twentieth century, the distinctions between the sexes that the advanced countries have done away with ... The woman also demands with her loudest voice to be restored her political rights, rights granted to her by the shari'à and dictated to her by the demands of the present.'[1]

It was not just by chance that Duriya Shafiq (1908-1975) founded another Egyptian women's organization called Bint al-Nil (Daughter of the Nile) shortly after Huda Sha'arawi's death. As a young pupil, Shafiq wrote to Sha'arawi asking to speak at a meeting of the Egyptian Feminist Union and with Sha'arawi's support went to study at the Sorbonne where she wrote a doctoral dissertation on the subject 'The Egyptian Woman and Islam'. Upon her return to Egypt in 1945, she founded a woman's journal which eventually included a political section. In 1948, the Bint al-Nil Union was established, a socially and geographically broader organization than its predecessor. Its main goals were combating female illiteracy and acquiring political rights for women. It functioned in the volatile political atmosphere of Egypt in the post-war period when a variety of revolutionary movements were competing for the support of politically active Egyptians. Bint al-Nil, like the Egyptian Feminist Union before it, also dedicated itself to the nationalist struggle, providing paramilitary training for women to participate in the popular movement against the British.

Most impressive was Duriya Shafiq's relentless struggle for women's political rights in the waning years of the monarchical period - when one thousand women broke into the parliament demanding the right to vote and stand for election; and after the 1952 revolution - when she headed a group of women in a hunger strike and threatened to starve herself to death if the government did not grant women the vote. After ten days, the President promised the women that the matter would receive serious consideration, and in fact, in the new constitution of 1956, women were given political rights despite an Islamic legal judgement (*fatwa*) by one of the chief religious authorities in Egypt. The achievement was all the more impressive because Bint al-Nil had been closed when political parties were dispersed by the revolutionary regime, and the free officers who ruled Egypt at this time were not amenable to independent political and social movements. In 1957, two women candidates (endorsed by the single, government party) were elected to the Egyptian parliament. One of the candidates, who had been an officer in women's commando units, countered the opposition to her as a woman by citing the wives of the Prophet. Duriya Shafiq, however, was placed under house arrest for her opposition to Abd al-Nasir's regime.

Nawal al-Saʻdawi (1931-) represents a new generation of Egyptian and Arab feminism building on previous achievements in women's rights, emerging in a new social and political reality, and influenced by the renewed international feminist movement of the 1960s. Saʻdawi is a psychiatrist by profession who began working as a physician in the rural areas of Egypt in 1955, and simultaneously published her first works of fiction. In 1972, while serving as Director-General of Health Education in Egypt, she published *Woman and Sex* which caused a furore and led to her dismissal. She started working for the United Nations and published additional books in Lebanon. In 1980, she returned to Egypt, and in the same year her best known book *The Hidden Face of Eve: Women in the Muslim World* was first published in Arabic (and subsequently translated into English and other languages).

In 1981, Saʻdawi was arrested along with many activists from the left and right-wing opposition to the government of Anwar al-Sadat. She was released by Husni Mubarak after Sadat's assassination as part of his liberalization policy. She returned to public life working to establish a new feminist organization and publishing a large number of books in Arabic and other languages.

The Arab Women's Solidarity Association was registered as an independent, non-governmental organization in Egypt in 1985 after Saʻdawi succeeded in overcoming the opposition of the government. She credits the support of Egyptian writers and intellectuals for this victory but the fact that the association was recognized as an advisory 'non-governmental organization' by UNESCO certainly influenced the Egyptian government's decision as well, and an association delegation participated in the UN international conference concluding the Decade of Women in Nairobi (in 1985). The importance of the Arab Women's Solidarity Association lies not only in its radical, feminist platform but in the fact that it is one of the first independent, political women's organization to appear after the governments of the Arab world co-opted the women's issue and women's organization for their own goals.

In 1986, the Arab Women's Solidarity Association held a conference in Cairo, and when difficulties were met in publishing rebuttals to attacks on the proceedings, it was decided to establish a publishing house and a journal. Most of the speeches delivered at the conference were subsequently published in English as *Women of the Arab World* edited by Nahid Toubia (London and New Jersey: Zed, 1988). It was not until 1989 that Nawal El Saadawi managed to overcome local opposition and publish the feminist journal *Nun* (the first letter of the Arabic word *nisaʼ* or women, but also as her detractors point out, the first letter of her own name). Nawal El Saʻdawi is undoubtedly the most well-known Arab woman in international feminist circles and this has clearly assisted her in her struggle during the last decade. One cannot but be impressed by her personal courage as a radical feminist functioning in the Arab world at great risk to her safety.

To what extent does the Arab Women's Solidarity Association appear to be an outgrowth of indigenous problems faced by women, and to what extent does it seem to be influenced by international feminist concerns? Why is funding discussed at such length in the following document, and what dilemmas does this issue raise? How do you understand the slogan: 'Lifting the veil from the mind'? How will greater democratization in the Arab countries affect nongovernmental women's organizations and the status of women in general?

A number of Doria Shafiq's writings have appeared in European languages: *La Femme et le Droit Religieux de l'Egypte Contemporaine* (Paris, 1940); 'Egyptian Feminism,' *Middle Eastern Affairs* (August, 1952); and 'Islam and the Constitutional Rights of Woman' (May, 1952) in the collection by Badran and Cooke. Earl L. Sullivan's *Women in Egyptian Public Life* (Syracuse: Syracuse University Press, 1986) summarizes the achievements of the women's liberation movement in Egypt and contains important chapters on Egyptian parliamentary women and women of the opposition.

Among Nawal El Sa'dawi's numerous publications translated into English, the following should be mentioned: *The Hidden Face of Eve* (1980); *Woman at Point Zero* (1983); *God Dies By the Nile* (1985); *Two Women in One* (1985); *Memoirs from the Women's Prison* (1987); *The Fall of the Imam* (1988); *Memoirs of a Woman Doctor* (1988);'Eyes,' (1988), Badran and Cooke; *The Circling Song* (1989); *Searching* (1991); *The Innocence of the Devil* (1994); and *The Nawal ElSa'dawi* (1997) including articles on a variety of subjects. A conversation with Sarah Graham Brown was published in *MERIP Reports* (March-April, 1981), and another with Fedwa Malti-Douglas and Allen Douglas held in August, 1986 appears in Badran and Cooke under the title 'Reflections of a Feminist.' Literary critic Fedwa Malti-Douglas has devoted a full-length study to *Men, Women, and God(s): Nawal El Saadawi and Arab Feminist Poetics* (Berkeley and Los Angeles: University of California Press, 1995.)

Nawal El Sa'dawi, The Arab Women's Solidarity Association

The idea of establishing the Arab Women's Solidarity Association was born with the 1970s. The idea emerged as a group of free-thinking Arab women became increasingly aware of and alarmed by the forms of subjugation suffered by Arab women and Arab peoples in general. The truth dawned upon us that the liberation of Arab peoples will never be accomplished unless women are liberated, while the liberation of women is by necessity dependent on the liberation of the land as well as liberation from economic, cultural and media domination. We firmly believed that solidarity was the only means to consolidate our power, for right without power is ineffective, weak and easily lost.

The solidarity of Arab women became a hope we exchanged whenever we met on any territory. We held a number of preparatory meetings in Egypt, Lebanon, Kuwait, Tunisia, Syria, Jordan, Morocco, the Sudan, Algeria, Yemen, and so on. In 1982, the foundations of the Association were laid. We applied for, and in 1985 were granted, consultative status with the Economic and Social Council of the United Nations as an Arab non-governmental organization. This organization was to be international, non-profit making, and aimed at the promotion of Arab women and Arab society in general, politically, economically, socially and culturally - and sought to consolidate the ties between women in all Arab countries.

Since 1982 a large number of Arab women, both those living in the Arab area and abroad, have joined the association. The following years, however, witnessed a setback for the rights women had acquired during the 1950s and 1960s. The fierce attack launched against women was but an integral part of the siege that (despite apparent differences in their attitudes) neo-colonialism, Zionism and Arab reactionaries laid against the Arab nation to stifle its voice and end its struggle for independence. Despite the involvement of religious fundamentalist movements in several battles against Israel and against Western influence, they have been hostile to the cause of women, because of their reactionary attitude towards democratic, social and even basic national issues.

It has become evident that many of the traditional standpoints adopted on issues related to Arab women and their rights are in opposition to the true development of Arab societies. The present situation calls for a deeper, more modern look into the role of women, both in society and the family, and for a clearer definition of the objectives of the Arab women's movement in its task of enhancing freedom and exacting justice for the millions of Arab citizens whose yoke is not easy.

General Objectives of the Association

The main principles and objectives of the association may be summarized as follows:

1. Women's active participation in the political, social, economic and cultural life of the Arab countries is a prerequisite for the exercise of democracy.

2. For the institution of social justice in the family and at the national level, all forms of discrimination on the basis of sex both in public and private spheres should be eliminated.

3. Guided by a scientific approach and an enlightened mind, efforts should be made, in a spirit of understanding of the real needs of women in the contemporary Arab environment, to promote the creative development of women and the emergence of their distinctive personality to enable them to criticize the ideas and values aimed at undermining their struggle for freedom.

4. To combine intellectual and practical endeavours in order to improve work conditions and the general quality of Arab women's lives and to take substantive and continuous steps to reach the broadest sectors of women in the poorer classes both in rural and urban areas.

5. To participate actively in projects aimed at intensifying the participation of women in political, economic, social and cultural activities at private and public levels; to explain to women the relationship between their problems and the problems of the society at large; and to open new fields of activities for the creative endeavours of women for the liberation of the mind and the stimulation of the capabilities of youth.

6. To open membership of the association to those men who believe that advancement of Arab society cannot be accomplished without the liberation of women.

Difficulties Encountered

Under the present conditions of dissent and fragmentation within the Arab nation, the establishment of an association for the solidarity of Arab women was no easy task.

Arab women are dominated by men in every area of life in the patriarchal family system: state, political party, trade union and public and private institutions of all types. It is not surprising, therefore, that the problems of Arab societies all reflect on the solidarity of Arab women.

Despite these difficulties, we have succeeded in drawing a large membership of Arab and Egyptian women who believe in their cause. We have also succeeded in registering the branch in Egypt after the Ministry of Social Affairs (as the competent body to approve the registration) had refused our application on the pretext that the State Security Police and the Criminal Control Department were opposed to the idea. Following support for our campaign by prominent writers and public figures including Fathy Radwan, Mustafa Amin and Salah Hafez, on 7 January 1985 the Arab Women's Solidarity Association was officially registered and came into being.

Activities of the Association

The association has participated in a number of activities for Arab women held at the local and international levels.

In 1985, it sent a delegation to the International Conference on Women in Nairobi, where it organized a seminar on Arab women and social values to which valuable studies were presented. Our delegation took part in the meetings and marches organized by Arab women during the conference and the association presented a Statement by the Arab Women's Solidarity Association which was circulated as one of the conference documents.

The association took part in the campaign launched against the setback to the position of women precipitated by the modification of the Personal Status Law of Egypt in 1985. In addition to holding meetings and issuing statements, the association submitted proposed modifications to the draft law to the People's Assembly.

Cultural seminars on the issue of women were held during the period 1982-87. During the first week of April 1985 the association also invited the Black American writer Angela Davies to Egypt. The programme of her visit included several meetings with a number of prominent women leaders in Egypt.

The association played a significant role in raising public awareness of the danger of certain drugs used as contraceptives. The Minister of Health was approached on the matter, articles were published by members and an urgent appeal was addressed to the Medical Syndicate.

The Conference

As the conference was conceived as a social and cultural as well as a scientific assembly, invitations were not restricted to academic specialists alone. The aim was to achieve a large gathering of Arab women to pledge solidarity and closer ties. Invitations were also addressed to certain men noted for their interest in the cause of women and the liberation of Arab thought.

The majority of the studies presented to the Conference on the Challenges Confronting Arab Women at the End of the 20th Century, held in Cairo from 1 to 3 September 1986, are contained in this book. The studies were discussed in plenary sessions and in four committees: the political, economic, social and cultural committees. The resolutions and recommendations resulting from its deliberations are set out in Chapter 16. The inaugural session was attended by 159 participants from various Arab countries.

The conference may be said to have realized its three basic objectives, namely:

1. To study the challenges confronting Arab women at the end of the 20th century in the political, cultural, economic and social fields.
2. To establish an assembly of a large number of Arab women intent on solidarity and co-operation to become an effective force for the liberation of themselves and of their Arab societies.
3. To convene the general assembly of the association; to elect its board of directors and its representatives to the United Nations; to modify certain of its statutory articles; and to approve projects for the forthcoming period.

The city of Cairo was chosen as a venue for the conference in view of its distinctive position in the Arab world, and its being the location of the Arab Women's Solidarity Association. The Arab League premises were to house the conference to emphasize Arab solidarity in the face of neo-colonialism and Zionism, as well as of the reactionary and fanatic movements pervading the Arab world in recent years which direct their blows particularly at women. Women, it should be noted, are the perennial and essential victims of all attacks launched against movements for the liberation of peoples and movements for the institution of human rights.

Preparations for the conference took a year and a half. Having decided to hold the conference in Cairo, we applied to the Ministry of Social Affairs for its approval, but received no reply. We then applied to the Ministry of Foreign Affairs, the competent authority for matters concerning Arab and international organizations, the association being an Arab international organization with consultative status with the UN Economic and Social Council. Our application was approved, and appended to it was a courtesy note from Foreign Minister Dr Esmat Abdel Meguid. The efforts of Mrs Mervat El Tillawi, Minister Plenipotentiary at the Egyptian Foreign Ministry, deserve special mention.

Financial Difficulties
Confronted by the lack of funds for the conference (our resources consisted of the annual subscription fees of 10 Egyptian pounds per member) the association approached certain Arab and Egyptian organizations for contributions. None of these proposed the funding, or responded to our request - even long after the deadline; the association, therefore, had no choice but to approach certain international organizations in Egypt. Of those approached by the head of the preparatory committee, OXFAM and the Ford Foundation in Cairo responded positively. Their contributions, though not very large, were unconditional, and on these grounds were accepted by the association as being in conformity with its statutes. Later, we also received small contributions from certain international organizations concerned with women, but the main

funding was provided by NOVIB in Holland.

The contributions we received covered the expenses incurred by a large number of researchers and association members from various Arab countries who were invited to the conference, there being no conditions attached to the funding apart from the understanding that it be used for conference purposes.

Conference Emblem

The conference adopted the emblem of the association: 'The Power of Women - Solidarity - Lifting the Veil from the Mind'. It appears on all the association's letterheads and publications, and on the invitation cards for the conference. The emblem is envisaged to combine the basic objectives of the association, namely solidarity, without which women cannot become a power, and awareness, which necessitates the lifting of the veil. It was conceived to have the largest appeal possible, drawing women from different political and conceptual trends, political parties, governments, trade unions, non-governmental organizations, etc. for how can anybody object to solidarity or to the freedom to think and exercise the powers of the mind?

Success of the Conference

The assembly halls of the Arab League headquarters witnessed for the first time a gathering of Arab women representing no government or party, and the walls resounded with the vigour and enthusiasm of a younger generation. During the three days of the conference, the four committees reviewed 24 studies; women's books on art and literature were on display. Coverage of the conference was undertaken by Egyptian, Arab and international media, a fact which brought many issues of a conceptual nature to the forefront. Some attempts were made by certain political movements to influence the course of deliberations and to attack the conference as well as the association, but these failed.

Attitudes of Certain Political Movements towards the Conference

Islamic 'Salafi' Movements

Most of these boycotted the conference from the beginning, considering that the emblem 'Lifting the Veil from the Mind' and 'Solidarity of Arab Women' to be a transgression of God's commands and a violation of religious law. Consequently they rejected the invitation and prohibited their female members from attending. Nevertheless, a number of women Islamic thinkers endowed with independent minds participated actively in the deliberations of the conference. Newspapers published by the Islamic fundamentalist movements made numerous and diverse charges against us, the least of which were infidelity and atheism. We were also charged with treason for having accepted conference funding from non-Islamic and non-Arab sources.

Traditional Rightist Movements

These too, boycotted the conference from the very start. For them, the Arab Women's Solidarity Association is a communist organization because we associate the domination of women as a class with patriarchal domination. The word 'class' is totally banned from the usage of such political movements. For them, we should assume the role of a women's charitable society to care for the sick and those with war disabilities, doing little more than distributing sweets. Political issues, historical perspectives or class conflict as they reflect on women are all domains into which we should never enter. In this context, traditional rightist movements said we were communists recruited by the Soviet Union to serve its interests.

Traditional Leftist Movements

These accused us of being agents of the USA and Zionism for having accepted a grant from the Ford Foundation. When these charges failed to produce the desired effect, however, we were attacked from another direction. The ideas put forward and discussed were said to separate the cause of women from that of the nation, or were concerned with the sexual aspect only and neglected the political and economic aspects, or were dividing the ranks by antagonizing men, and so on.

The Government

The Ministry of Social Affairs completely ignored the conference by not responding to our invitation. Some members of the government press attacked the conference and pressured the authorities to inspect the association's records. The Ministry of Foreign Affairs, however, adopted a positive attitude by approving the convening of the conference and making possible the booking of the necessary facilities of the Arab League premises.

The Crisis of Democracy and the Press

The articles sent to national and opposition newspapers in answer to the attacks and charges heaped on the association were for the main part refused publication. The few articles which were eventually published were meddled with in one way or another, with sections deleted or titles changed. In spite of the fact that Egyptian law provides for the right to reply in the same newspaper, on the same page and in the same space, we were, without exception, denied this right by all newspapers in Egypt.

This situation, however, should cause no surprise because for the press, as in politics, 'might makes right'. In the world of the media, rights are taken, never granted.

The very first draft resolution adopted by the association at its latest general assembly held on 1 September 1986 called for the establishment of a publishing house and the issue of a newspaper or magazine to propagate the views of the association. This book is the first fruit.

Arab Women's Solidarity Association, Cairo
January 1987

Notes

1. Badran and Cooke, p. 338.

THE STORY OF A CONTEMPORARY WOMAN

MYSTIC

[Fatima Mernissi, *Doing Daily Battle: Interviews with Moroccan Women* trans. Mary Jo Lakeland (New Brunswick, N.J.: Rutgers University Press, 1989), pp. 126-44, 213-7.]

The mystic women of the past, such as Rabi'a al-Adawiyya, are not so much concrete, historical figures as timeless role models whose words and deeds live in the popular culture of Muslims today. Conversely, some contemporary Muslim women report mystic experiences which changed their lives in a manner similar to those of the daughter of Umm Hassan. Access to the life-stories of contemporary female mystics requires overcoming barriers of values, culture and class, and is one dimension of the methodological debate about the anthropological and sociological validity of interviews.

The historical value of interviews is the subject of disagreement. The conservative view is that information about an individual's lifetime (which may span a century) may be carefully elicited in an interview. Others put credence in orally-transmitted information over generations, particularly in non-literate societies. But interviews aiming to collect data on contemporary issues have their fair share of methodological problems as well. How were the interviewees selected and how did the interviewer gain access to them? Was a closed, questionnaire format used or open-ended questions? What barriers of misunderstanding separate the interviewer from the person interviewed? Published interviews with women have become increasingly prevalent in recent years to represent the silent voices of women, particularly lower-class women. The question invariably arises as to the extent the interviewer is presenting his or her own views rather than those of the women interviewed.

Fatima Mernissi, a radical, feminist Moroccan sociologist, openly challenges the research techniques of the social sciences such as representativeness, objectivity, and control of the interviewing process. Her anthology *Doing Daily Battle* comprises eleven interviews from a total of one hundred collected since 1970 of women remembering their childhood in the harem, factory workers, housemaids, emigrés, etc. She tried to be sensitive to the narrative pace of illiterate women, intervening and editing as little as possible. She also aimed to preserve the rambling style, confused sequence of events and inconsistencies of the narrative. While the selections in the book are obviously a product of Mernissi's views about Muslim women (which have been forcefully presented in many publications the most influential of which is *Beyond the Veil: Male-Female Dynamics in a Modern Muslim Society),* the ultimate test of her research technique is how realistic the interviews are, how open to differing interpretations.

The story of Habiba the Psychic was clearly selected to convey certain messages. What are they? What kind of a woman is Habiba? How did her mystic experience change her life? What do we learn in her narrative about the relations between men and women in the mystic environment?

Similar first-hand life stories of Middle Eastern Muslim women may be found in: Elizabeth Warnock Fernea and Basima Qattan Bezirgan, *Middle Eastern Muslim Women Speak* (1977); Nayra Atiya, *Khul-Khaal: Five Egyptian Women Tell Their Stories* (1982); Elizabeth Fernea, *Women and the Family in the Middle East: New Voices of Change* (1985); Michael Gorkin, *Days of Honey, Days of Onion* (1991); Bouthaina Shaaban, *Both Right and Left Handed: Arab Women Talk about Their Lives* (1991); and Lila Abu-Lughod, *Writing Women's Worlds: Bedouin Stories* (1993). Steven Barboza has done the same for American Muslims in *American Jihad* (1994).

Fatima Mernissi's, Interview with Habiba the Psychic[1]

A peasant father

Q: *Tell me about your life from the time you were a child. Tell me what your father did, where the family lived, where you were brought up, and so on.*

A: When I waš born, my father was a soldier. He had enlisted in the Spanish army.

Q: *Were you born in the Spanish zone of Morocco?*

A: When my mother died, we were still there. My father was fed up with his job. He left the army and came to live in this area [the interview took place in Rabat]. We were eight children.

Q: *Were you the oldest?*

A: No, I wasn't the oldest. There were six girls and two boys.

Q: *Your mother had eight children in all ?.*

A: Without counting those who died. My father brought us to this area and went back to farming.

Q: *Did he work on farms or did he have a little piece of land?.*

A: He worked for other people. You know, my father always worked in farming. He always worked the land. Even when he was in the army, he was assigned to farming; he worked the land for the army. Then he brought us here and in order to support us, he worked the land. After my mother's death, he married a very good woman who was very kind to us. My father and my stepmother are dead now.

Q: *Did your stepmother have children by your father?*

A: Yes, she had three; one died and two are still living. We are all married, except one daughter who is handicapped. The poor thing, and God gave her no help! She also, like me, had seizures.[2] The seizures struck her during the wedding of one of our younger sisters. My father had married her off very young, when she was seven years old. He had put her in the care of a woman who was supposed to protect her until the age of ten, that is, to prevent the consummation of the marriage before my sister was ten years old, to prevent the husband from coming near her. But this woman did not keep her promise. At any rate, my little sister stayed with that man just long enough to persuade him to give her a divorce. Then she remarried and had children with another man. After that, it was my turn to get married. I was married before I met this man [the interview took place in Habiba's living room, in the presence of her husband and children].

Q: *How old were you when you got married?*

A: I was fourteen.

Q: *People got married young at that time.*

A: I got married without a licence, without anything. I got married just with the *fatiha*.[3]

Q: *In Rabat?*

A: At that time my father was living in Sidi Slimane in the Gharb and my husband in Sidi Kacem, not very far away. My husband was originally from our part of the country [that is, the Sahara]. But Allah did not let that marriage succeed. I had two children with my first husband, but the marriage quickly turned sour. My husband mistreated me, and I left him. I remained a divorcee for four years, and then Allah arranged for me to meet this man, and I married him. He is also from our people.

Q: *The second time, did you get married in Sidi Kacem?*

A: No, I got married in Rabat to this man you see here.

Q: *Your children are from your first husband?*

First signs of 'seizures'

A: Yes. Unfortunately Allah has not given me children by my present husband. As for my present condition, that began when I was a small child. My brothers and sisters would begin to tickle me and I would black out. I wouldn't regain consciousness until they put my hand in water or had me inhale something that had been burned in fire. If someone tickled me, I would run away from there like mad. My father, may Allah rest his soul, would yell at the children, ordering them to stop: 'Leave your sister alone, don't tickle her any more', he told them over and over.

Q: *How old were you when it began?*

A: I was ten or eleven. You see, I was very young. There wasn't much of a gap between us, and people used to believe that we were twins. There was an animal that had a terrible effect on me, worse even than the tickling: I mean frogs. I was terrified of frogs. It was enough for someone to say the word in front of me for me to go crazy. If I had something in my hand, I threw it; I became aggressive, chased other people. Yes, I became crazy. I began to scream like a mad person, screaming until I lost consciousness. My poor father tried to prevent this from happening, to protect me. He forbade my brothers and sisters to torment me. And because of all that, this thing that I have began to get worse. I remember one day when I was invited to visit my brother. My son Muhammad was still a baby. Someone said the word *'jrana'* [frog] in front of me. I fell upon my baby and I nearly killed him. I lost consciousness. My brother was so upset that he swore that from then on he would take to court anybody who tried to excite me: 'You know perfectly well that my sister has an attack when she hears that word, so avoid saying it in front of her!'

Q: *Was your first husband aware of the situation?*

A: Yes, I used to have attacks when I was living with him after our marriage, if someone upset me. But, you see, he didn't believe in it; he used to say to me, 'You are crazy.' He didn't have faith, he didn't believe at all in that. So when he saw me having a seizure, he would cry out, 'I think this woman is crazy.' In fact, he was rather inflexible; he didn't believe at all in the power of the djinns.[4] He was a very ordinary man; I never understood him. He had an odd manner about him. I stayed with him for five or six years.

Q: *He didn't believe in those things?*

A: He didn't believe in them at all. But when I had an attack, you see, I have to admit that he did take care of me. But he had a sort of pride, it was as if he was ashamed in front of others when this happened to me. We lived on a farm in the country, and he didn't want people to see me in that state or to know about it. When there were strangers in the house, he would lock me up and ask neighbouring women to take care of me.

Q: *And your second husband? What is his attitude about the djinns? Did you tell him about it before you got married?*

A: Yes, he knew all about it when he married me. You see, although he doesn't have any legs, he helps me when I have an attack. If the seizure comes upon me when I am near a puddle of water, he throws himself on top of me, tries to pull me away, and calls people to my aid. He gets them to carry me to a clean place; then he washes off my clothes, rubs me with benzoin,[5] puts my head on his shoulder, and calms me. Life went on like this until I got pregnant. I got pregnant two or three times with him, but it always came to nothing. You see, he had been married before meeting me. The parents of his first wife came and threatened me in order to make me leave him and thus force him to return to their daughter. They threatened me with a knife, and that incident made my seizures worse.

Q: *Did they attack you?*

A: Yes, they attacked me. They burst into the garage where we were living at that time in the Hassan neighbourhood of Rabat.

Q: *Was your husband there?*

A: Yes, he was there, but not in the same room. They locked themselves into the garage with me, where it was very dark. They attacked me once in the stomach with the knife and once in the neck. And then my condition got worse: I was beset on one side by the 'spirits', and on the other by fear. Just before my periods, my belly would swell up. I went to see a doctor and had an operation to make it possible to have a baby by this man, but up to now God has not granted our wish, and we continue as we are. You see, the djinns made a pact with me; they gave me to understand that I could never have children if I didn't pay a visit to the shrine of Mulay Ibrahim, and up to now I haven't been able to.[6]

Q: *You still haven't been able to go? Then how were you initiated into your work as a psychic? How did you become a psychic?*

The calling becomes clear

A: The day that I began to work, that was it. I became a *shuwafa,* a psychic.

Q: *Were you with your first husband or your second?*

A: I was with my present husband. You see, we have been together for a good long time.

In short, before the time that I became a psychic, I had begun to have visions;

it was on the eve of the Prophet's birthday.

[Habiba describes her visions, predictions and her feelings that she should visit the tomb of Sidi Ali.)

The journey of initiations

As soon as I could, I made the pilgrimage to Sidi Ali's shrine.[7] I said to my husband, 'I must go.' 'But where are you going? he asked me. My older sister was supposed to accompany me, but she let me down at the last minute.

Q: *Did you give up the idea of leaving then?*

A: No. I left, but all alone. I went out of the house and I began to ask the way. I came to the place where they sell bus tickets, and I bought one. There was a crowd at the ticket window. It was the height of the pilgrimage season. I hesitated, and then I decided to leave even if I were never to return. Was I perhaps going to be doomed to wander from one saint to another? I would follow the decisions of Allah, whatever they might be. So I left. I arrived at the shrine of Shaikh al-Kamal.[8] There I found the ritual procession going toward the shrine of Sidi Said, may God increase his glory![9]

Q: *Did that happen the same day that you left Rabat?*

A: Yes, the same day. When we arrived, with the pilgrimage in full swing, the town-crier came on to the bus to announce to us: 'Beware! Don't wear black. You might have trouble.' I was dressed entirely in black from head to toe. My *djellaba* was black, and my veil also.

Q: *You hadn't known about it?[10]*

A: No, I really hadn't. It was the first time I had heard of it. And just imagine: I have always loved wearing black. When I see people dressed in black, I stare at them and can't look away; I want to jump on them and take their clothes. When the bus arrived, I got off, but I didn't know where to go, what direction to take. I met two young men, one about the age of my son and the other a little older. I said to them: 'I beg you, take me to the saint; show me the way.' They told me that I should wait there for another bus which would take me. So I remained there until nightfall. The taxis which usually carried people for two and a half dirhams began to double their price. They took advantage of people's impatience. While I waited for the bus, I heard people around me saying that every year during the pilgrimage there is a bus that is cursed and breaks down, never gets repaired and never gets its passengers to their destination. It seems that somebody had once committed a shocking act during the pilgrimage. Having heard these rumours, I looked around me. I spotted a man sitting there, and I approached him and asked him where he was going. 'To Sidi Ali', he answered. He told me that he lived nearby. When the bus came, I boarded it at his side; he was the only person in the group in whom I felt any confidence.

But when we were settled in the bus, they asked us for five dirhams. Everybody then left the bus, except for that man and me; we were the only ones who agreed to pay double the normal price. When we arrived at Sidi Ali, it was already quite late at night. He asked me where I was going and if I knew where the shrine was. I begged him to take me to the door of the shrine, telling him, 'I don't know where I am. I have never before left Rabat to go further than to Kenitra. Please help me. I am a stranger here; I don't know where to go.' He agreed, and then added, 'If you want to stay the night at my house, you are welcome.' I accepted with pleasure, and went to his house. He had brought a table and some utensils with him on the bus. He walked along and I followed him. It was a very dark night. To tell the truth, I was very afraid of him. I said to myself, 'He is going to lead me somewhere and cut my throat.' But, on the other hand, I was deeply convinced that I was following a preordained path and that no harm could come to me. My objective was right and good: to visit the saint's shrine. So I followed him. Along our route someone greeted him, calling out, 'Good evening, sharif.' 'Well,' I said to myself, 'he is a sharif, so nothing can harm me. 'When we arrived at his wife's house, she caused quite a scene. She woke her children up and said to them, 'Come and see what your father has brought from the market; he has brought a woman. He forgot to buy the things we needed because his mind was on something else; he has brought back a woman. That's what interests him the most!'

I was very humiliated and upset by this scene as it was on my account that the man had got into this quarrel. I turned to the woman and said to her: 'Give me a sheepskin, I beg you.' She asked me who I was, and then prepared a very unappetising meal for us. I couldn't swallow a mouthful of it, but I told myself that if I didn't eat, her suspicions would grow. So I took some eggs out of my bag and laid them on the table with half a loaf of bread and some cakes. I also gave the mistress of the house some money - ten or fifteen dirhams, I can't remember exactly. I told her, 'Please accept this contribution for the food.' In spite of all that, I still kept on my djellaba. The mistress of the house showed me a place where I was supposed to sleep, then went with her husband into another room to sleep. Before I fell asleep, she came to me and asked: 'Do you intend to rent?' I answered,'Madame, I will do what you want. If you want me to rent [the sleeping space], I will rent. You see, I have come to visit the saint. It's the first time I have come, and I don't know what is customary.' The next morning I got up, washed, and said my prayers. Since the daughter of my host and hostess was leaving for school, I asked her to take me to visit the saint's shrine. I left all my things at their place: my bag, the blanket I had brought from Rabat, my towel, my sheet - in short, I left everything I possessed at that woman's house. I told her, 'I am leaving all my things with you; if I succeed in finding this house again, I will fetch them; otherwise they are yours, you can keep them.' She asked me again if I intended to rent space in her house, and I answered that I didn't know yet what I was going to do.' I have to go to the saint's shrine to find some people that I know.' In fact, I didn't know anybody; I wasn't supposed to meet anybody. I just said those words, like that; I don't know why.

Pilgrimage to Lalla Aisha

So I left that house and went down with the daughter toward the saint's shrine. She pointed out to me the grotto of Lalla Aisha:" 'There is Lalla Aisha, if you want to visit her, and the saint's shrine is at the foot of the stairs.' I thanked the little girl and gave her some money. Then I 'visited' Lalla Aisha. But people told me, 'This is not the time for the visit to Lalla Aisha! This is not when they hand out the henna.' They asked me why I had come. 'I am a person possessed and I have come to visit.' A woman then advised me to come back at sunset: 'That is the time for visiting this place, when hens and cocks are sacrificed here.' So I went on to the saint's shrine. I pressed my head against the wroughtiron grille and broke into sobs. All the events of the previous night came back to me - the humiliations, the insults of that woman. I was overcome with sorrow as I remembered it all. I had been weeping for some time when a woman approached me and said: 'Why are you crying? Don't cry any more.' For a long time I couldn't say anything. I shook my head like a mute person, as though I were telling her to let me take care of myself, to let me cry, and I continued crying until I felt better. 'What's the matter?' she resumed. 'Well, Madame', I began, and I told her all that had happened the night before, finishing by saying, 'I came, and now I no longer know where to turn.' 'Welcome', she told me. 'My husband is the *muqaddam.*¹² We are camping in a tent, and we eat at the sharif's table. Our food is brought to us from the *zawiya* [Sufi lodge]. You are welcome to join us.' 'Where are you from?' I asked her. 'I am from Rabat, and where you do you come from?' she replied. 'I am from the Sahara.' She welcomed me with open arms. Her husband had two other wives. One of them had stayed at home, and the two others had accompanied him to the shrine. Her husband decided that I should be welcomed as a guest; he forbade me to do any of the house-keeping chores. They gave me food that was all prepared, and all I had to do was eat it. I wanted to do the washing up; sometimes I tried to wash and cut the mint bouquet, but each time someone stopped me. Allah is great. The blessing of the ancestors and saints was with us. I stayed with them until the last day of the pilgrimage. On only one evening did they let me pay for the cost of dinner; otherwise I was completely taken care of. One of the wives of the *muqaddam* was a psychic. We went together to perform the ritual dance of possession. The day of the ritual procession, we went to the saint's shrine, taking the *dabiha*. Each group had its own special ritual. So we left with the procession going to Sidi Ali Ibn Hamdush, then to Sidi Ahmad Dughughi. We walked the whole route of the procession in bare feet.

Q: *Were there just women, or men and women together?*

A: We marched in the procession together. The announcers called out to the crowd: 'Barren women, enter the shrine!' They entered and stretched out on the ground, and the procession marched right over them. Some were very well dressed, wearing a caftan of thick felt, but they lay down like the rest. To all those who had a malady they wanted to be cured of, the *muqaddam* called out: 'Come forward, ye who are halt and lame; approach, ye who have pain in the back.' The *muqaddam* got so excited that his saliva sprayed out. The march was accompanied by the music of bagpipes. Meanwhile, if the crowd of those performing the dance of possession saw someone passing with a goat, they wrested it from him, brought it into their midst, tore it into shreds, and ate it raw.

[She describes the ritual in detail: trance-like dancing, special dress, the procession of the two saints on the seventh day, self-inflicted injuries and receiving the bread as a sign of receiving the vocation.]

He said: 'You have come from very far. You are going to succeed. You are going to get what you want.' I placed a candle like everybody else. The man said to me: 'Go forward, march on. You are going to begin to work and you will not want for anything. You will return many times to this shrine.' He kept on speaking and speaking, and listened as if everything he said was going to come true. I had confidence in myself; all that was going to happen.

Q: *And did you begin to work after your return?*

A: From the moment I got back to Rabat I began to work.

Q: *How did it take piace? One morning you woke up and began to 'see' things?*

Doing the work of a psychic

A: No. I began to see things after having made the 'blood sacrifice'. I bought a cow for 800 dirhams without giving a thought to the price. I invited the *muqaddam,* who came accompanied by fourteen people, not counting the women.

Q: *Where did the muqaddam come from? From the shrine of Sidi Ali?*

A: No, he came from Kenitra. The first time he visited me, he had said, 'You must prepare yourself. When you are ready, come and tell me, and I will arrange the celebration, the *layla'*. So they came and they stayed at my place for seven days. We danced for seven days, and I never got enough of it. The day they wanted to leave, I threw myself on the ground in front of the door. I didn't want them to leave me. They began to pray.

Q: *They stayed seven days with you?*

A: Yes, seven days eating and drinking, thanks be to God. The *muqaddam* stayed a whole month with me. He left very satisfied.

Q: *You began when he left?.*

A: He left me after my inauguration. His wife came to join him; she herself was a *muqaddama,* an initiator. They put the banner on my door.[13] The *muqaddama* made a *tabaq* for me.

Q: *I have visited lots of psychics who don't have a banner. Have the ones who have a banner on their door, like you, carried out the celebration and made the sacrifice, or what?*

A: Of course. There has to be a blood sacrifice. You have to receive the approval of the *muqaddam*. You see, afterwards, you must make blood sacrifices on specific occasions: in the month of Sha'ban and for the Prophet's birthday. If you don't, you go in fear of your life. You don't have to observe the Hamdushi celebration; you can do the Ganawi or the Jilali, if you prefer. Each person must dance for their own master. Each can operate through a saint who is particularly close: Mulay Abd al-Qadir Jilali, al-Ganawi, al-Hamdushi, al-Issawi, or al-Sarqawi. You know, there are several kinds of spirits. We leave people free; we try to be flexible with them; but in fact each person is possessed by their own *malik,* their own master spirit. Each one of us, the possessed, dances their own dance: one handles fire, another pours water on the head to feel well, and still another must tear their clothes to find relief. Another, seeing a person they don't like, runs after him and hits him. That's the way it is in our world. When I had carried out the celebration and danced and cured some people, I began to receive others. For the next Prophet's birthday, I paid the expenses of a Ganawi celebration. The tray that I offered to Lalla Malika[14] cost me 200 dirhams; I had to put on it a variety of things, such as *siwak,* watermelon seeds, figs. The piles of things must be placed on this tray so that there will be *hajba*.

Q: *What does hajba mean?.*

A: Hajba means that the tray must be isolated in a room which no one goes into, especially children. You cover the tray, which has been very carefully arranged. If someone enters the room and takes something without permission, they put their life in danger. One of my nieces, who was seventeen years old, was touched that night. She didn't know what was going on, the poor thing. Now she is touched, she too.

Q: *She went into the room where the tray was?*

A: No, it happened when we put the scarf on the horns of the cow.

Q: *When the cow was being sacrificed? At that moment?*

A: Yes, just then. When she saw the cow with the scarves, she let out a crazy laugh. Then 'they' struck her. Now she dances more than I do. I stopped after a certain time; she, the poor thing, continues. I have really tried to intervene with 'them' to free her, but in vain. One time a participant at the Hamdushi ceremony that I had organised got up to dance. In twelve years Lalla Aisha had never made an appearance to her. That night Lalla Aisha came. I begged her to free my niece:[15] 'Why has my niece been chosen?[16] She is only a child. It is right for you to choose me, who is beginning to age, who has lived a long time and has accepted life's hard knocks. But she is a girl; she still knows nothing of life.' She replied to me: 'We want our family to grow. You don't want to be our only kin, do you? That's why we are going to keep her among us.' So my niece was obliged to pay all the expenses necessary for the ceremonies; she had to finance all the activities for healing, and today she is still possessed. She 'sees' everything. She sees everything just as I see everything.[17]

Q: *Does she practice as a psychic, like you?*.

A: No, she doesn't 'see' for others. She sees imaginary beings. Sometimes she sees Lalla Aisha beside her; she sees herself travelling with Lalla Aisha, accompanying her everywhere. As soon as she sees her, she laughs in her face. She has never recovered, the poor thing.

Q: *Didn't you ever take her to see someone to help her?[18]*

A: We didn't take her to see anyone. She went to pay a visit to Sidi Mi'mun, in God's name, at El Ksar, and her mother arranged a blood sacrifice - she made all the arrangements for the black ceremony.[19]

Q: *And is she better now?*

A: She is better when she dances. For example, after the Sha'ban ceremonies,[20] she feels better during the following months. But she quickly relapses again into her old condition. She just has to see someone crying and she has a seizure. You know, this is not acting.

No, it's not acting. You know, one day I was visited by a client, a young woman who was very self-assured and full of youth and health. I thought she didn't believe at all in our world. She had to come to see me because she had some problems. I conducted a séance for her. *The jawads* told her everything: 'You were once engaged, there was a dispute', etc. That day I had the *muqaddam* and his wife at my house, and there were some ceremonies in progress. The young woman appeared at the door and she didn't respect us. I thought that she didn't believe in our world, that she must be laughing at us. Well, do you know what happened to her? She fell down right in front of the grocer's across the street from my house. They picked her up; her foot was sprained, her toes twisted; she couldn't walk. The grocer and the neighbours, who knew me, understood what had happened. They told her: 'Go back to the *sharifa* and ask her for forgiveness. ' She returned to my house, limping, and said: '*Sharifa,* I am limping ...' 'My daughter, ask to be forgiven, make obeisance, and never again laugh at us, at all these people, the *jawads.'* I pulled at her toes, and then she left, walking on both feet, as if nothing had happened. Afterwards she became a habitué; she came and brought everything that was necessary. She is a wonderful young woman.

Q: *How long have you been practising as a psychic?*

A: Three years.

The visit of the young black man ...

Q: *You began by charging two dirhams for a séance?*

A: Yes, exactly. The day that Allah willed that my resources be augmented, I saw a young black man, black as that young man there across from you.[21] He was like him, very similar in appearance, except that his hair stood on end.

Q: Did you see that young man in a dream or in reality?[22]

A: I saw him in a dream. Latifa, a 'teacher' like me, was here. She had just come to tell me that someone was at the door and wanted to see me. I opened the door and found myself face to face with this young black man. We greeted each other, and then he said at once: 'Are you the woman who uses the *ladun?*[23] 'Yes', I answered. Then he put me to a test: 'What do you do for someone who comes to you sick?' 'If you want to see what I do, then come in. I will show you. If you are a believer,[24] you are welcome.' I was very afraid of him. 'Why are you afraid?' he asked me. 'Master, people are afraid of me, and I am afraid of you. In the name of God, who are you?' 'I am the Master of the *Ladun.*' I grabbed him by his clothes and pulled him with all my strength to the sofa where I pushed him down. 'How do you use the *ladun?*' he asked. 'I give it to my visitor to hold in the hand; then I throw it in the fire, and then in cold water. Afterwards I look into it, and I see.' 'Next time do the same thing, but on the head of your visitor, like this', he said, acting out his words. Then he ordered me to 'do' the *ladun* on him. I began by passing the *ladun* over his head with my right hand. He grabbed my hand in his, saying, 'Very good, seventy rials [three and a half dirhams], and you really deserve it.' You know, I remember every detail of that dream. It was five months ago that I met that man in my dream, but the dream remains engraved in my memory in its smallest details. ... and its consequences.

The next day I didn't dare announce the new fee to my visitors. At the beginning I used to accept any donation at all, even just a bit of benzoin. I was embarrassed to announce this rise in my fee to my visitors. I could already hear what they would say: 'You know our Morocco.' Once their tongues were loosened, if they decided to attack me, they would not try to look for the reason that had impelled me to act. So the day after that dream, I was unwilling to announce the rise to my clientele. That same evening a black woman appeared to me in a dream. She wore three rings, one in her nose, another in her ear, and a third was hanging from her lower lip. She made them clang against each other and lashed out at me: 'You refused to obey orders. You refused to announce to people that your fee would be seventy rials from now on. You will see what is going to happen to you now. You will suffer the consequences of your act. We are going to burn you. You were more afraid of people than of us. We are going to burn your mouth. Your wound will linger for a year.' I was terrified. I had already been suffering for a year from a wound in the foot that wouldn't heal. And now I was supposed to have committed an offence against 'them'! I had already lost a finger in this business. So, with these threats, I was terrified and had to announce the new fee to my clientele.

One day, at eleven o'clock in the morning, there was a knock at the door. There was no one there, just thirty rials on the ground. I called to my daughter, 'You are irresponsible, dropping coins with the face of His Majesty Hassan II on the ground.' But it was not she who had put that money there. I realised then that it had to be the spirits, because the thirty rials was the amount of the rise in my fee. So I announced my new fee to everyone. To those who protested, I said that I was not going to put my life in danger and there was nothing I could do for them. I showed them the marks of the three burns on my leg, three scars as big as a rial, which appeared after the dream. I still have those marks. Here, look. [Habiba then showed me her leg, where the traces could actually be seen.]

Now people come to me from all over, from all sections of the city. The other day a woman came. She had dreamed of Lalla Aisha. She had had an accident - a moped had crashed into her in the street because she was on her way to attend some séances without having done her ablutions and anointed herself. Her face was all swollen. The people in the street told her to come and see me, to come and light some candles for Lalla Aisha. She came and brought some henna. She put it right here and lighted the candles in honour of Lalla Aisha. That very evening Lalla Aisha visited her. You know, I built a shrine for Lalla Aisha.

A shrine for Lalla Aisha

Q: *Where did you build the shrine?*

A: Right here in this house. The day that we began to dig the foundation, the *muqaddam* and his aides, who were in charge of the ritual of the installation ceremony, sacrificed a cow before setting to work. They found the spot where the blood gushed hot from the beast. I asked the *muqaddam* the meaning of this, because it was my sister who was helping him dig, and it was she who had seen it. The *muqaddam* answered: 'That means that God has made you rich. You can build a shrine to Lalla Aisha in your house' We bought the necessary bricks and cement, and a black bird that was offered in sacrifice at the same spot.

Q: *Did all that happen right here in the house?*[25]

A: Yes, right here in the house. I regularly placed the henna. People came to visit the shrine; they came from far away with their problems and asked Lalla Aisha for help. But you have to believe in it, obviously, if you want this to work for you. If you believe in it, Lalla Aisha comes to visit you in a dream; she tells you what has to be done, how to begin, and the order of the steps to be taken. Lalla Aisha tells you to come to see me; she will make your wishes come true through my mediation.[26] Do you know that a woman who had never heard of me came the other day from Tabriket [Sale]?

Q: *Then how did she know your address?*

A: She had come once, but she didn't know that the shrine existed. She dreamed that it was as it is. She told me: 'I saw the door with a green plant falling over it.' Come see if this is the door you saw in your dream.' She f ollowed me and recognised what she had seen in her dream. She brought some benzoin, bread, olives, and candles, and made her wish. She wanted to 'find a key', that is, she was looking for an apartment. She has not yet found what she wants. But she came from Tabriket without knowing the route and by asking along the way.

Q: *What did she ask?.*

A: She asked the people she met: 'Do you know a black woman who has made a shrine for Lalla Aisha?' One child told her that he knew a black woman living in this neighbourhood, but he didn't know if she had built a shrine or not. 'Only Allah knows. You will have to go and ask her yourself.' When she came to my door, I had her come in and led her to Lalla Aisha. She broke out in sobs: 'I was looking for this place without knowing the address.' I did for her what I could. You know, some people refuse to pay the seventy rials. It happens and I can't do anything about it. It is not my fault. When I see that a woman is really poor, I let it pass. I even give her back part of the money for bus fare. You see, when a woman is very poor, I have to reduce the fee. I can't let her be lost.

An illiterate woman writes charms

Q: *And writing charms, how does that go?*[27]

A: It depends on the age of the client. If it's for a sick child, I write it for 200 rials. If it's for a grown-up, I charge double, 400 rials. Sometimes people simply have to burn a selection of things in a brazier at home; the smoke is supposed to be purifying and dissipates the *thiqaf*. They give me money - it is not a fixed sum - and it is I who then buy them the necessary items. The other day two men came to see me.

Q: *For a charm?*

A: Or course, for a charm. I have a *faqih*[29] who writes for me, but just in the evenings. I never write a charm during the day, except in very urgent cases, for someone very ill who is really suffering. In that case, I write the charm during the day. But normally, it is the *faqih* who writes for me.

Q: *How is it done? Do you write while awake or asleep?*

A: I write while awake, but in fact it is not I who writes. My hand moves by itself, as if it were connected to a machine, in the space of a few minutes. I can write forty or fifty charms very easily. But it is not I who writes. All I do is carry out the orders of my *faqih,* whom I obey and in whom I have total confidence. It is he who writes for me. I write charms for different problems: to help a young girl get married, to solve work problems, etc. I write charms in the evening. It is my *faqih* who instructs me; he reveals things to me, shows me things I don't know about.

Q: *So, a person orders a charm one day and then comes back to get it the next day?*

A: Yes. You know, not everybody necessarily needs a charm. It depends on what *the jawads* demand. For some people they demand the *tabkhira* for others the *kitab,* and for still others the *ladun,* for a certain period of time - three to seven days - and your problem can be solved. Sometimes it happens that people come back a few days after having visited me to tell me that things are going better. A woman went out just before you came in. She told me: 'I dreamed about you two nights in a row. So I decided to come. The last time - just yesterday - I said to myself, 'I must go to see her.' 'If you don't believe me, ask my husband, ask anybody.[29]

Notes

1. Habiba was born in 1927 in a village in the Spanish zone of Morocco. This interview took place in 1977 in Rabat, when I undertook the study on psychics. The other interviews in this book date from 1974 onwards. Originally taped in colloquial Arabic, they were translated into French by Said Binjallun, with the exception of this one, which I translated myself. In order to make Habiba's story understandable, I have included some notes on the quasi-mystical vocation of a *shuwafa* (female seer or psychic). Some of these consist of my personal reflections based on visits I made to twenty-two shuwafas during the spring and summer of 1976, which I hope will lead to a future analytical study of sorcery.

2. The seizures are supposed to be due to the possession of an individual by spirits.

3. Since the enactment of the 1957 Family Law, marriage has to be registered with the government. Recitation of the *fatiha* is no longer sufficient.

4. That is, he was not a 'believer' in the djinns, in order to neutralise what was thought to be their fierce, destructive power.

5. Benzoin is supposed to calm the spirits and please them. Under its effect, they release their victim, or, at any rate, loosen their hold on her.

6. Mulay Ibrahim is a saint of the southern part of Morocco, and one of the patron saints of psychics.

7. Sidi Ali is the patron saint of the Hamdushi sect. Like Mulay Ibrahim, he plays an important role in magic practices and initiations, and the activities linked to sorcery. He offers the advantage, for a woman living in Rabat, of being accessible (because nearer) than Mulay Ibrahim, whose shrine is in the environs of Marrakech. Sidi Ali's shrine is near Meknes, 130 kilometres from Rabat.

8. Shaikh al-Kamal is the patron saint of the Issawi sect. The pilgrimage to his shrine at Meknes takes place during the first week of the celebration of the Prophet's birthday.

9. The shrine of Sidi Said is located a few hundred metres from that of Shaikh al-Kamal and is an important centre for rituals and processions.

10. The ban on wearing black during Shaikh al-Kamal's ceremonies is well-known even in circles which are not particularly interested in the world of the spirits.

11. This refers to Lalla Aisha Qandisha, one of the most important female spirits in the supernatural world.

12. In this context, the *muqaddam* is the local figure in charge of initiating the novices and conducting the ritual.

13. The psychics whom I visited in the shantytowns surrounding Rabat-Salé and Casablanca often had a banner on their door to publicise their vocation. Those who lived in the residential quarters of the cities were more discreet. Habiba is an exception: she lives in one of those residential quarters, but has a banner on her door.

14. Lalla Malika is a spirit like Lalla Aisha, but each spirit has its own distinct speciality.

15. She makes her appeal not to the participant who is physically present, but to the spirit that possesses her - in this case, Lalla Aisha Qandisha.

16. That is, chosen as the victim.

17. She 'sees' future events, as well as perceiving beings who do not have a physical existence. The gift of psychic powers is supposed to be one of the compensations enjoyed by those who are possessed by the most powerful spirits and who, as a result, suffer the

most violent seizures.

18. I didn't dare say the word 'doctor'.

19. Each important spirit has its own colour, black being one of the most violent. After the ceremony, the patient will have a particular rapport with that colour.

20. The month of Sha'ban, like Ashura (the tenth day of Muharram), is a period of great importance for those who, in one way or another, deal with the spirits. This is true whether they are people who make use of the assistance of the spirits for earning a living, like Habiba; or whether they are passive victims, like her nieces; or whether they resort to them to solve a specific problem.

21. The whole family was present during the interview, including two teenage friends of her son. Habiba was very dressed up for the occasion, wearing a green veil on her head. The family and all their friends were dark-skinned. In the world of the spirits, having a very dark skin is a great asset. Contact with the south, with deepest Africa, is a dominating factor and point of reference. Let us remember the Senegalese visitor at the beginning of the interview.

22. This clumsy, but necessary question revealed to me that the fundamental distinction between the real and the imaginary has no validity in the world of the spirits. The beings in the dream are as present as the real beings. The borderline between dream and reality, between the imaginary and the real, is meaningless, unimportant in the structure of Habiba's world.

23. The *ladun* is a chunk of lead that serves as a prop during the séance. The psychic gives the 'client' the *ladun* after the latter has deposited the amount of money agreed upon as a fee. The client takes the *ladun* in the palm of the hand, tries to concentrate on it and infuse it with his or her wishes, before returning it to the psychic. The latter then throws it into a brazier where it burns in a spectacular fashion. She then plunges it into a bucket of water, takes it out, and, while concentrating on the twisted shape of the burned metal, details the client's problems and anxieties. The *ladun* is very frequently used among the psychics of Rabat-Salé, the only ones whom I visited during my intensive research in 1974 (twenty-two in four months).

24. She means a 'believer' in the spirits, not in Islam.

25. I had become a little confused about space and time in Habiba's narrative. I was no longer sure which events had taken place in real time and space, and which belonged to the realm of dream or the imaginary, as mentioned in note 28.

26. Habiba agreed to be interviewed in connection with the making of a film. The interview took place while she was being filmed carrying out some typical operations. As I used to come to see her fairly often and as I was having the *ladun* séance done for me (the film producer had handsomely paid for it), Habiba very subtly tried to push me to get more involved and make some specific demands of Lalla Aisha through her, demands that cost some hundreds of *dirhams*. However, as she was afraid of losing me as a 'journalist', she did not insist on this, since she was already earning a lot of money as things were, with the additional possibility of more publicity. Her refusal to either describe or show me her shrine to Lalla Aisha seemed to be just a way of exciting my curiosity and of drawing me into a closer and more costly relationship with Lalla Aisha. In the end I never was able to visit the shrine. During the *ladun* séance, she told me that my emotional life left something to be desired and that I had an emotional block as a result of a previous magical operation.

The prognosis of course involved intervention by the *siyadna,* 'our masters', as will shortly be seen.

27. The word for 'charm' in Arabic is *al-kitaba,* literally 'the writing'. A charm then is a written formula designed to bring about the desired result. The production of charms, like access to Lalla Aisha, brings in thousands of *dirhamu.* The initial séance (three and a half *dirhams)* only identifies the problem and establishes the prognosis. The psychic directs this process by using the *ladun* or the *tabaq.* She asks questions which one must answer, and usually the 'client' gives all the information she needs in order to divine the nature of the problem. Often the rituals which accompany this séance (benzoin fumes, a veil concealing the head of the psychic, loud burping and other strange noises by the psychic) are only devices to put the client in a favourable mood for participation. As for what happened to me, I had to furnish her with the details of my marital status in response to three short questions. The séance ended (as was the case with each of the twenty-two psychics with whom I had a session as observer-participant in 1977) with a diagnosis of total failure on my part: I was a failure in my professional and emotional life, and I had a block, a *thiqaf.* Once the failure was identified and the block duly noted, the séance was at an end. One then either chose to remain stuck in the dead end which the psychic had sketched out as one's life, as I did, or decided to take action, which amounted to asking her to do what was necessary to nullify the famous *thiqaf.* At that moment, one gets involved in the second stage, where the price of the operations is not fixed, where she is going to try to 'do something': write up charms or something which is even more costly and without any limits whatever, planning magic operations around Lalla Aisha and her shrine. These operations can stretch out over months or years and require prompt payments which can vary, according to my research during 1977, from 200 to 2,000 or 3,000 *dirhams.*

28. *Faqih* in this context refers to a guiding spirit.

29. At this point, Habiba's invitation for me to get a little more involved than I had been until then was no longer ambiguous.

22

NEO-ISLAMIC RESPONSES: FATIMA EMPOWERED;

A CONVENANT FOR ISLAMIC RESISTANCE

[Ali Shari'ati (1933-77), *Fatima Fatima Ast,* trans. Marcia Hermansen, in 'Fatimeh as a Role Model in the Works of Ali Shari'ati,' *Women and the Revolution in Iran* ed. Guity Nashat. (Boulder: Westview Press, 1983), p. 93. *The Islamic Covenant,* trans. Reuven Paz (Tel Aviv: The Dayan Center for Middle Eastern and African Studies, Shiloah Institute, September, 1988), pp. 34, 38-40.]

A young woman in full Islamic dress careening down a water slide is one of the images which pointedly raises questions about Islam and gender in the contemporary Middle East. Neo-Islamic movements is a neutral term for a variety of ideological, organizational, social and political manifestations of Islamic responses to the challenges of modernization. In the Arab world, the Society of Muslim Brethren founded in Egypt in 1928 served as a model for religious revivalism and political activism. Associations styled Muslim Brothers were established in Syria, Jordan and among the Palestinians but organizational links to the mother movement in Egypt seem to be tenuous.

In Iran, opposition to the regime of Muhammad Reza Shah Pahlavi between 1953 and 1979 encompassed a variety of ideological streams including left-wing movements, liberals and Islamists. An Islamic tone, however, was dominant in mass demonstrations, with the black *chadur* or proper Islamic dress serving as a symbol of the struggle for women. Many observers have wondered why women in the hundreds of thousands, including educated women, actively supported a movement which appeared to curtail their rights. The answer is complex but one crucial factor was the mobilization of young, educated women and men to a new Islamic vision by Ali Shari'ati.

Ali Shari'ati (1933-77) was a Sorbonne-educated sociologist and Islamic theoretician whose ideas influenced and continue to influence millions of

Muslims not only in Iran but in other countries as well. Twice jailed by the Shah's government, he was allowed, in 1977, to travel to Europe where he died under mysterious circumstances. Shari'ati's popular, activist interpretation of Islam was at one and the same time an important tool to mobilize masses and a threat to any government that does not maintain his high standards of justice and equality. Shari'ati's best-known work in the Western world is *On the Sociology of Islam* (translated by Hamid Algar and published in 1979), a brilliant, original analysis of the struggle between popular forces in Islamic society and corrupt Islamic rulers and leaders.

Shari'ati's works originated as lectures to young people at the College for the Propagation of Islam (during the years 1965-73) and they continue to be disseminated as audio cassettes and simply-printed pamphlets. His use of poetry is in the best Middle Eastern tradition and facilitates oral communication. Shari'ati has re-interpreted the lives of Ali, Husayn, Zaynab and other Shi'i figures as well as Fatima, the daughter of the Prophet.

Shari'ati presents Fatima as a role model for young Muslim women who reject the traditional ways as well as the modern, Western life-style, and are searching for their own path. In his book *Fatima is Fatima,* he presents an alternative reading of the dry facts about Fatima's life. He emphasizes her close relation with her father, her strength in the face of poverty and suffering, her courage in standing up to Abu Bakr and Umar. Fatima is depicted as politically knowledgeable, capable of interpreting the Quran, and socially responsible. Her protest against the materialism which had begun to spread in Islamic society is a clear hint at contemporary problems in Iran at the time of the Shah. The message becomes even clearer when Shari'ati says 'Muhammad had to bear the heavy burden, and Fatimeh had to demonstrate in herself the character of the new, revolutionary values.'

In Shari'ati's view, Fatima is an independent woman who must learn to face adversity, not a passive figure whose powers come from God. She was first taught by the Prophet himself that she is unique but her uniqueness entails a special burden. Muhammad also warned her that being the daughter of the Prophet is not sufficient; she must transform herself with her own powers into the noble Fatima. The individual Muslims must intellectually and spiritually internalize their faith and take their destinies in their hands.

Shari'ati ends the book with a seemingly simple poem that gradually builds up to an emotional identification with Fatima.

What traditional materials and media has Shari'ati used in his appeal to Muslim women? In what ways does his message differ from classical Islamic views? What avenues does Shari'ati's alternative reading of the Islamic primary sources open for contemporary Muslims?

Although neo-Islamic movements in the Arab world have received a great deal of scholarly attention in recent years, their ambiguous and changing positions on women's roles in Islamic society has only begun to be studied. Internal contradictions may be drawn from alternate readings of Islamic sources juxtaposed with varying modern influences and practical exigencies (as illustrated in the excerpts from the Hamas covenant below). Moreover, there is great variety in the theoretical stance of different neo-Islamic idealogues and movements on specific gender issues, and differences between theory and practice. The Ayatullah Khomeini initially opposed the Shah's granting suffrage to women, but after the revolution, women participated in the referendum to establish an Islamic republic and were allowed to vote and be elected to the republic's new institutions. Similarly, members of one Egyptian militant Islamic group expressed relatively egalitarian views on gender but did not accept female members. Conversely, another group was more conservative on the theoretical level but allowed women to join their ranks. Perhaps the group which originated at the Egyptian Military Academy was influenced more by this bastion of male military norms than by an interpretation of women's right to participate in a jihad.

The Hamas is the offspring of Islamic societies similar to the Muslim Brothers which existed in Gaza and the West Bank. From 1967 to 1987, the neo-Islamic forces among the Palestinians devoted most of their efforts to education, recruitment and building a network of social-service organizations, and therefore, did not come into conflict with the Israeli authorities. About one-half year after the beginning of the Palestinian uprising *(intifada)*, the Covenant of the Islamic Resistance Movement - Palestine (Hamas) appeared in Gaza. This document aims to present the platform of the militant branch of the Palestinian Muslim Brothers and a counterpoint to the Palestine Liberation Organization covenant.

The Covenant of the Hamas is a fairly short document consisting of thirty-six articles divided into an introduction, five chapters and a conclusion. The chapter titles are: the movement; the goals; the strategy and the means; attitude towards other Islamic movements, other Palestinian movements, the Arab and Islamic states and their governments, adherents of other religions; historic proof [of our way]. The subject of women is addressed briefly in two sections: one dealing in general with the obligation of fighting in a holy war (jihad); and another relating directly to women's role in the political struggle.

How can the contradictory messages in the two excerpts below from one relatively short document be reconciled? What can we learn about the 'genuinely Islamic' attitude towards gender issues from this seeming contradiction?

In practice, the Hamas' position on women's participation in actual attacks has been ambivalent. In the political organization, a number of female kin of male activists seem to have some role, and a woman's auxiliary has been established. It is in the less political, more social areas, such as education, that large numbers of women participate. In fact, the Hamas as well as other neo-Islamic movements appear to have targeted the education of women as part of their theory and strategy for implementing Islamic gender relations.

Zaynab al-Ghazali (1917-) -'mother of the Muslim Brothers' in Egypt - is the most prominent female Muslim activist. In 1936 (at the age of eighteen), she established the Muslim Women's Association, dedicated primarily to philanthropic and educational work. In the late 1930s, as the association grew, Hasan al-Banna asked Ghazali to merge her organization with his Muslim Brothers, but she refused. In 1948, when the Muslim Brothers were supressed by the Egyptian government, Ghazali pledged her personal loyalty to Banna but maintained the independence of her organization.

After the 1952 revolution, Ghazali's political involvement grew when she and her organization (numbering 119 branches) provided needy Muslim Brotherhood members with food, medical attention and other services. But since the links between the Muslim Women's Association and the Muslim Brothers were secret (and perhaps because of the 'insignificance' of a women's philanthropic society), Ghazali's organization was not harmed even after the Association of Muslim Brothers was declared illegal in 1954. On the contrary, the Muslim Women's Association gained official recognition under the auspices of the Ministry of Social Affairs in 1957.

In the late 1950s, after the attempted assassination of President Abd al-Nasir and the subsequent government crackdown, Ghazali and another member of the Muslim Brothers were given permission by the leader at the time to reorganize the Brothers as an underground movement. At this time, her home became a meeting-place for the younger members. These underground activities led to her arrest in 1965 along with many other members. Sayyid Qutub and another leader were executed for attempting to overthrow the government. Ghazali received a twenty-five year sentence and the Muslim Women's Association was banned.

In 1971, Ghazali was released after serving six years in prison together with a number of her colleagues when the new President Anwar al-Sadat made overtures to leaders of the neo-Islamic movement (as a counterweight to leftists and Nasserists). Since her release, Zaynab al-Ghazali has continued to disseminate her neo-Islamic message as a teacher, lecturer and publicist. She would not call herself a feminist and preaches to women to restrict themselves to domestic, subservient roles but in practice she has subverted her family life to her public activities.

Zaynab al-Ghazali wrote of her six-year imprisonment in a book titled *Ayam min hayati (Days of My Life,* 1982). This work has been analysed by Miriam Cooke in an article in *Die Welt des Islams* (1994). Earlier, Ghazali's views were expressed in a fascinating interview to Valerie J. Hoffman which appeared in *Women and the Family in the Middle East: New Voices of Change* (Austin: University of Texas Press, 1985).

More information on Ali Shari'ati's views on Muslim women's roles may be found in Marcia Hermansen, 'Fatimeh as a Role Model in the Works of Ali Shari'ati,' in *Women and the Revolution in Iran* ed. Guity Nashat (1983); Adele K. Ferdows, 'Women and the Islamic Revolution,' *International Journal of Middle East Studies* 15 (1983); and in particular, Edward H. Thomas, 'Ali Shari'ati on the Role of the Muslim Woman,' *The Muslim World* 81 (1991) a translation of a talk given by Shari'ati at a mourning ceremony in Iran in honour of a couple who were martyrs in the struggle against the Shah, shortly before he left for England. A number of other short pieces by Shari'ati are available in English, and a political biography by Ali Rahnema has been published in 1998.

At least six volumes have appeared on the subject of women in Iran and countless articles have been published on this and related subjects. Aside from the Nashat collection cited above, they are: Eliz Sanasarian, *The Women's Rights Movement in Iran: Mutiny, Appeasement and Repression From 1900 to Khomeini* (New York: Praeger, 1981); Azar Tabari and Nahid Yegan eh, eds *In the Shadow of Islam: The Women's Movement in Iran* (London: Zed, 1982); Farah Azari, ed. *Women of Iran: The Conflict with Fundamentalist Islam* (London: Ithaca, 1983); Fathi Asghar, ed. *Women and the Family in Iran* (Leiden: E. J. Brill, 1985); M. Afkhami, *In the Eye of the Storm: Women in Post-Revolutionary Iran* (1995).

On women in the neo-Islamic movements, see: Saadeddin Ibrahim, 'Anatomy of Egypt's Militant Islamic Groups: A Methodological Note and Preliminary Findings,' *International Journal of Middle East Studies* (1980); and Kimberley Faust, 'Young Women Members of the Islamic Revival Movement in Egypt,' *Muslim World* (1992).

Ali Shari'ati's, 'Fatima is Fatima'

I wanted to say, Fatima is the daughter of noble Khadija.

I saw, this is not Fatima.

I wanted to say, Fatima is the daughter of Muhammad.

I saw, this is not Fatima.

I wanted to say, Fatima is the wife of Ali.

I saw, this is not Fatima.

I wanted to say, Fatima is the mother of Hasan and Husayn.

I saw, this is not Fatima.

I wanted to say, Fatima is the mother of Zaynab.

Still, I saw that this is not Fatima.

No, she is all of these but all of these are not Fatima.

Fatima is Fatima.

The Covenant of the Islamic Resistance Movement - Palestine Filastin (Hamas), 1 Muharram 1409 - 18 August 1988

Chapter Three: The Strategy and the Means

The Homeland and Patriotism from the Point of View of the Movement in Palestine

Article Twelve: From the point of view of the Islamic resistance movement, patriotism *(wataniyya)* is part of religious belief. There is no greater and deeper patriotism than a situation in which the enemy takes over Muslim land. Then, the jihad turns into a religious obligation for every Muslim man or woman. The woman goes out to battle without her husband's permission and the slave without his master's permission.

The Muslim Woman's Role

Article Seventeen: In the campaign for liberation, the Muslim woman has a role which is no less important than that of the man because she creates the men. Her role in the guidance and education of the younger generation is great. Our enemies also understand this and they believe that if they could educate her and lead her away from Islam, they would win the campaign. Therefore, they invest great efforts in the media, films and educational materials through their creations - the Zionist organizations which have different names and forms, such as the Freemasons, the Rotary clubs, espionage networks and so forth, which are all nests of destruction. These Zionist organizations have huge material resources which enable them to penetrate societies in order to fulfil Zionist goals and to spread the ideas which serve the enemy. While these organizations are active, Islam is missing from the field and foreign to its people. The Islamic [activists] must fulfil their role against the plans of these powers so that some day Islam will direct life and liquidate these organizations which are enemies of mankind and Islam.

Article Eighteen: The woman in the home and in the combatant family, whether as mother or as sister, has an important role in caring for the house and raising the children by the moral values and concepts drawn from Islam. She must educate her sons to fulfil religious duties in preparation for the task which awaits them in the jihad holy war for Islam. Thus, the schools for girls must be cultivated so there will be righteous mothers who are conscious of their role in the campaign for liberation.

The woman must have sufficient consciousness and understanding to manage household matters, and to be thrifty within the limits of the difficult circumstances which surround us. She must know that money is like a drop of blood which must flow through the arteries for life to continue.

> Lo! men who surrender unto Allah, and women who surrender, and men
> who believe and women who believe,
> and men who obey and women who obey,
> and men who speak the truth and women who speak the truth, and men
> who persevere (in righteousness) and women who persevere,
> and men who are humble and women who are humble,
> and men who give alms and women who give alms,
> and men who fast and women who fast,
> and men who guard their modesty and women who guard
> (their modesty),
> and men who remember Allah much and women who remember - Allah
> hath prepared for them forgiveness and a vast reward.
>
> [Quran] Al-Ahzab Chapter [33], 35

23

MODERN POETRY: A DAUGHTER OF THE

GALILEE CHALLENGES MEN

[Bint al-Jalil (Najat Aqari), 'Record: I am a Woman,' *Al-Ittihad,]*

Verse was one of the most popular means of expression in Middle Eastern society and culture at least from the time of the pre-Islamic Arabs, possibly because it facilitated oral transmission of information, attitudes and feelings. Couplets were interspersed in genealogical works and battle stories before the advent of Islam. The Quran is composed in a form of Arabic rhymed prose whose very language is regarded as divine work. Arabic poetry, both religious and profane, flourished both in rulers courts and mystic circles. It was interspersed in practically every literary genre (as we have seen), and expression in verse was not restricted to professional poets but was a common practice.

In the twentieth century, poetry has remained a mass art form of the Arabic language; more poets than novelists and short-story writers are published in the Arab countries. Also, since World War II, Arabic poetry has slowly but surely freed itself from the great tradition of classical conventions and evolved new forms. Much of modern Arabic poetry has focused on nationalist and social themes, and this often limits its universal appeal.

Another aspect of Arabic poetry is that it is not the exclusive domain of a cultural elite. Westerners are often surprised to find that 'ordinary' Arabs who do not consider themselves artists nor do they aspire to literary careers write poetry. In this sense, a poem cannot be considered representative of a particular political or social movement but rather a personal voice. Once the poem is published, however, and the forums in which it is published may determine to what extent it is taken up as an expression of popular feelings.

Najat Aqari is a relatively unknown young woman from the Galilee village of Araba who published the poem 'Record: I am a Woman' in the Arabic daily *Al-Ittihad* under the *nom de pen* Bint al-Jalil. Her poem is a play on a very famous poem by the Palestinian poet Mahmud Darwish, 'Identity Card' (first published in 1963). Nabila Ispanioli, a radical feminist from Nazareth, read the poem and was impressed by its powerful simplicity. She translated it into Hebrew, and it was published in *Noga: A Women's Magazine* (1993).

In the poem 'Identity Card,' Darwish placed himself opposite an Israeli government bureaucrat (and by extension Israelis in general) and stated the essential items of his identity. Opening with the words 'Record: I am an Arab,' Darwish goes on to express feelings of humiliation, pride and anger at the situation of the Arabs in Israel. The poem is written in a simple, modern, yet powerful style. The last verse concludes:

Then, record on the first page:

> I do not hate people and I do not attack people,
> But. ... if I am starving, I will eat the flesh of my usurper *(mughtasib)*
> Beware ... Beware ... of my hunger and my wrath!!

The next to the last line caused quite a stir among Jewish Israelis who debated how far the poet had meant to go in his metaphor.

In addition to the traditional village venue, Najat Aqari's poem strikes a familiar note among Arabs most of whom are familiar with Darwish's work. In this sense it reflects the culture of Arab men and women. The poem, however, may also be read as a universal, feminist warning.

In reading the poem, some thought should be given to the following questions. Who does the poet address, when she says 'Record'? Is her poem an extreme feminist statement? Does it speak to non-Arab readers?

Bint al-Jalil, Record: I am a Woman

Record:

I am a strong woman.

Discrimination does not crush me and racism does not weaken me. I demand my equality to you in the name of justice and freedom, Because I have proven myself in every field of life, And when I emerged into the world, I decided to change the basis of my
      education.

Record:

My father, from a patriarchal village not from a modern city,

Teaches me blind obedience before reading and writing.

Do you like my female words?

Then, record on 'the first page'

I do not hate men and do not accuse anyone falsely,

But if I am raped 'I will eat the flesh of the rapist' *(mughtasib)*
'Beware .. beware .. of my uprising and my wrath'!!

Record:
I will live and die strong.

EPILOGUE: WOMEN AND ISLAM IN THE
TWENTY-FIRST CENTURY

Although it has been less than a decade since the first edition of *Women in Islam and the Middle East* was completed, global events have intensified interest in the questions raised in the book. At the same time, Middle Eastern women have been elevated to the top of the region's agenda, and primary sources as well as historical precedents have received more widespread and more innovative attention. The war in Afghanistan, in which the customary local *burqa* functioned as a prominent symbol for the United States-led coalition, transformed Muslim women's dress into an issue of international relations. Middle Eastern governments, NGOs, feminist, liberal and even Islamist groups, as well as the Middle Eastern media, have reacted to Western criticism of the status of women in Islam; but they have also been impelled by internal needs to view women's progress as a corollary of human and economic development and even democracy. Islamic terminology, such as sharia and madrassa, have entered everyday Western parlance in a pejorative sense, while scholars try in vain to explain the manifold meanings of these terms. Concurrently, Islamic feminists and liberals, as well as Islamists, have each interpreted and employed gender norms in the foundation texts of Islam in line with their own views.

The development and dispersal of electronic media and information technology have resulted in a virtual revolution for specialists and the general public interested in Islam and the Middle East and have brought important texts and images to our desktops. The Muslim Students Association of the University of Southern California pioneered the use of the internet to make primary Islamic works accessible, as mentioned earlier. They have now made three English renditions of the Quran available on the web, side by side to facilitate comparative reading of each verse. They have also posted serious English translations of Bukhari's *Sahih* and Malik's legal compendium (*al-Muwatta*) from which readings in this volume have been taken. The multinational, bilingual film biography of the Prophet

Muhammad – *The Message/al-Risala* – is now available on DVD and the reader can view how the late Syrian–American producer and director Moustafa Akkad, after reading the text, rendered the battle of Uhud on the screen. The reason that this proviso is added is that cinema is such a powerful medium that once one has seen a film version, the impact is so great that it overshadows the written text. The Islamic Society of Rutgers has posted the work of thirteenth-century Shafi'i Muslim legal scholar al-Imam al-Nawawi, which may be compared with Malik's eighth-century work and Maghinani's twelfth-century Hanafi guide excerpted in Chapters 7 and 8. This opens to the English-reading audience a chance to examine changes in Islam law over time and across differing legal schools (Maliki, Hanafi, Shafi'i; *The Muwatta of Imam Muhammad al-Shaybani*, one of Abu Hanifa's two leading pupils, has been translated by Mohammed Abdurrahman and Abdus Samad Clarke, but is not available on the web).

Dr Ali Shariati's official website includes texts in English of some of his works on women (including the one in Chapter 22) as well as the Persian original and numerous translations into European and Eastern languages. Multilingual websites such as AlJazeera.net, Islam Online and that of the popular Egyptian television preacher Amr Khaled provide information on gender in the Arab and Islamic worlds as well as insights into the dissemination of varied gender messages via new media. The increasingly sophisticated search engines facilitate reaching these and other websites dealing with Islam, women and the Middle East. Some guidance, however, is necessary, since a search for 'Women in Islam' will bring up more than 40 million sites. The worldwide web has become an important vehicle through which contemporary Muslims can present their views of fundamental Islamic issues whether liberal, Islamist or Islamic feminist. As such, the web provides access not only to secondary material but, as we have seen, to primary sources as well. These should be read as critically as the primary sources included in this volume and, as far as possible, placed in context. Some studies of the implications for Middle Eastern women of the revolutions brought about by the electronic media are Fatema Mernissi's 'The Satellite, the Prince, and Scheherazade: The Rise of Women as Communicators in Digital Islam', http://www.tbsjournal.com/mernissi.htm and Deborah L. Wheeler's 'Blessings and Curses: Women and the Internet Revolution in the Arab World', in Naomi Sakr (ed.) *Women and Media in the Middle East: Power Through Self-Expression* (London: I.B.Tauris, 2004), pp. 138–61.

Although Islamic feminism was already presented and defined in the first edition of this book, there is no doubt that this ideological and practical movement has greatly expanded in the last decade and generated a debate about its efficacy.[1] The Quranic verses in the first chapter are still central to Islamic feminists' efforts to read the Quran in the most liberal fashion possible. Some critics doubt the sincerity of some of the advocates of Islamic feminism, arguing that their change of heart is a ploy to appeal to the masses and counter the popular influence of Islamist movements. Others argue that attempts to base feminism on any religious beliefs are bound to fail. Still others claim that Islamic feminism is a lost cause and its influence is limited. The emergence of what I would term 'second generation Islamic feminism' – namely Islamic feminists who no longer need to return to the primary sources but rather can rely on the pioneering work of the first generation – is another interesting development.[2] Also, there are signs that Sufi Islamic mysticism may be a basis for Islamic feminism, based, I would argue, on the beliefs of primordial Sufis whose search for gnosis is gender blind.[3] True, to the extent that Sufism becomes institutionalized, women may defer to male shaykhs and teachers. But the use of Sufism as a platform for Islamic feminism is still a promising avenue for exploration. Adding excerpts to this reader reflecting Sufi gender attitudes would link up nicely with the selections on 'Sufi hagiography: Devout Women' and 'The Story of a Contemporary Woman Mystic' that already allude to women's unusual role in the world of Islamic mysticism.

The analytic term gender has firmly entered popular and scholarly language although not all who use it are sufficiently aware of the meaning of the concept. Gender is not merely a politically correct synonym for women, but rather an analytical concept, like class or race, that refers to the socially constructed relations between women and men.[4] As a social construct, gender is a function of time and space. In other words, relations between women and men differ over time, and studies of women and gender by Middle Eastern historians during discrete time periods (referred to below) flesh out the somewhat flattened image that may emerge from this reader. Also, the changing definition of gender relations in different venues is extremely relevant to understanding Middle Eastern social reality. In the United States, for some time, only women shopped for food and 'real men' proudly declared that they did not even know their way around the supermarket. In the Middle East, on the other hand, men did the food shopping. Does this mean that Middle Eastern women lived with more liberated men? Certainly not. The 'patriarchal bargain', as Deniz Kendiyoti has dubbed it,[5] differs in the USA and the Middle East. Women in the USA agreed to be in charge of the food shopping – often receiving the 'food money' in cash – because they knew that by thrifty shopping they could put some funds aside in the cookie jar for use at their own discretion. In the Middle East, men believed that by not letting their respectable women shop in the market, they would protect their reputation. Moreover, by doing the shopping themselves they maintained control of the money and dictated the menu. How did Middle Eastern women deal with this patriarchal bargain? The answer to that has been passed down from mother to daughter over time, much like the 'cookie jar' manoeuvre.

In the last decade an important development in the study of women and Islam in the Middle East has been the bringing to light of differing gender relations in various areas of life, fine-tuning the general extremes of empowered or victimized women. This multiplicity was addressed in the first edition, though perhaps not explicitly enough. Rachel Simon, for example, has shown that although Jewish women in nineteenth and twentieth-century Libya began working outside their homes and as a result acquired education, their status within the family and the community remained unchanged.[6] Similarly, classical Muslim scholars, most of whom were men, accepted the legitimacy of women as transmitters of *hadith* traditions, but the legal scholars were wary of women's ability to bear witness in court cases.[7] In an in-depth and careful study, Margaret Meriwether has demonstrated how differently economic changes in nineteenth-century Syria affected upper-class women, property owners, lower-class urban women and rural women in the city of Aleppo and its environs.[8] The result of the focus on differing, specific areas of life is the revision of the eternal, loaded question: is the status of women in Islam and the Middle East lower than in the (Christian) West? The question raised today is how and in what areas does women's status in Islam and the Middle East differ from other cultures? What are the causes of these differences? What can be learnt about Middle Eastern societies and cultures over the centuries by examining different aspects of gender relations? How can unique Middle Eastern gender relations contribute to the development of general theories on gender?

An issue that began to emerge from the readings in this volume but was not fully articulated is gendered space in Middle Eastern societies and cultures. The separation of women and men has been regarded as a defining factor of Middle Eastern societies. A growing body of evidence, however, prescribes a more sophisticated analysis of this social construct. Secondary and primary sources in this volume show that some women played a part in preserving the text of the Quran, as well as the sayings of the Prophet

Muhammad (among the fundamental texts of the Islamic religion), and transmitting it to prominent men who were not necessarily their kin, seemingly invading male scholarly space and mingling with men. Women participated in battles in the tribal and urban milieu in various supporting roles, and in dire circumstances, even as combatants. When institutionalized armies became dominant, as in the Umayyad period, however, a woman sending her man off to battle (as in Chapter 5) – a more common gender image – replaced the woman involved in the fray. Women also went out into the public sphere to attend performances of the *ta'ziye* passion plays, bringing their children along as well. Not surprisingly, women surrounding powerful men in the Middle East as elsewhere often played a crucial 'behind the scenes' role in political affairs, particularly succession, as related in the chronicles of the Abbasid period. Nizam al-Mulk's rules for kings in Chapter 10 reflect the fear that this involvement of women in higher politics was a violation of the male domain of politics. In the writings of male legists and theoreticians, tensions between the legitimacy of women's transmission of information on the one hand, and the desire to protect their privacy as well as prevent situations in which men would be subordinate to women on the other, created a variety of problems for gendered space, which are highlighted in Chapters 7, 8 and 9. Devout women were reported as mingling with men without any negative implications both in the classical period of Islamic mysticism and in the contemporary Middle East (Chapters 11 and 21). Learned women met male teachers and students; women appeared in court over domestic problems, economic transactions and issues connected with *waqf* endowments. Among the lower classes, women lined up in public to receive meals from public kitchens. Poor Juha had to endure his wife going out to visit neighbours in the evening and attending talks by popular preachers, and was a battered husband at that. Aisha the carpenter's daughter managed to outwit the prince even when he tried to incarcerate her after their marriage. All this anecdotal information and other similar reports do not seem to fit the image of the traditional secluded Middle Eastern woman.

The documented scope of women's public social and economic activities has raised the question of the meaning of measures taken to guard women's privacy or modesty in public, such as wearing the *hijab* and a face veil, and being accompanied by a male family member. Also, formal or informal division of public space by gender was maintained, but it is unclear how these conventions were upheld. Certain areas indoors (household domains, *hammam* public bathhouses) and outside (terraces or riverbeds where laundry was done) were defined as women's space, either permanently or at specified times. Nevertheless, there is evidence of men spying on women washing or engaged in other mundane activities.[9] The voyeuristic conceit holds that women were naive and unaware, believing they were sheltered from men's view. It is highly unlikely that women were not equally aware that gendered boundaries of space could be violated, and made use of this knowledge for their own purposes. Moreover, gendered space may also be literary and representational, whether in the voices and gazes of female and male writers and visual artists or in symbols and metaphors. The human body has also been revealed as a field of gendered space.

Some scholars have attempted to move from describing specific cases to proposing middle range theories that may elucidate Middle Eastern gender relations. Nikki Keddie, for example, has advanced the hypothesis that women were better off in tribal societies or societies ruled by elites of nomadic origin.[10] Leila Ahmed proposed a thesis that marginal and popular socio-religious groups emphasized an ethical, egalitarian gender message, while the political, religious and legal establishment (in the Abbasid period) enforced a pragmatic, hierarchical approach of which the influence is evident to this day.[11] Similarly, I have suggested that the growing bureaucratization of the Islamic scholarly establishment caused the rise in the prestige of the holders of tenured positions in higher education – positions that women did not hold – at the expense of prominent female and male scholars who functioned in informal frameworks.[12] In contrast to Keddie's view that more limitations are imposed on women in periods of economic scarcity, Miriam Hoexter concluded that women entered the property rental market in the city of Algiers in the early nineteenth century because of the economic depression, when a demographic decline was accompanied by a rise in the quantity of properties for rent.[13]

Participants in an international conference on Gendered Space in Middle Eastern Societies and Cultures (2002) linked the degree of segregation of women and men to time, place and a variety of other circumstances.[14] Ayesha ar-Rifa'i suggested that the issue is related to historical circumstances along the lines of Leila Ahmed's thesis – the advent of Islam was revolutionary and carried an egalitarian message that was later corrupted, a view that many Islamic feminists and some experts on Islam and Middle Eastern history supported. Rachel Simon holds that the ecological setting – town vs. village, centre vs. periphery – may be the key. Ruth Kark and Roy Fischel hypothesize an association in Ottoman and mandatory Palestine between women's land and property ownership and their ethnic and religious affiliation. Khuloud Dajani viewed education as the key to women's agency (crossing ethnic and religious boundaries) and has massive contemporary quantitative data to support this assertion. Yet, Laila Abed Rabho found that formal education was not a necessary variable to determine whether a Muslim woman in a dysfunctional marriage would have the information and courage necessary to appeal to the authorities. Perhaps, aside from formal education, which can be measured quantitatively, women's informal knowledge, transmitted orally, is still important. Brenda Geiger studied Arab and Mizrahi women who resisted abuse – to the point of criminality – in societies in which the majority of Israeli men and many women as well still believe that women's abuse should be suffered silently at best or is the woman's fault at worst. What gave these abused women the strength to go to such lengths – unusual in all patriarchal societies – to challenge the system?

As Judith Tucker suggested in her important book on *Women in Nineteenth Century Egypt* (cited in the Introduction), perhaps a class dimension should be added. She demonstrated that economic necessity forced lower-class women to challenge gendered space to support themselves and their children, even at the price of social opprobrium. To Tucker's work may be added the notion that upper-class women (and men perhaps) may have regarded separation from the public and concealing clothing as a perquisite of their status, and could afford this luxury. Also, upper-class women and men had other ways of dominating public space, such as establishing large foundations and buildings that often led to whole neighbourhoods being named after them. The Khasseki Sultan complex in Jerusalem, described in the endowment deed of the favourite concubine (and later wife) of Suleyman Kanuni the Magnificent, portrayed in Chapter 14, is an example. The middle strata would inevitably wish to copy the ruling class and might even have applied the rules of gendered space more stringently to emphasize their distance from the masses, but they might also have been forced to compromise on social norms in order to maintain their economic status.

The analysis of specific instances of gendered space by experts from various fields of study raised a variety of conclusions about the physical and symbolic separation of women and men. Some reinforced the common view that women were relegated to a separate sphere and their interaction with men was severely limited, although this division could produce remarkable Middle Eastern women's social frameworks and cultural productivity. Others emphasized the entry of women into areas considered male domains whether by subtle measures such as negotiation or by more direct means of subversion and outright challenging. The overall view that emerges of Middle Eastern women is as active members of society and culture engaged in what one author terms 'cooperative conflict' with the boundaries of gendered space.

Mainstreaming the study of Middle Eastern gender has been viewed with suspicion by those who fear that including one class on 'women', in general courses or books on the Middle East and Islam, will undercut the development of the field of Middle Eastern gender studies. My own aim (which I have explicated elsewhere) is to take Middle Eastern gender studies out of the harem and prove that no subject in the field, no matter how 'masculine', can be truly understood without gender analysis. Perhaps the best example is the study of military strategy and tactics – certainly a male-dominated field – through gender lenses. I have argued that by examining the role of women and other non-combatants in violent conflicts – from the Prophet Muhammad's alternate proposals to the Muslims to fight the pagans in the city of Medina or on the battlefield of Uhud (Chapter 2), to the relative popularity and institutionalization of the Palestinian intifadas – sheds light on the overall plans and stratagem of battle.[15] It is for this reason that most of the selections in this reader have been taken from existing English translations. The readers can turn from the excerpt to the entire work in order to place the role of women in a broader context.

The expansion of the role of the state into increasing areas of society during the twentieth-century has also brought state feminism to the fore in the Middle East. State feminism may be defined as the adoption by the ruling elite – frequently authoritarian rulers – of a policy of promoting women's progress for their own purposes, along the lines of their own agenda and most importantly, to the exclusion of autonomous feminist movements. State feminism in the Middle East has been motivated most frequently by nationalist aims to advance the nation, but has also been part of socialist and even Islamist government policies. The issue of state feminism has become more topical as various Arab governments have attempted recently to improve the internationally perceived status of women in their countries by government fiat. In an attempt to evaluate the prospects of state feminism, it would be valuable to read an original programmatic statement or visual representation of Turkish Kemalist feminism from the 1930s as well as recent articles in the Arab media (Al-Jazeera Net in English provides a good source) on Saudi government or Palestinian National Authority attempts to improve the situation of women. These documents frequently reveal the problematic of state feminism. A comparison of Turkey and Iran reveals the chasm between the use of state pressure and state force for change of gender norms through various regimes. Gender analysis of Middle Eastern governmental websites is an excellent and convenient method for examining the overall interest of state decision-makers in women's issues and the context in which women's advancement is viewed. (These may also be compared with online statistics on indicators of women's actual advancement such as education and political participation.)

The study of Islamic or Middle Eastern sexualities was a natural outcome of similar developments in the Western world. Well-meaning researchers of homosexuality and homoeroticism aimed to expand the study of sexualities to non-Western societies including the Middle East.[16] These initiatives were met with sharp criticism from researchers and Middle Easterners alike who felt that traditional Western stereotypes about the 'depraved' sexuality of the Middle East were resurfacing. Clearly, the seriousness of studies of sexualities in Islam and the Middle East will determine the contribution this sensitive yet crucial line of enquiry will make to understanding gender complexities in the region. While several selections in this volume relate to female and male sexuality, it would be valuable both to hear female voices on these subjects and have a selection or two on lesbianism, a subject that has not yet been studied properly.

The impact of globalization on Muslim and Middle Eastern women is frequently regarded as a contemporary issue. In fact, the Middle East from the time of prehistoric woman and man has been a crossroads for tribes and military forces, bringing with them 'global' influences. The custom of female circumcision seems to have travelled east and north from Africa to the Arabian peninsula in pre-Islamic times and migrated with the Sinai bedouin to Palestine and perhaps parts of what is today Israel, Palestine, Jordan and Syria. India in the East has been the source of new religious movements, whether mystic or reformist, that have influenced the lives of women and men in the Middle East. Muslim pilgrims, scholars, students and merchants – women and men – travelled from one end of the Muslim world to the other bringing with them ideas and customs, at least since the Middle Ages. Perhaps the best pre-modern example of this phenomenon as it effected everyday life was the changes of dress of women and men based on fashions that were brought from North, South, East and West. Yedida Kalfon Stillman pioneered the study of this phenomenon,[17] but as the 1908 lecture of Bahithat al-Badiya (Chapter 19) demonstrates, even in the early twentieth century Cairene upper and middle-class women were adopting fashions from the women of Istanbul, who most likely took them from French fashions of the time.

Similarly, the development of the public sphere (sometimes called civil society) has until recently been regarded as a modern Western phenomenon that accompanied liberalization. A collaboration of leading scholars in the fields of sociology, Islam and Middle Eastern history has produced a volume of analytical studies that demonstrate empirically the existence of diverse and changing types of public spheres in pre-modern Middle Eastern societies and polities – albeit not the formal intermediate structures that developed in western Europe and were precursors to liberalism – that suggest new understandings of the role of religion in society and politics.[18] Common wisdom notwithstanding, Muslim women participated in public spheres in the pre-modern Middle East and continue to do so. Women taking part in various Islamic public rituals and communal religious duties that have social and even political ramifications – such as the mosque and the pilgrimage – are worthy of further examination. Similarly, women have been full or partial legal individuals in the Islamic courts whether in giving evidence or in matters of inheritance, representation and contracts. Women's participation in the political contract (*bay'a*) is cited in classical Islamic sources from the time of the Prophet, although the transformation of the early Islamic community into an institutionalized state and empire seems to have decreased women's role in the polity. Women's position in warrior societies is, as we have seen, a subject that certainly deserves further thought. Women's involvement in guilds or other socio-economic frameworks in the Middle East has been documented, but it is unclear to what extent these were gender specific guilds (professional singers, dancers, prostitutes and perhaps others).[19] The central government's view of women as members of taxable households rather than individual taxable subjects is an excellent indicator of the degree to which women are regarded as fully-fledged members of the polity. Moving from specific dimensions of the public sphere, it may be possible to evaluate the variables that impinge on the extent of female participation in public life, such as the ecological setting (nomadic, rural, urban), political organization, general religio-political climate and discrete events threatening the socio-political order, economic structure and external cultural influences. Some contemporary Islamic and Middle Eastern feminists link the development of civil society to the emergence of autonomous women's organizations, following the maxim that 'women's rights are human rights'.

Elizabeth Fernea has been a pioneer in the study of children in the modern Middle East, as she was in the study of women earlier.[20] With perfect hindsight, what she recognized is clear – childhood and adolescence are crucial corollaries of gender relations in Middle Eastern societies. The importance of the representation of gendered childhood is already evident in the memoirs of Halide Edib in Chapter 18. The plethora of autobiographies written by Middle Eastern women and men (many of which have been translated into English) may be juxtaposed with Middle Eastern cinematic renditions of childhood as well as studies of formal and informal education in the region. Pre-modern Islamic attitudes toward children and childhood have begun to be studied[21] and are worthy of further attention based on massive textual and extant visual material.

In this book I use the term medieval, as is customary for a long and varied period of Islamic history that has been defined by European chronology. Subsequently, when I had a chance to work with colleagues who specialize in Christian and Jewish women in the European Middle Ages, I began to question the relevance of European periodization to Islamic history. Today, I would suggest a breakdown of the history of the Islamic Middle East into five periods: the formative phase of Islam from the time of the Prophet to the height of the Abbasid dynasty; the classical era of the eight and ninth centuries when Islamic sacred history, law, general history from an Islamic viewpoint and political structures were crystallized; the middle ages – a period of political and social fragmentation following the classical Abbasid age; the rise of the great Islamic empires in the sixteenth century from North Africa, through the Middle East and Persia to India; and finally the modern period. Women's history and gender in the Islamic Middle Ages is the most difficult to study because political fragmentation influenced the generation of written materials. The communality of medieval Islamic scholars, their frequent travels and their common language of Arabic, however, undoubtedly created a certain uniformity of gender prescriptions if not practice. Marghinani's legal guide (Chapter 8) and Ghazali's 'Book on Etiquette of Marriage' (Chapter 15) are probably good examples of Islamic medieval works with widespread influence on gender regulations in their own time and until today.

Among the primary sources that would enrich this volume is a selection from W. M. Thackston Jr, translated as *The Tales of the Prophets of al-Kisa'i*, either on Eve, the primordial mother of humankind in the Quran as well as Islamic tradition, or the story of Joseph, a very popular narrative that appears in the Quran and has captured the imagination of Muslims through the ages. Both these narratives as they appear in the popular collection of

Kisa'i and other influential sources have been revealed as misogynist reworking of the Quranic source in the study by Jane I. Smith and Yvonne Y. Haddad cited in Chapter 10 and in Merguerian, Gayane Karen and Afsaneh Najmabadi, 'Zulaykha and Yusuf: Whose "Best Story"?', *International Journal of Middle East Studies,* 29 (1997), pp. 485–508.

Among the Islamic legal sources that are beginning to be studied for women's studies are the collections of judgments or *fatwas* handed down by prominent Muslim jurists. Interestingly, although the dominant opinion among Muslim authorities follows Mawardi (Chapter 9) that women may not be judges, women were recognized as capable of handing down *fatwas*, although only four women in all Islamic history have achieved the title of jurisconsult (*muftiyya*).[22] Judith Tucker's groundbreaking work *In the House of the Law: Gender and Islamic Law in Ottoman Syria and Palestine* (1998) demonstrated the new insights on family life that could be elicited from the study of legal opinions of three prominent eighteenth-century jurisconsults. A single opinion by a famous eighteenth-century Palestinian *mufti* permitted a woman to kill an abusive ex-husband who was still attacking his ex-wife. The strict, Hanbali fourteenth-century jurisconsult Ibn Taymiyya, who is a guiding light to contemporary Islamists on political issues, produced a very large number of legal opinions on women that are published in numerous editions to this day. Among the most interesting for their misogynist conclusions are his opinions on female circumcision (*khitan al-mar'a*), which may be placed in context by reference to Jonathan Berkey's 'Circumcision Circumscribed: Female Excision and Cultural Accommodation in the Medieval Near East', *International Journal of Middle East Studies* (1996). Ibn Taymiyya also wrote an illuminating *fatwa* that dealt with the relative importance of a woman's fasting and prayer when they come in conflict with her sexual obligations to her husband. This issue has financial ramifications for the wife, for if she is declared a rebellious wife (see Quranic verse in Chapter 1) for refusing to meet her husband's sexual demands, under Islamic law she will lose the material support that the husband is required to provide her. Modern legal opinions, such as Muhammad Abduh's view that the Quran actually does not permit polygamy (mentioned in Chapter 19), are also worthy of further examination. Today, interactive sessions on the internet, allow Muslims to request legal opinions from Muslim scholars on websites with separate sessions devoted specifically to women's issues and family problems.

The growing public interest in women in Islam and the Middle East has reinforced stereotypes via political statements, the press and cyber legends.

On the other hand, there is an increasing thirst for reliable information on the complexities of the theoretical and practical aspects of women's lives in Islamic societies and the Middle East. The sources excerpted in this reader have become, if anything, even more relevant to current affairs.

Select References

One aspect of the boom in the study of women in Islam and the Middle East is the outpouring of material on the subject – often also available in digital media. The following review, therefore, aims to present some general reference works on women in Islam and the Middle East and update the original references provided after each selection. A survey of all the works that have appeared on the subject in the last decade would require a separate project.

One of the signs of the flowering of learning on women in Islam and the Middle East is the appearance of a high-quality *Encyclopaedia of Women and Islamic Cultures* (*EWIC*) in four hefty volumes edited by Suad Joseph along with a team of some of the top scholars in the field. This reference work deals with sources, methodologies and paradigms in the study of Islam from its advent to the present that are relevant to the study of women, as well as a wide range of subjects from law and politics to sexuality and family life. In addition, two scholarly journals have appeared dedicated to publishing new studies on women in the Middle East – *Hawwa: Journal of Women in the Middle East and the Islamic World* and *The Journal of Middle East Women's Studies*.

Among the foundations of Islam, the focus of Muslims as well as non-Muslims has naturally been on the Quran as a source for Islamic gender norms. The editor of the *Encyclopaedia of the Quran* deemed this subject important enough to devote an entry to 'Women and the Quran'. Barbara F. Stowasser has made an important contribution to understanding *Women in the Quran* (1994) by expanding from the text deemed by Muslims to be the revealed word of Allah to the interpretation of the text by fallible, human, male scholars. Her article 'The Hijab: How a Curtain Became an Institution and a Cultural Symbol?' in A. Afsaruddin and A. H. Mathias Zahniser (eds) *Humanism, Culture and Language in the Near East* (1997) is a welcome addition to the references cited in Chapter 1. Stories in the Quran embody gender role models for believers, but as several experts have shown, the messages of the Quranic narratives have frequently been subverted by Muslim male classical scholars. Eve's role in the garden has been reinterpreted to make her culpable for the sins of Adam and all mankind, and the story of Joseph has been reworked as well, as we have seen above. Similarly, the development of the image of Mary, mother of Jesus, has been developed in J. D. McAuliffe, 'Chosen of All Women: Mary and Fatima in Qur'anic Exegesis', in *Islamochristiana* (1981) and J. I. Smith and Y. Y. Haddad, 'The Virgin Mary in Islamic Tradition and Commentary', in *The Muslim World* (1989). The legal material in the Quran – so important for matters of marriage, illicit sexual relations, divorce, inheritance and other gender issues – had to be developed by Muslim jurists into the classical Sharia using other sources and various methodologies. A relative who arranges the nuptials in the name of the bride, for example, is referred to in the Quran (2: 237), but the technical term *wal* (often translated guardian) and its precise legal definition were later derived from traditions of the Prophet. The laws of inheritance, on the other hand, are specified precisely and in great detail, leaving little room for interpretation (Q 4: 7–18, 175). The inheritance rules provide women with a crucial source of income, even if less than for men who have a similar relationship to the deceased.

Modern versions of the biography of the Prophet Muhammad have become the subject of my own special interest in recent years. Among the cases I have studied are an illustrated version by a French Orientalist painter who converted to Islam; a drama by the foremost Egyptian playwright; an allegory by Nobel laureate Naguib Mahfouz; a series of popular essays by an Egyptian female scholar and novelist; lectures by the founder of the Syrian Muslim Brotherhood; Arab films from the 1950s through the 1970s; and an Algerian Islamic feminist.[23]

The *hadith* sayings of the Prophet remain a difficult subject to study except for specific subjects. One of the topics selected in Chapter 3 is women's participation in public prayer. Since then, Asma Sayeed has demonstrated that the majority of jurists concluded that women should avoid mosques despite the numerous *hadith*s that indicate that they did attend the mosque at the time of the Prophet. Architectural evidence as well as illustrations and paintings support the view that women attended mosques despite the majority of legal opinions. Moreover, the queries to jurisconsults throughout Islamic history attest to women's attendance at the mosque.[24] Classical Islamic illuminations, mosque architecture and modern illustrations document a variety of arrangements for women to attend the communal prayer.[25] Anecdotal contemporary information suggests that customs still vary from place to place.

Islamic law has been the focus of much scholarly attention in recent years.

Not surprisingly, two doctoral dissertations have been devoted to the evolution of the Islamic rules of ritual priority.[26] Also, the selection on whether women may be judges from Abu al-Hasan al-Mawardi's *al-Ahkam as-Sultaniyyah* has now been translated into English by Asadullah Yates. An outpouring of studies based on Ottoman Islamic court records have dealt with gender issues, aside from the economic transactions documented in Chapter 13. One of the most outstanding works in this field is Leslie Peirce's *Morality Tales: Law and Gender in the Ottoman Court of Aintab* (2003).

For the long period dubbed 'medieval' in this book, a number of important works should be added to those referred to a decade ago. The representation of outstanding women, which I have dealt with in the context of biographical collections, has been addressed in depth in Hilary Kilpatrick, 'Some Late 'Abbasid and Mamluk Books about Women: A Literary Historical Approach', *Arabica*, 42 (1995), pp. 56–78. The study of devout women has been greatly enriched by Rkia E. Cornell's unearthing and translation into English of a crucial volume on *Early Sufi Women: Dhikr an-niswa al-muta'abbidat as sufiyyat* by Abu 'Abd ar-Rahman as-Sulami (1999). More information on traditional female professions may be found in Maya Shatzmiller, 'Women's Labour', in *Labour in the Medieval Islamic World* (1994). Shlomo Dov Goitein's *A Mediterranean Society* was based on Jewish documents, but he argues that in economic affairs Jewish and Muslim women did not differ much. Valuable information may therefore be elicited from his sections on 'Professions of Women' (1: 127–30); 'Female brokers' (1: 161); and 'Women in economic life' 3 (1978) pp. 324–32, 346–52. Eva Baer, 'Muslim Teaching Institutions and their Visual Reflections: The Kuttab', in *Der Islam*, 78 (2001) pp. 73–102 contains unique visual evidence of girls and boys attending traditional primary schools together, albeit separated in the classroom by gender. Baer's illustrations verify that Halide Edib's description in Chapter 18 was not specific to nineteenth-century Istanbul.

The bulk of new research on women in Islam and the Middle East has been devoted to the long twentieth century – from the innovations in attitudes toward women's status in society to concrete changes in education, the advent of women's journals, first public lectures by women, dress and legal reforms. Changes in women's education have been documented quantitatively and qualitatively. Ottoman data on women's education (Chapter 17) demonstrate that new women's education preceded the First World War and the colonial regimes that followed. Ela Greenberg, has shown that Islamic institutions provided new types of education for Muslim girls that were not that different from the missionary and state schools. ('Educating Muslim Girls in Mandatory Jerusalem', *International Journal of Middle East Studies*, 36 (2004) pp. 1–19). The dilemmas that rapid development of state education for girls and women have in Saudi Arabia have been analysed by Eleanor Doumato in the volume she edited with Marsha Pripstein Posusney, *Women and Globalization in the Arab Middle East* (2003). Current trends in women's education in the Middle East in comparison with other regions of the world may be seen in statistics collected by the UN and posted on websites: http://hdr.undp.org/reports/global/2004/pdf/hdr04_HDI.pdf Table 26 'Gender Inequality in Education'.

Since the first publication of this book, there has been an outpouring of Middle Eastern women's autobiographies appearing in English and this genre has become a subject of study and analysis. Since many of the writers of memoirs are literati as well, it is often difficult to draw the line between self-invention and biographical fiction. Moreover, women film makers also write screenplays and direct films that are based to one degree or another on their own life experience. Moufida Tlatli's film *Silences of the Palace* (Tunisia, France, 1994) provides a fascinating insight into the lives of lower-class domestic servants at the time of Tunisia's independence in 1956. Although the director clearly aimed to make a feminist statement about the sexual victimization of lower-class women and the closed atmosphere of the grand palaces, she also reveals the camaraderie among working women and the ways in which the outer world does in fact penetrate the walls of seclusion.

Women and gender in Iran has been the subject of a virtual flood of scholarly books and articles, and only a few can be cited here.[27] Two noteworthy books on Iranian women during the twentieth century are Parvin Paidar, *Women and the Political Process in Twentieth-Century Iran* (1997) and Cameron Michael Amin, *The Making of the Modern Iranian Woman: Gender, State Policy, and Popular Culture, 1865–1946* (2002). A brilliant, pioneering work with ramifications far beyond the study of Iran is Afsaneh Najmabadi's *Women with Mustaches and Men without Beards: Gender and Sexual Anxieties of Iranian Modernity* (2005).

The subject of women and gender in Iraq, on the other hand, has been neglected. Because of this, Noga Efrati's recent gender studies of twentieth-century Iraqi history are a unique contribution. Efrati casts a new light on the early Middle Eastern women's liberation movement in 'The Other "Awakening" in Iraq: The Women's Movement in the First Half of the Twentieth Century', *British Journal of Middle Eastern Studies*, 31 (2004) pp. 153–73. She also studies contemporary gender developments in Iraq against the background of the position of women during the monarchical period when Iraq was in the British sphere of influence, and socialist Baathi Iraq.

Nawal El Saadawi continues to promote her independent, radical, feminist agenda through her actions, writings and most recently her website. Government threats against her have elicited worldwide support through the powerful new tool of the e-petition. Similarly, an attempt by Egyptian Islamists to force her husband to divorce her for her alleged blasphemy failed. Her latest high-profile effort was to run as a candidate for president against the incumbent Husni Mubarak. In Afghanistan, radical feminists have been active against the US occupation and to further women's issues using a multilingual website http://rawa.org/. Similarly, Iraqi radical feminists have re-emerged after exile abroad (www.iraqiwomenleague.org) and new groups have sought expression through the web (see, for example, http://www.equalityiniraq.com/english.htm). Noga Efrati, in 'Negotiating Rights in Iraq: Women and the Personal Status Law', *Middle East Journal*, has placed the efforts of Iraqi women rights activists of various political persuasions against recent attempts to abolish the Iraqi Personal Status Law, in force since 1959, in the historical context of women's participation in shaping the law over time.

Life stories of Middle Eastern women (as in Chapter 21) continue to be an important anthropological, sociological and even political tool to elicit narratives that have not been recorded in other manners. Rosemary Sayigh's 'Palestinian Camp Women as Tellers of History', *Journal of Palestine Studies*, 27 (1998), based on open interviews with Palestinian women in refugee camps in Lebanon, contains interesting insights into the important issue of women's roles in time of war. Assia Djebar used the cinematic medium to project women's narratives of the Algerian struggle for liberation from French colonial rule in *La nouba des Femmes de Mont Chenoua* (Algeria, 1977). The recollections of mountain women provide a good counterpoint to the more famous Algerian women fighters depicted in *The Battle of Algiers* (Italy, Algeria, 1965). In the film, Djebar suggests that elderly women become the keepers of 'tribal' historical memory that spans more than a century and that they pass it on to the youngsters, alluding to an endless chain of oral history. Annelies Moors has taken women's narratives one step further by combining open interviews with written documentation to analyse *Property and Islam: Palestinian Experiences, 1920–1990* (1995).

Experts have adopted the North African term Islamists for what I referred to as the neo-Islamic movements that are still widely called fundamentalist, and recently have elicited even harsher rhetoric. The influence of Ali

Shariati's messages on the role of women in Islam and in the Islamic revolutionary struggle have been perpetuated and disseminated in various Islamic languages as may be seen in the impressive website dedicated to his heritage. A challenging book on Iranian women in the revolutionary movement is Haideh Moghissi, *Populism and Feminism in Iran: Women's Struggle in a Male-Defined Revolutionary Movement* (1996). Events in Iran, often reflected in women's space, are in a constant state of flux. Nevertheless, a study that may assist in understanding current events is Ziba Mir-Hosseini, *Islam and Gender: The Religious Debate in Contemporary Iran* (1999).

The influence of Islamist movements in Syria seems to have increased as the Ba'th regime appears to be weakening. Suzanne Stiver Lie and Karl Vogt's 'Islamization in Syria: Gender, Education and Ideology', *Journal of South Asian and Middle Eastern Studies* (2003) sheds light on an important and neglected area. My work on the founder of the Syrian Muslim Brotherhood, Mustafa al-Siba'i (*Middle Eastern Studies*, 2006), showed how much emphasis early Islamist movements placed on women's active role in the missionary endeavour to bring society to 'true' Islam. Similarly, the functions fulfilled by the women of Hamas have been reviewed in Kai Adler's article subtitled 'Islam Protects Us' (*Qantara*, 2006) and in Victoria Firmo-Fontan's 'Power, NGOs and Lebanese Television: A Case Study of Al-Manar TV and the Hezbollah Women's Association', in Naomi Sakr (ed.) *Women and Media in the Middle East: Power through Self-Expression* (2004).

This volume concluded with a modern poem by a 'daughter of the Galilee' writing under a pseudonym. Women have composed Arabic poetry from before the advent of Islam, most notably the elegies of al-Khansa'. In classical Islamic works, sacred and profane verse ascribed to women was recorded (as we have seen in Chapter 2) although their words were mediated by men who compiled the collections in which they appear. Islamic biographical dictionaries also contain original couplets by female poets and singers as well as devout women.[28] Little has been done, however, by way of gender analysis of this poetry. Kemal Silay has recovered not only the biographical notices but also the voices of female Ottoman poets.[29] Silay's analysis of the works of four female Ottoman poets of the fifteenth, eighteenth and early nineteenth centuries shows that some educated, upper-class Ottoman women were able to break into the male literary elite. They did so, however, by trying to write like men and mimic classical poetry rather than attempting to express a female poetic tradition. Only in the nineteenth century would women authors write of an explicitly male beloved in their poetry. From the nineteenth century as well, women's poetic voices were heard (in Arabic as well as Turkish). Kuwait and Lebanon have appeared on the international consciousness in connection with wars and the hesitant attempts to include Kuwaiti women in the political process and further democracy. Kuwaiti female poet Suad Sabbah has berated Arab men and her message has been magnified by the Lebanese singer Majida al-Rumi[30]:

> Be my friend.
> This will not diminish your manhood.
> Even though the Eastern man is not content with any role except
> the leading role.

Ruth Roded
Jerusalem
September 2006

Notes

1. Valentine M. Moghadam critically analyses the complex debate among Iranian women in Iran and in the Iranian diasporas regarding Islamic feminism, suggests a differentiation between Independent and State Islamic feminists in the Iranian context, and views 'Islamic feminism as one feminism among many'. See 'Islamic Feminism and its Discontents: Toward a Resolution of the Debate', *Signs: Journal of Women in Culture and Society* 27 (2002) pp. 1135–71.

2. Ayesha ar-Rifa'i's presentation 'Exegesis of Women's Rights in Islamic Tradition' at the International Conference on Gendered Space in Middle Eastern Societies and Cultures in Jerusalem, June 2002, exemplifies this trend, which is most likely very widespread in view of the sales of first-generation Islamic feminist works.

3. On Sufism as a basis for women's empowerment, see Ruth Roded, *Women in Islamic Biographical Collections: From Ibn Sa'd to Who's Who* (Boulder: Lynne Rienner Publishers, 1994), pp. 91–114. Ayesha ar-Rifa'i as her name implies comes from a Sufi background. The film *Bab al-Sama Maftouh/Door to the Sky* (Morocco, 1989) directed by Farida Ben Lyzaid tells the story of a Frenchified Moroccan woman who returns to her homeland and under the influence of a popular shaykha, turns her father's home into a shelter for battered women.

4. Joan Wallace Scott, 'Gender: A Useful Category of Historical Analysis', *Gender and the Politics of History* (New York: Columbia University Press, 1988), pp. 28–50, 206–11.

5. Deniz Kandiyoti, 'Islam and Patriarchy: A Comparative Perspective,' in N. Keddie and B. Baron (eds) *Women in Middle Eastern History* (New Haven: Yale University Press, 1991) p. 26.

6. Rachel Simon, *Change within Tradition among Jewish Women in Libya* (Seattle: University of Washington Press, 1992).

7. Roded, *Women in Islamic Biographical Collections*, pp. 78–80.

8. Margaret L. Meriwether, 'Women and Economic Change in Nineteenth-Century Syria: The Case of Aleppo', in Judith Tucker (ed.) *Arab Women: Old Boundaries, New Frontiers* (Bloomington: Indiana University Press, 1993) pp. 65–83.

9. See the work of French-Algerian Orientalist painter Etienne Dinet, Denise Brahimi, *La Vie et l'œuvre de Etienne Dinet, Les Orientalistes*, vol. 2 (Paris: ACR Editions, 1991); Ruth Roded, 'Modern Gendered Illustrations of the Life of the Prophet of Allah – Étienne Dinet and Sliman Ben Ibrahim (1918)', *Arabica* (2002) pp. 325–59; the realistic novels of Tawfiq al-Hakim and Naquib al-Mahfouz, and the Tunisian film *Halfaouine: Boy of the Terraces* directed by Ferid Boughedir (1990).

10. Nikki R. Keddie, 'Introduction: Deciphering Middle Eastern Women's History', in Nikki R. Keddie and Beth Baron (eds) *Women in Middle Eastern History: Shifting Boundaries in Sex and Gender* (New Haven: Yale University Press, 1991).

11. Leila Ahmed, *Women and Gender in Islam* (New Haven: Yale University Press, 1992).

12. Roded, *Women in Islamic Biographical Collections*, p. 72.

13. Miriam Hoexter, 'The Participation of Women in Economic Activities in Turkish Algiers' (unpublished paper).

14. International Conference on Gendered Space in Middle Eastern Societies and Cultures, the Truman Institute for the Advancement of Peace Research, the Hebrew University of Jerusalem, June 2002.

15. Ruth Roded, 'Mainstreaming Middle East Gender Research: Promise or Pitfall?' *Middle East Studies Association Bulletin*, 35 (Summer 2001) pp. 15–23.

16. Derek Hopwood, *Sexual Encounters in the Middle East* (New York: Ithaca Press, 2000); Leslie Peirce, *Morality Tales: Law and Gender in the Ottoman Court of Aintab* (Berkeley: University of California Press, 2003); Afsaneh Najmabadi, *Women with Mustaches and Men Without Beards: Gender and Sexual Anxieties of Iranian Modernities* (Berkeley: University of California Press, 2005); Khaled Al-Rouhayeb, *Before Homosexuality in the Arab-Islamic World, 1500–1800* (Chicago: University of Chicago Press, 2005); Dror Zeevi, *Producing Desire: Changing Sexual Discourse in the Ottoman Middle East, 1500–1900* (Berkeley: University of California Press, 2006). I would like to thank Dror Zeevi for updating me on this important subject.

17. Yedida Kalfon Stillman, *Arab Dress from the Dawn of Islam to Modern Times* (Leiden: Brill, 2000).

18. Miriam Hoexter, Shmuel N. Eisenstadt and Nehemia Levtzion (eds) *The Public Sphere in Muslim Societies* (Albany, NY: State University of New York Press, 2002).

19. Gabriel Baer, *Egyptian Guilds in Modern Times* (Jerusalem: Israel Oriental Society, 1964); Maya Shatzmiller, 'Women's Labour', in *Labour in the Medieval Islamic World* (Leiden, 1994), pp. 347–68; Amnon Cohen, *The Guilds of Jerusalem* (Boston: Brill, 2001).

20. Elizabeth Warnock Fernea (ed.) *Children in the Muslim Middle East* (Austin: University of Texas Press, 1995); *Remembering Childhood in the Middle East: Memoirs from a Century of Change* (Austin: University of Texas Press, 2002).

21. Avner Giladi, *Children of Islam: Concepts of Childhood in Medieval Muslim Society* (New York: St Martin's Press, 1992).

22. Roded, *Women in Islamic Biographical Collections*, pp. 80–4.

23. 'Gendered Domesticity in the Life of the Prophet: Tawfiq al-Hakim's Muhammad', *Journal of Semitic Studies*, 47 (Spring 2002) pp. 67–95; 'Modern Gendered Illustrations of the Life of the Prophet of Allah: Étienne Dinet and Sliman Ben Ibrahim (1918)', *Arabica* 49 (2002) pp. 325–59; 'Gender in an Allegorical Life of Muhammad: Mahfouz's *Children of Gebelawi*', *The Muslim World*, 93 (2003) pp. 117–34; 'Bint al-Shati's *Wives of the Prophet*: Feminist or Feminine?' *British Journal of the Middle Eastern Society*, 33 (2006) pp. 69–84; 'Lessons by a Syrian Islamist from the Life of the Prophet Muhammad', *Middle Eastern Studies*, 42 (2006) pp. 69–84.

24. Asma Sayeed, 'Early Sunni Discourse on Women's Mosque Attendance', *ISIM Newsletter* (2001) p. 10.

25. Kalfon Stillman and Zeren Tanindi, *Siyer-i Nebi: An Illustrated Cycle of the Life of Muhammad and its Place in Islamic Art,* English translation by Maggie Quigly-Pinar (Istanbul, 1984); E. Dinet et Sliman Ben Ibrahim, *La Vie de Mohammed, Prophète d'Allah* (Paris: Piazza, 1918).

26. Marion Holmes Katz at the University of Chicago and Zev Maghen at Columbia University.

27. Liora Hendelman-Baavur of Tel Aviv University, who has studied the women's press in Iran, keeps me updated on the most important works on gender in Iranian history.

28. Roded, *Women in Islamic Biographical Collections*, pp. 95, 125–6. Only the phenomenon of female poets was documented in this study; the verse was not analysed.

29. Kemal Silay, 'Singing his Words: Ottoman Women Poets and the Power of Patriarchy', in Madeline C. Zilfi (ed.) *Women in the Ottoman Empire: Middle Eastern Women in the Early Modern Era* (Leiden: Brill, 1997) pp. 197–213.

30. My colleague Dr Nadera Shalhoub-Kevorkian brought the forceful statement of Majida al-Rumi to my attention. Ms Osnat Ibrahim picked up the gauntlet to undertake a study exploring the Lebanese singer's role in disseminating nationalist as well as feminist messages.

INDEX